AF521685

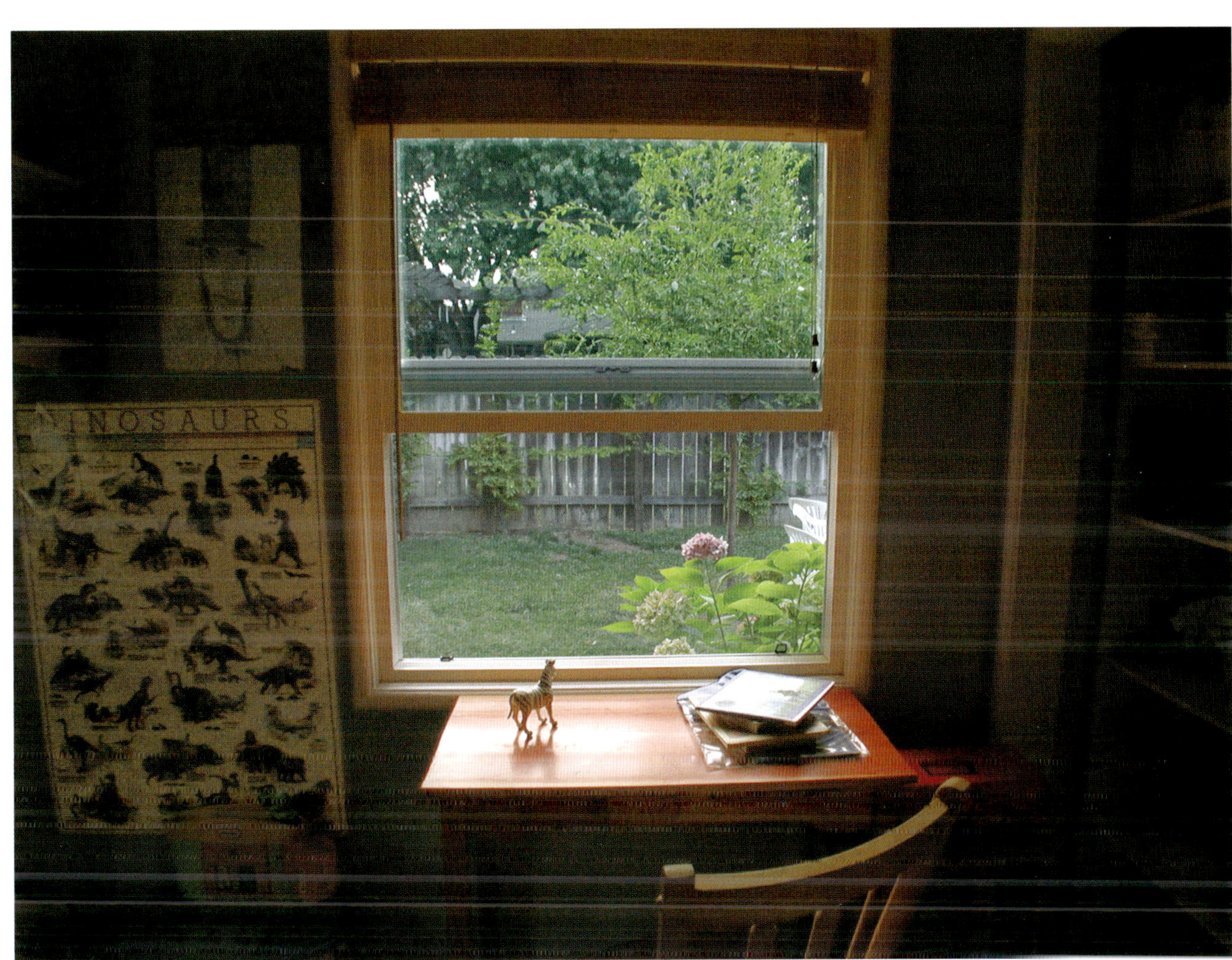
INOSAURS

# everyday

a yearlong photo diary

**by byron wolfe**

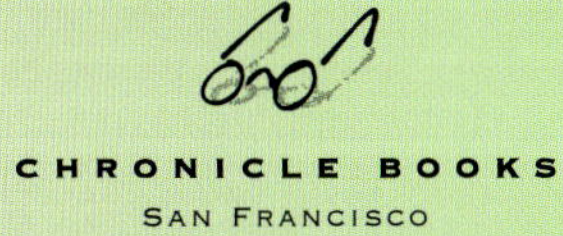

CHRONICLE BOOKS
SAN FRANCISCO

Library of Congress Cataloging-in-
Publication Data available.
ISBN-10: 0-8118-5527-9
ISBN-13: 978-0-8118-5527-3
Manufactured in China.
Designed by Iza Dar.
Distributed in Canada by
Raincoast Books
9050 Shaughnessy Street
Vancouver, British Columbia
V6P 6E5
10 9 8 7 6 5 4 3 2 1
Chronicle Books LLC
680 Second Street
San Francisco, California 94107
www.chroniclebooks.com

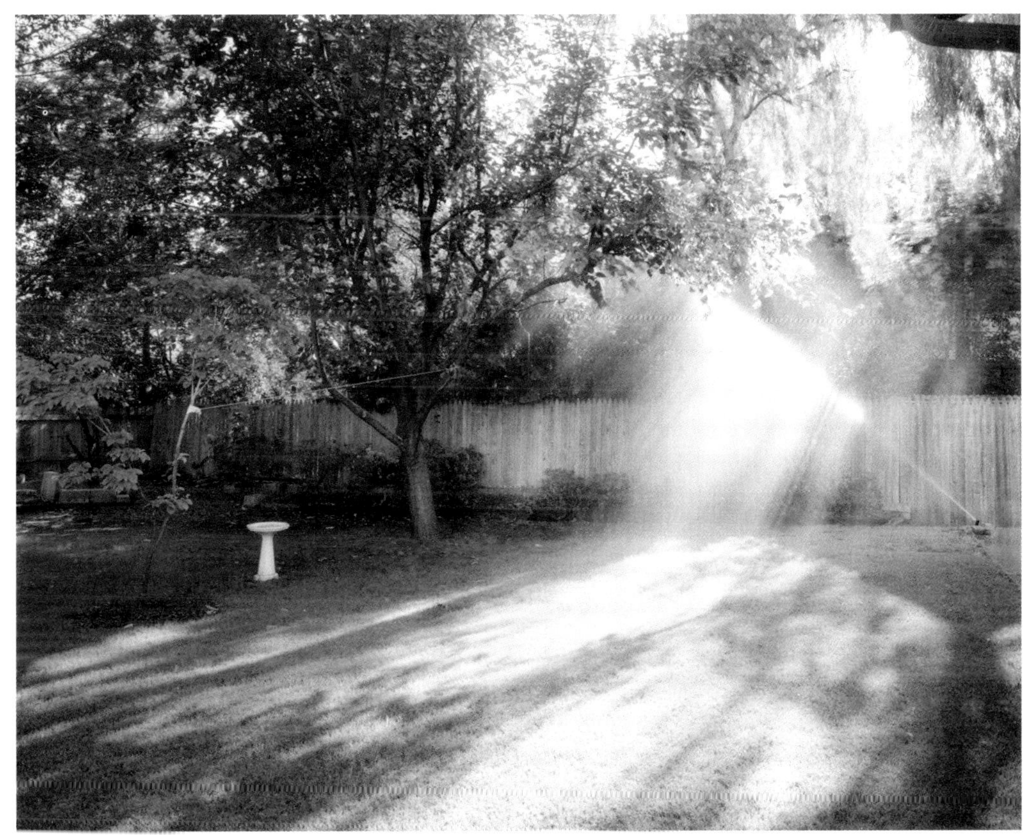

Summer solstice in my parents' backyard, June 1997.

## dear reader,

Every day between my thirty-fifth and thirty-sixth birthdays, I tried to make at least one completely new and compelling photograph. The idea was to create a narrative that was attentive to place, change, and the meandering pace and flow of life. For practical reasons (family, job, sleep), the pictures emerged from my daily activities. I used a digital camera and worked quickly, usually generating scores of photographs in a matter of minutes. Each night before going to bed, I chose a single image and often wrote an accompanying caption.



The idea of making daily pictures was one I'd considered for years, but in the pre-digital era, it was a notion that was prohibitively expensive, if not logistically impossible. As a college professor and a professional photographer, I also had serious doubts about what could even come from such an effort. The basic concept was certainly a little nutty—after all, how could the endeavor possibly warrant the time and attention that it would require? And who would ever want to see the results? Eventually, a series of events justified the idea until I not only felt that I had something worthwhile to say in this way, but also became desperate to say it. The following is a rough account of how I came to carry a camera everywhere and why I didn't go to sleep at night until I'd made my picture.

### what goes in the box

I'm a typical dad: I have a camera and I'm not afraid to use it, especially around the house. For years, I memorialized traditional family events, but I rarely made the kinds of pictures that normal people would want to paste into their scrapbooks. I tended to photograph such things as the halo of crumbs left after a flurry of plastic forks had obliterated a birthday cake, or the kids' tears following the inevitably popped party balloon. I thought that these kind of images were more engaging and truer to the experience of the occasion than a blinding "just-say-cheese" flashbulb moment, even though many of my pictures required an awkward account of their origin ("I know it looks like a mound of crumpled wrapping paper, but it was our son's birthday party"). My wife, who is a kind and understanding person, was usually untroubled by the shortage of pictures we

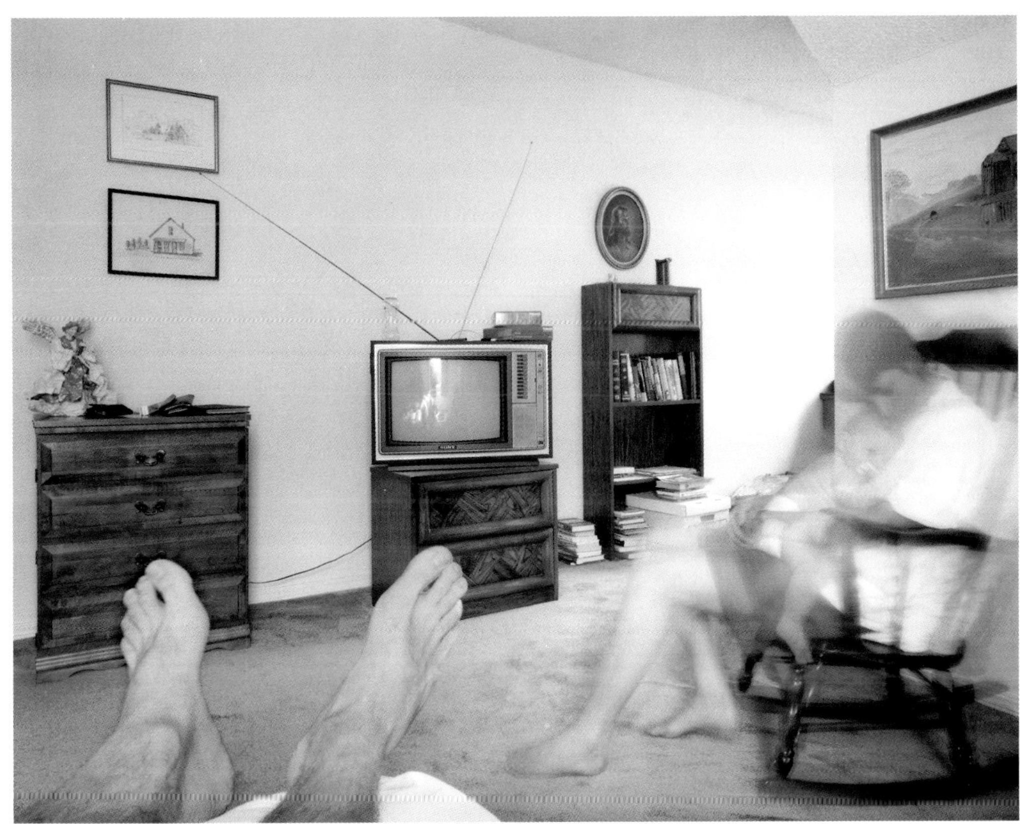

Rocking our first son to sleep in the bedroom of my youth, June 1997.

could confidently send off to relatives' refrigerators. Unless I had explicit instructions to do otherwise, I made family pictures so offbeat that they went straight into a box, safe from the light of day or any need for an apologetic explanation.

## desperately standing still



On other occasions, I made pictures around the house that commemorated ordinary mileposts. Captions for those photographs included "When the car turned 200,000 miles" and "Our annual wedding-tree picture, year seven: spraying to kill a fungus." These pictures honored events we valued—they were serious and simple elegies that chronicled a young couple's shared life and lamented the passage of time. They were also an effort to somehow slow the pace of our rapidly accelerating lives, which were increasingly filled with work, school, and kids.

Because the pictures were mostly about the world that my wife and I inhabited, we were rarely visible in them. We weren't characters in a play; instead, the play was onstage before us, and we tried to pay attention as its stories emerged. More often than not, though, these pictures, made for an audience of two, were just as likely to land in the box of photos that needed explanation.

## pictures as bookends

I was thirty-three when my grandmother died on a bitterly cold day in late December. I traveled alone across a blizzard-shocked country from my home in Northern California to attend her funeral in Indiana with my parents, siblings, and relatives. Like all such occasions, the entire experience was intensely emotional, but in one especially profound moment, I glanced at a photograph of her as a young wife and then saw her as an elderly woman lying in a casket. These two bookends of her life brought forth an explosion of mental images, a jumbled mix of my own experiences (recalled vividly as the family pictures I'd been making and putting in the box) and my memories of the black-and-white snapshots I'd seen in my father's photo albums. In a flash, the fullness of my

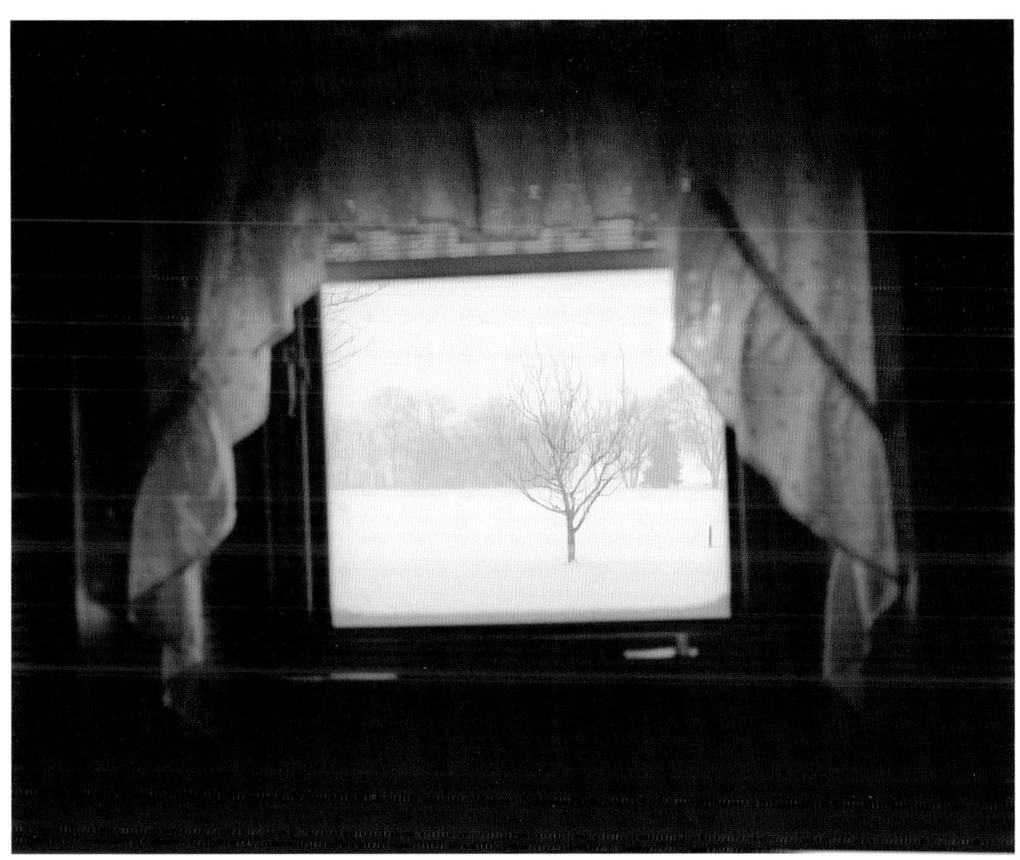

Maple tree in a blizzard: from my grandmother's kitchen window on the day of her funeral, January 2000.

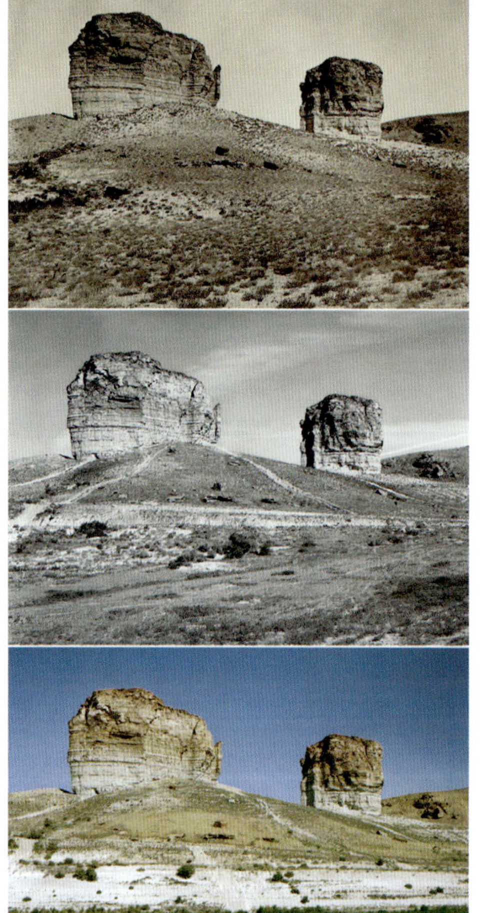

From *Third Views and Second Sights: A Rephotographic Survey of the American West* book and DVD: Three views of the Teapot and Sugar Bowl, Green River, Wyoming; Timothy O'Sullivan, 1872; Mark Klett, 1978; Mark Klett and Byron Wolfe, 1997.

grandmother's life arced between two distinct points, and the real and imagined scenes fused together and imprinted themselves on my mind.

### rocks, trees, and clouds

My ideas about how photographs can work as bookends, and my need to distill seemingly insignificant moments into emblematic images, weren't simply accidental or the result of a quirky personality; I'd been trained to think this way. For several years, I had been roaming the American West with a band of like-minded photographers, making new versions of nineteenth century landscape views from precisely the same vantage point. In our case, we were re-doing what had already been done in the 1970s, so we tacked an updated third view onto the existing pair, effectively creating time-lapse landscape studies.

These sequenced rephotographs are useful as ways to visualize time and change on a scale that transcends generations, and they're often engaging because differences between linked pictures—or even the lack of any discernible difference—suggest a narrative. What any given location's narrative might be is often anyone's guess, so we tried to rough in some missing details by connecting the sequenced pictures to contemporary human stories. This required talking to people who lived in the contemporary space of an old picture, or collecting on-site "artifacts" (discarded photo albums, old magazines, unraveled cassette tapes, rusted and decaying toys) that revealed something of the place's character. We also made our own pictures that addressed our personal experiences. Collectively, these attempted to find specific and personal emblems that stood for something far more universal. By linking old photographs of rocks, trees, and clouds to new pictures and collected junk, we tried to tell stories about where we'd been, and possibly even speak to where we were headed.

An especially confounding aspect of rephotography is that there is no guarantee you'll end up with a new picture that is even remotely interesting when considered on its own. It's the historical photograph—the very first in the series—that guides you on where to

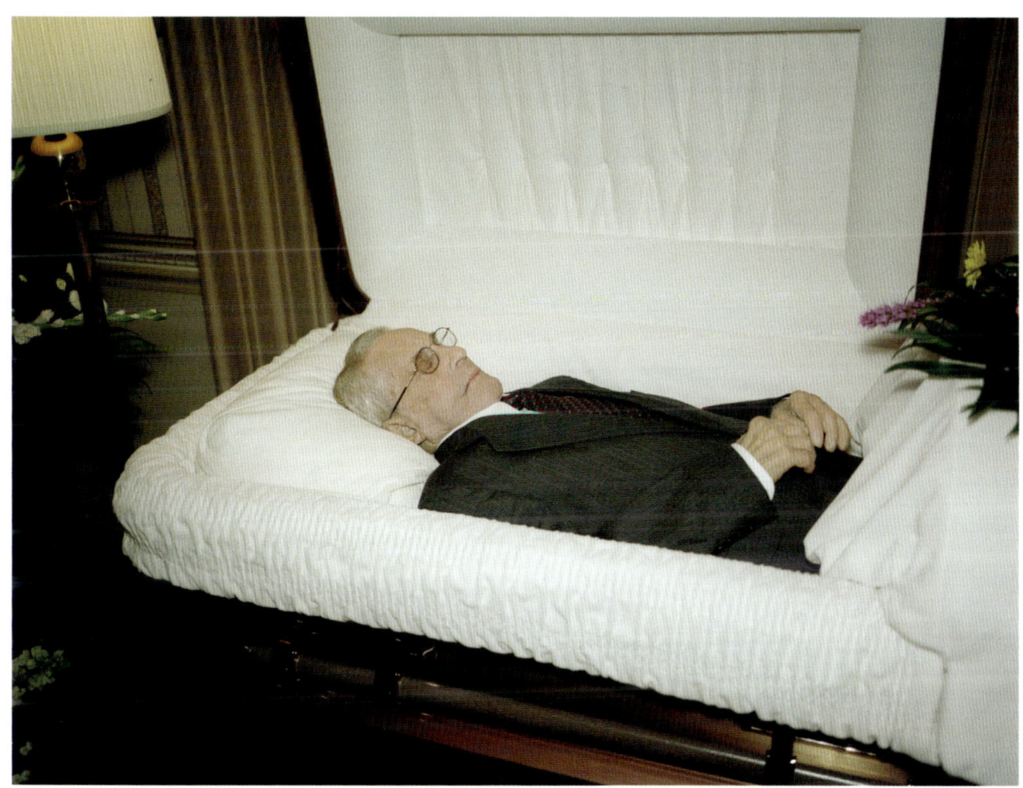

06.27.02

**Maynard L. Wolfe, my grandfather**

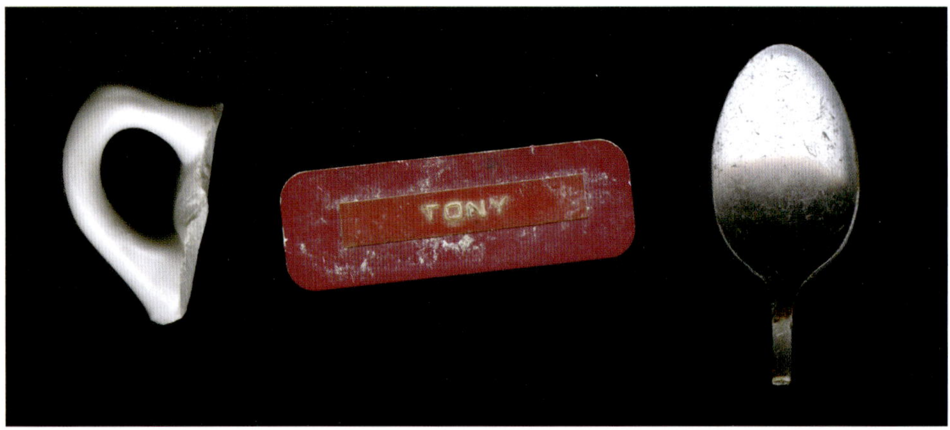


**Artifacts discovered at the base of the Teapot and Sugar Bowl, 1997.**

stand and when to press the shutter, so rephotography's seemingly random results require acceptance of that which is unexpected and often less than aesthetically ideal. It requires suspension of the expectation for singularly defining images. Moreover, understanding a rephotograph is largely dependent upon knowing that it's part of a larger sequence.

### food on the table

As someone who makes his living teaching photography, I've spent a lot of time looking at the very first pictures that students have ever made. For reasons I have yet to divine, fire hydrants, aluminum miniblinds, and skateboarders are disproportionately represented in the pantheon of new student pictures. Looking at so many of these first pictures inevitably leads me to consider a basic question: What really deserves to be photographed? It's a simple question that beginners and experts alike must continually answer.

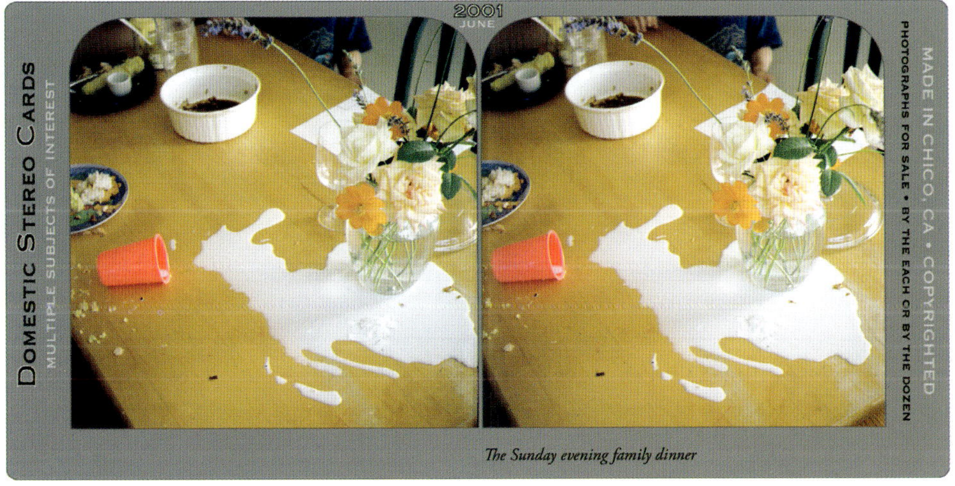


**The Sunday evening family dinner, June 2001.**



The teacher in me tries to help my students answer the question by calling on an old writers' adage: "Write about what you know." It's a statement that translates easily to photography, but it's difficult to put into practice when you're just starting out. It's hard enough to know "what you know," let alone learn how to use an intimidating machine with dials, buttons, and flashing lights to turn an experience into an image that resonates with meaning. Yet there is another adage that's just as valid: "Write to discover what you think." It's a variation on what I like to call the "document everything" method, in which everything (including fire hydrants, miniblinds, and skateboarders) deserves attention and one can begin to uncover ideas and opinions by sifting through the photographic evidence.

Seeing my students try to decide where to point their cameras has helped shape my own answers to the question of what deserves to be photographed. Once in a while, and often by accident, my students give me a glimpse of the world through *their* eyes, and I get to see *their* friends, families, homes, and jobs. These are pictures usually made on a whim and with little forethought. But they are also the pictures students hold in reserve and later present with an apology because they're just too embarrassing, personal, unimportant, or quirky, or they're outside the bounds of a given assignment. If my students kept boxes of photographs that they were reluctant to show, these would be the pictures they'd toss in first.



Several years ago, I became so intrigued with these pictures that I asked my students to carry their cameras everywhere and to consider photographing what was literally and figuratively close to home. Finding unexplored territory, I argued, has more to do with changing perception than with seeking exotic locations. Plus, taking your camera everywhere is now easy to do, since new digital models are smaller than ever, give instant results, and cost virtually nothing to operate. Making at least one picture a day seems like a reasonable expectation and fundamentally good practice. Musicians and athletes practice every day, so why shouldn't photographers?

Yet asking my students to make pictures everywhere and every day was a disingenuous request, and I knew it. I didn't carry my camera with me everywhere, and despite a genuine desire to do otherwise, I reserved my picture-making primarily for vacations and special occasions.

### unrelenting sadness

Then, 9/11 happened. In a very short time, we were swept up by a rolling cloud of fear, anger, and overwhelming sorrow. As the days progressed, we collectively yearned for life to return to normal, and we felt an urgency to value the basic and the routine. This was a longing that went beyond ordinary sentimentality and nostalgia; amid the intense and unrelenting sadness, that which was simple became revered as essential.

Standing in the emotional shadow of 9/11 made me, like so many others, reconsider a number of ideas. I thought a lot about my box of family pictures that needed explanation (by this time, I'd figured out how they were like rephotographs, making sense only when they could lean on one another). I recalled the power of the real and imagined photonarrative of my grandmother's life, suspended between two fixed points in time. I confronted my unsettled feeling that I was asking something of my students that I wasn't doing myself. I decided that there was value in photographic subjects I'd sheepishly dismissed as unimportant and maybe even a little self-absorbed. In my mind, all of these disparate thoughts and ideas pointed to one thing: I absolutely had to do what I'd long considered—practice making *my* pictures, every day, no matter what.



**reassuringly unoriginal**

I chose my birthday as a starting point, mostly because the date falls in the summer, which is the best time for me to establish a healthy working routine. Plus, that date is more about marking personal time than are the other, arbitrary, days of the year running from January to December.

When I began, I only had one or two ideas for pictures, though I was generally aware of the boundaries within which I expected to bounce around. To be sure, it was an unnerving undertaking, and even today I have to remind myself, as I often did then, that I just had to try to make one picture a day, and not all of them at once. Despite this, I had to constantly relearn the lesson that the more pictures I made, the more ideas I generated. For me, ideas usually came from doing work—not the other way around. But I was always searching for inspiration, which I found equally among the works of poets, painters, writers, musicians, and photographers

Because I generally employed the "document everything" approach, genuinely surprising themes emerged, and I learned to pay attention to things I'd not previously considered important. But what was most surprising—and reassuring—was learning that the paths I was following were anything but new. I was comforted by the reminder that for centuries, some of the most serious creative work has come from the most ordinary things: children, pets, fruit trees, seasons, and the passage of time.

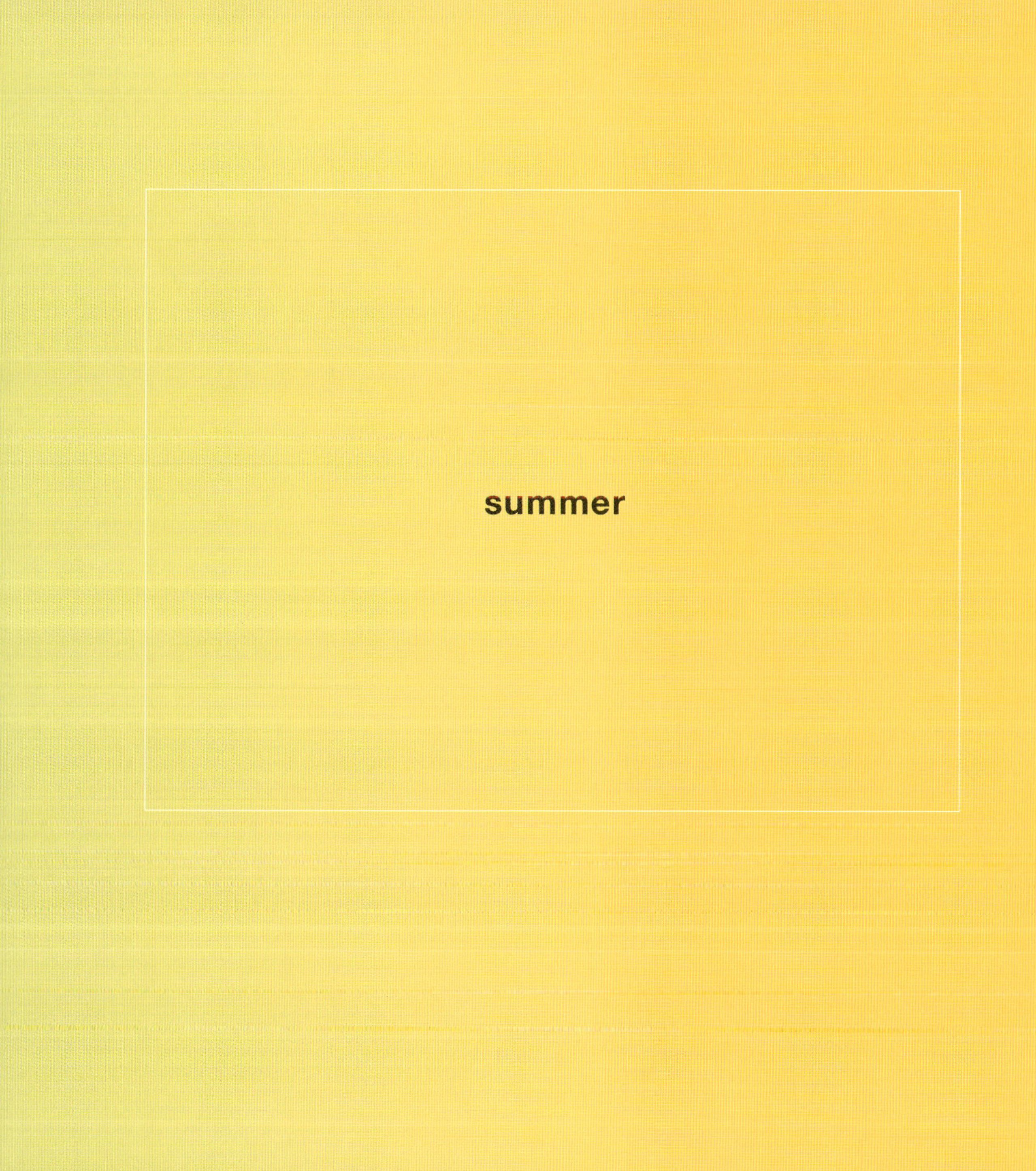

summer

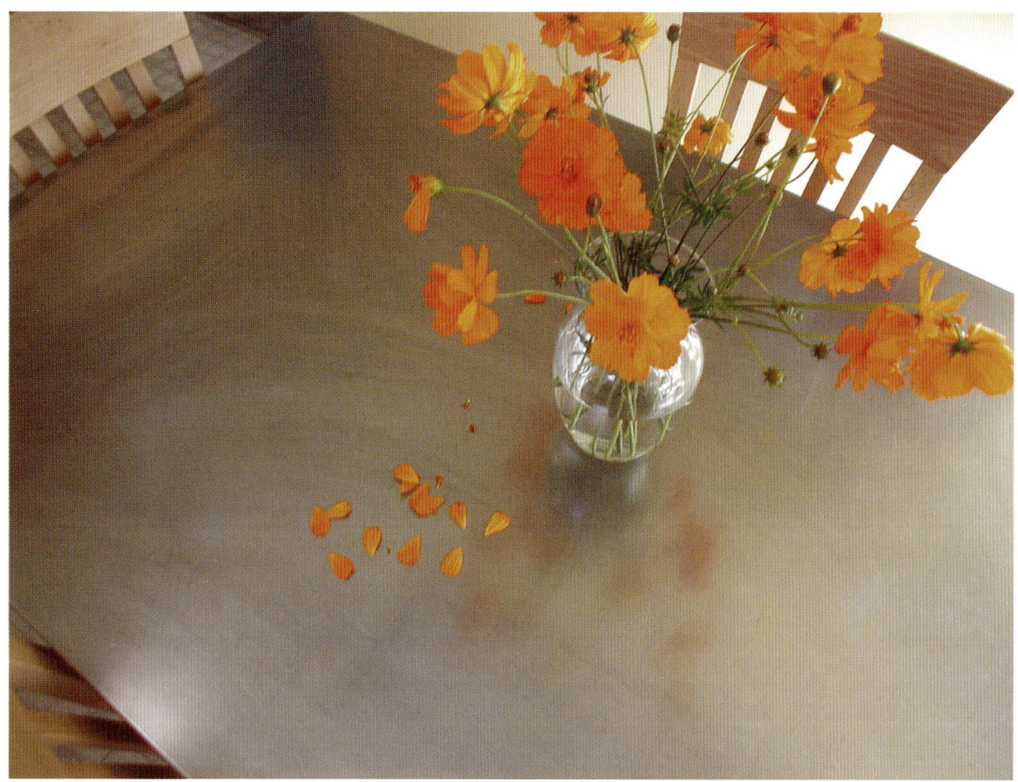

06.23.02

**First day: my grandfather died and I turned thirty-five**

06.24.02

**Traditional family portrait, made to share at the funeral**

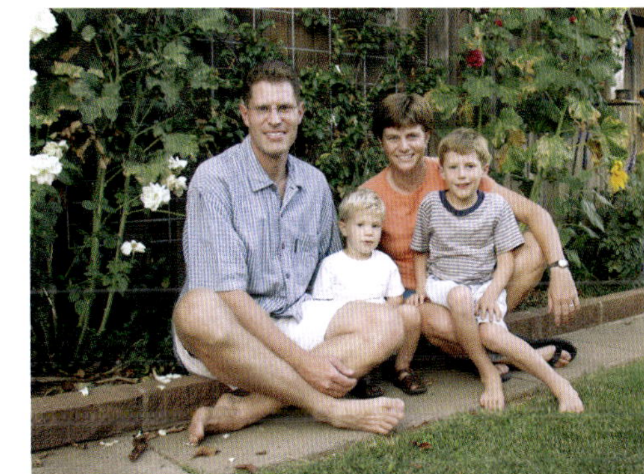

06.25.02

**Traveling cloud**

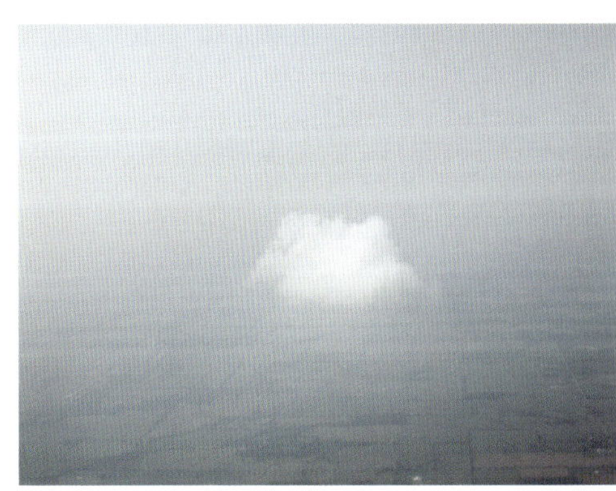

06.26.02

**View from my grandfather's barn: lightning storm above Lincoln County, Indiana**

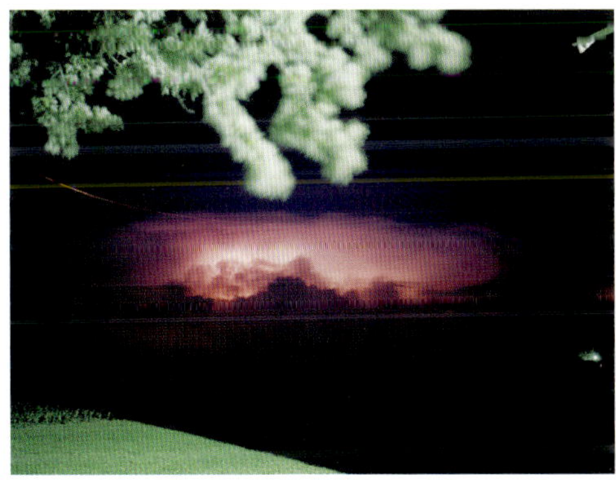

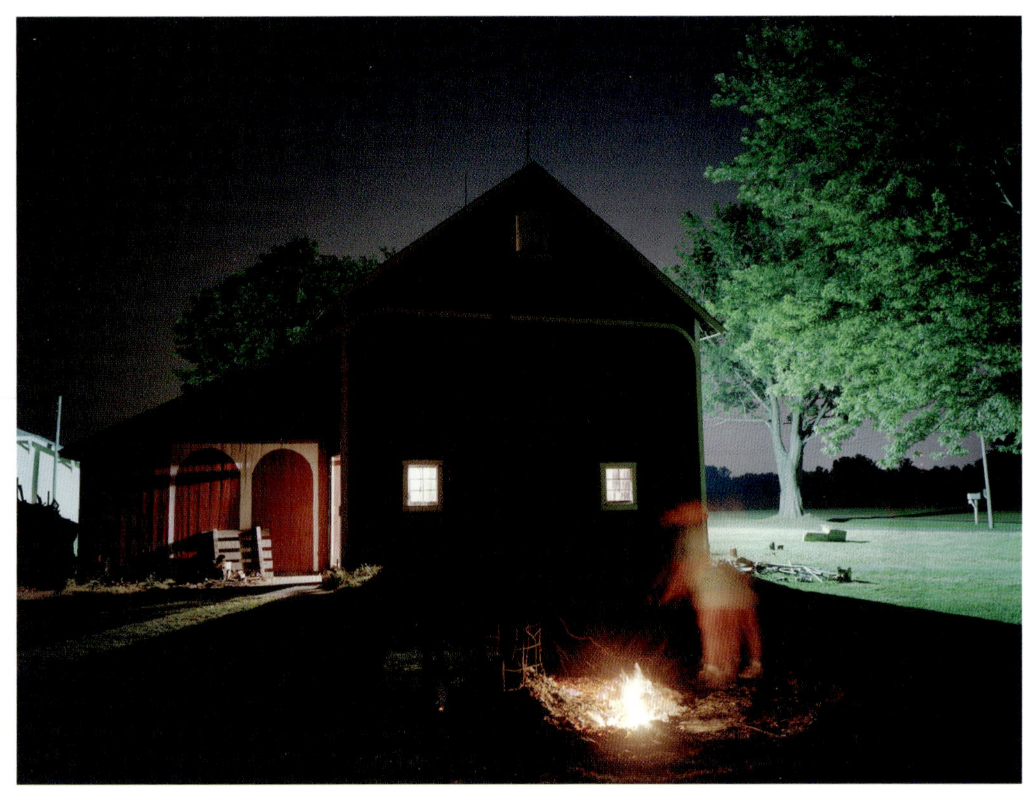

06.28.02

**After the funeral, cleaning out his barn**

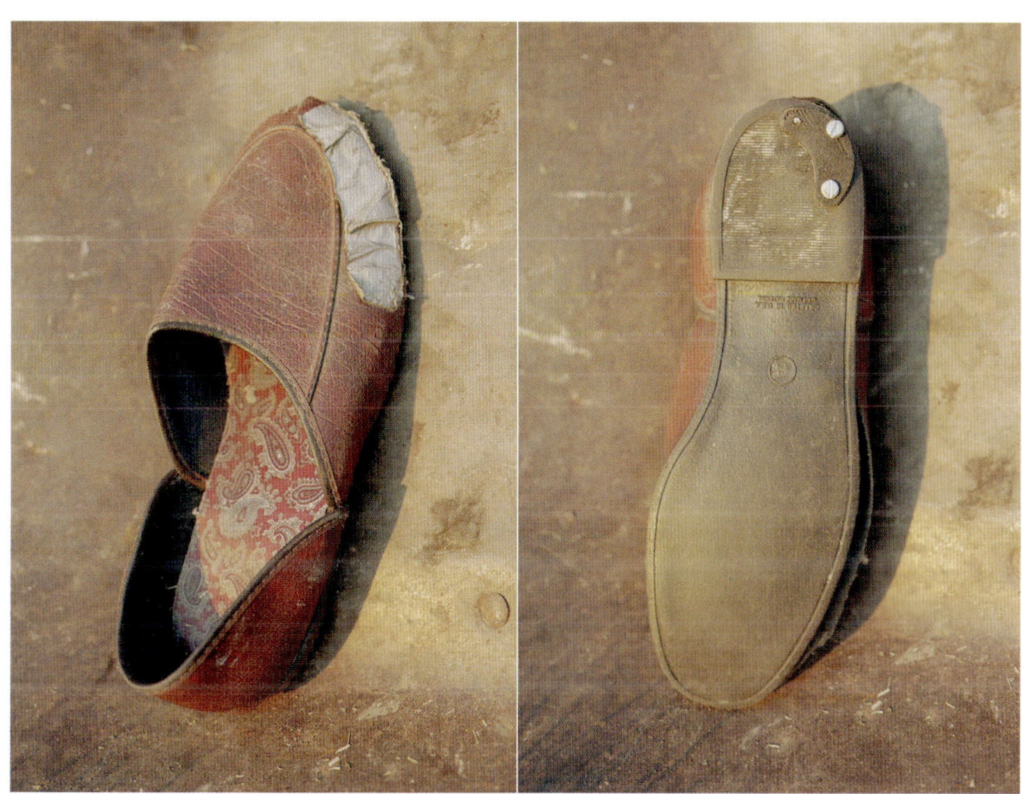

06.29.02

**My grandfather's favorite slipper**

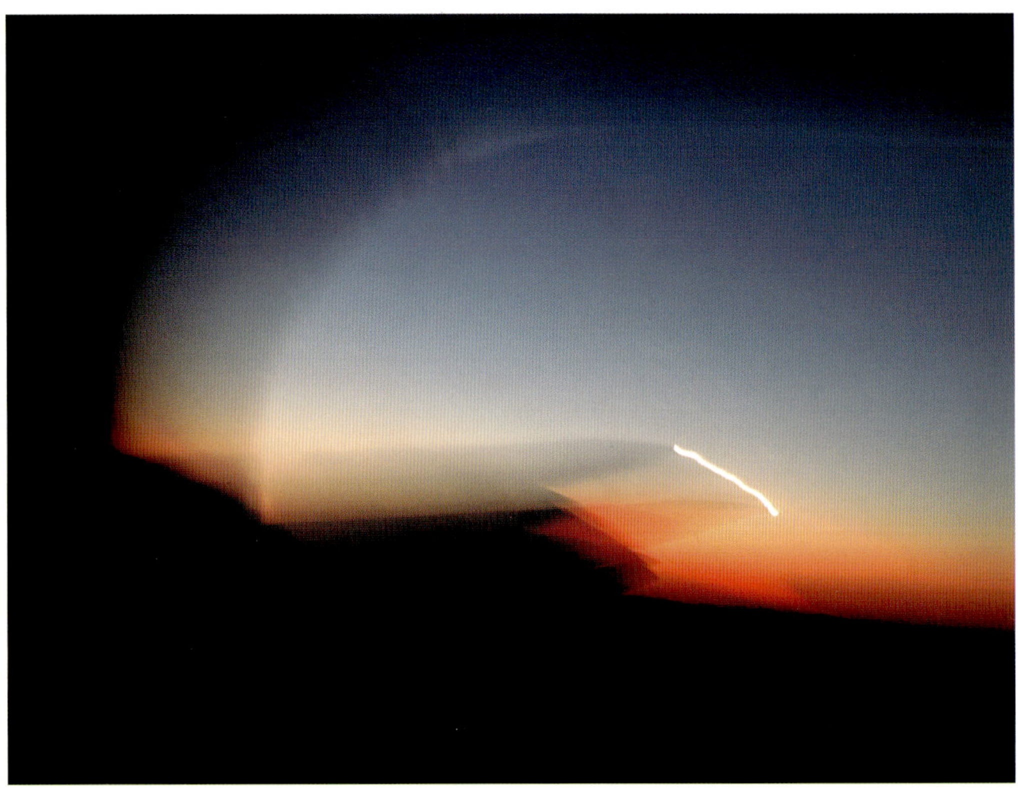

06.30 02

**Final descent, returning home**

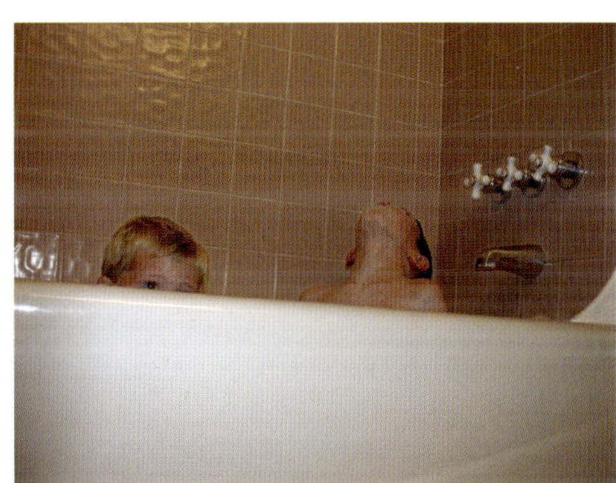

07.01.02

**Back home in Chico**

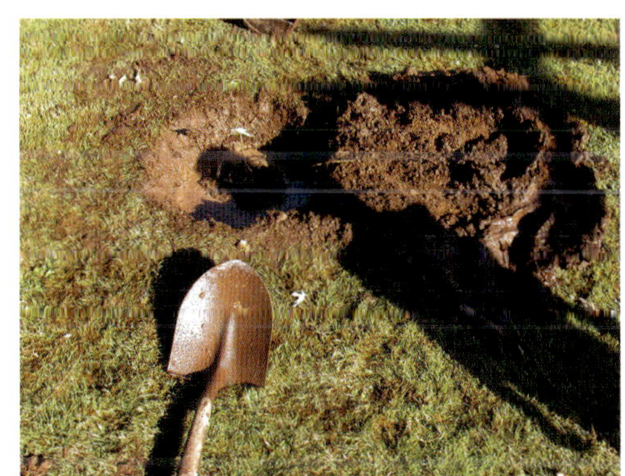

07.02.02

**A maple seedling transplanted across 2,200 miles and four generations**

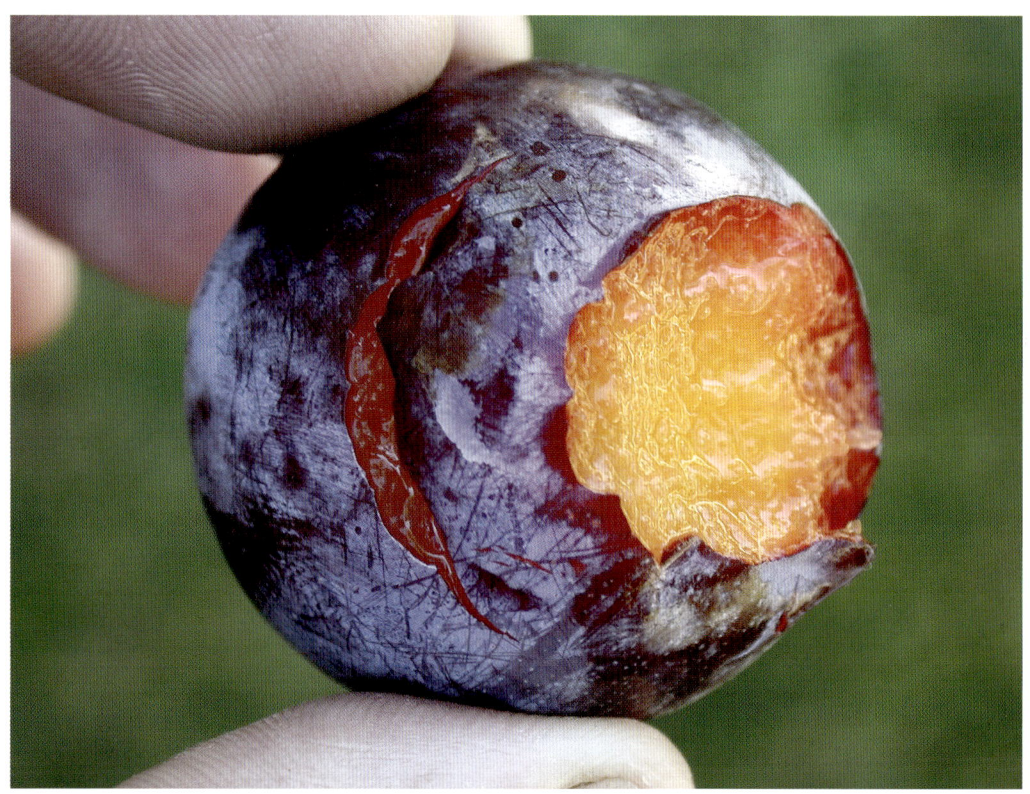

07.03.02

**From our favorite tree (the Weeping Santa Rosa)**

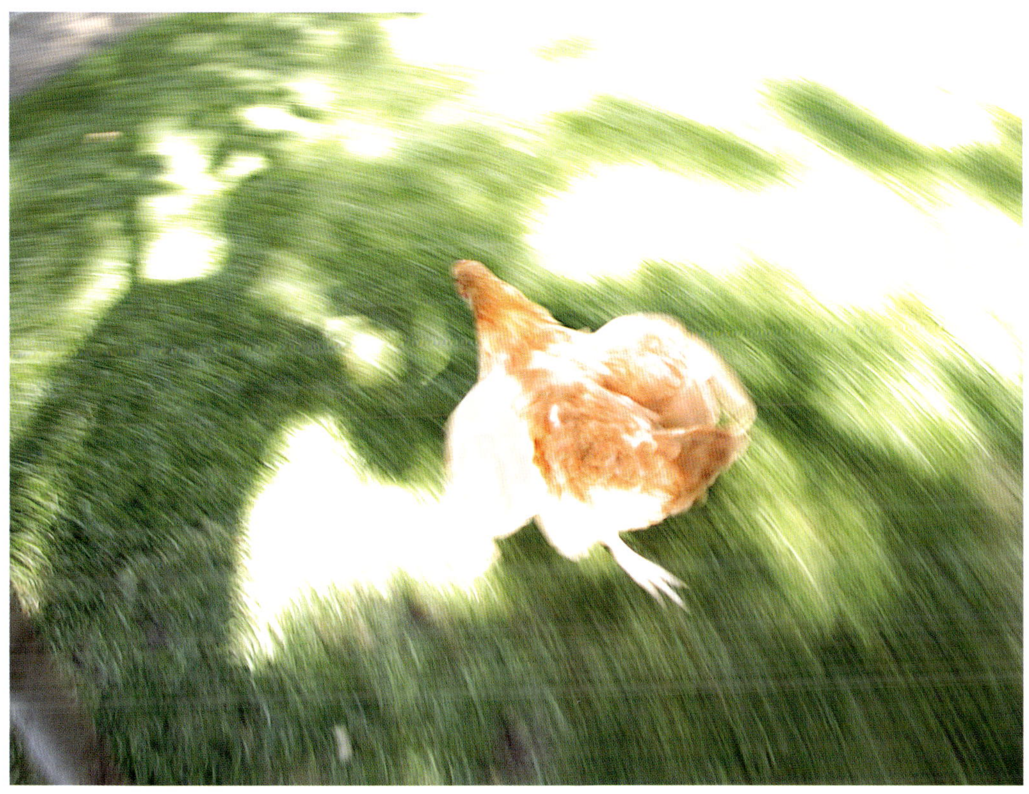

07.04.02

**“Yellow,” our most faithful hen**

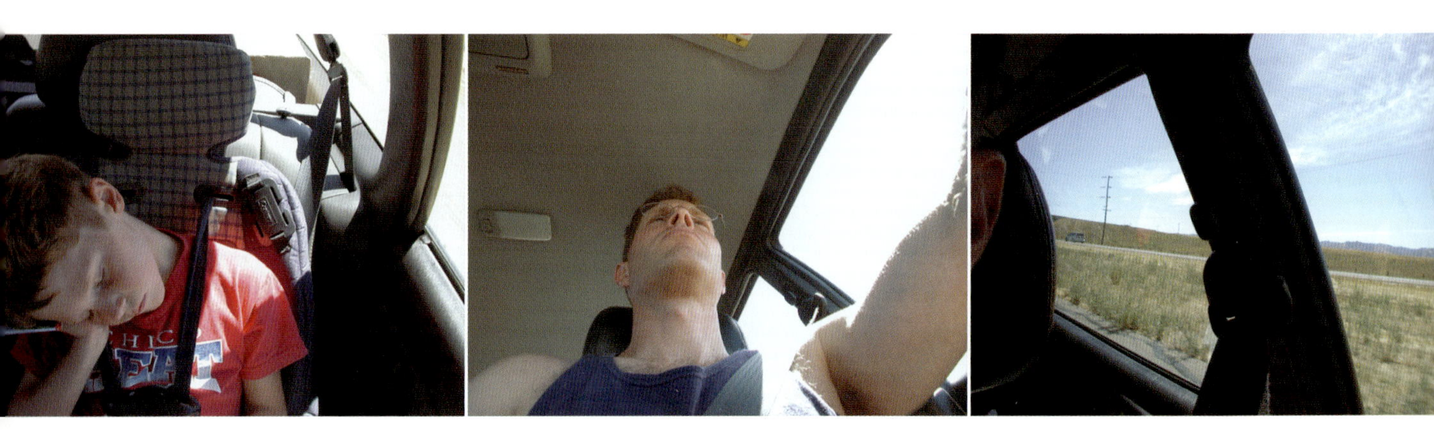

07.05.02–07.06.02

**Family portrait spanning two days and 450 miles**

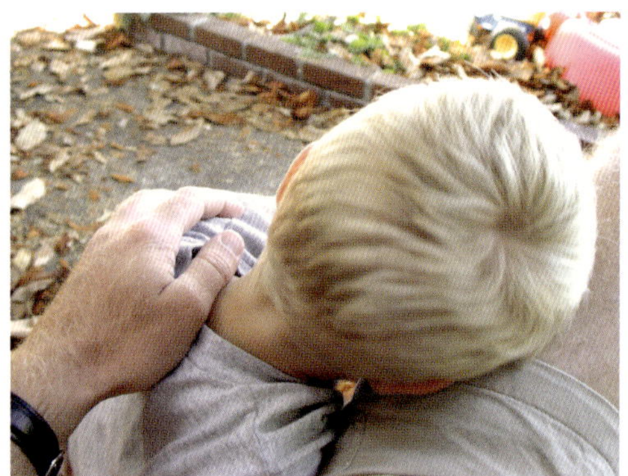

07.07.02

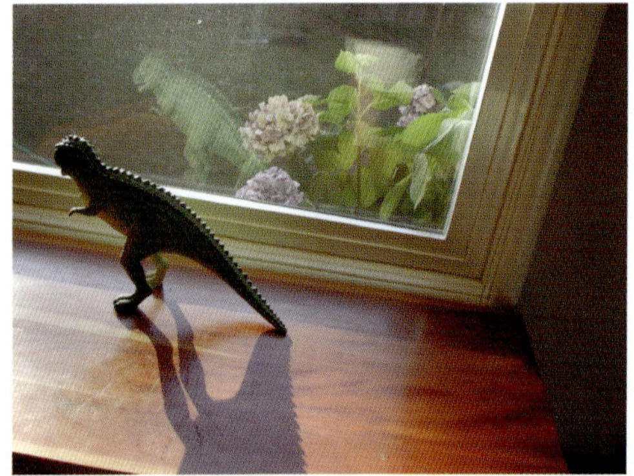

07.08.02

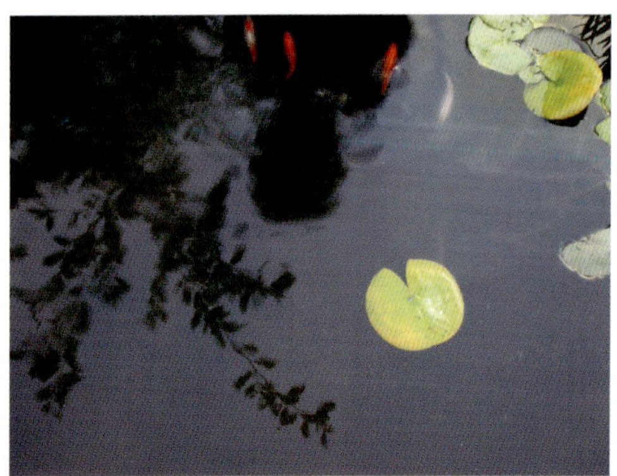

07.09.02

07.10.02

**105° at 8:00 PM**

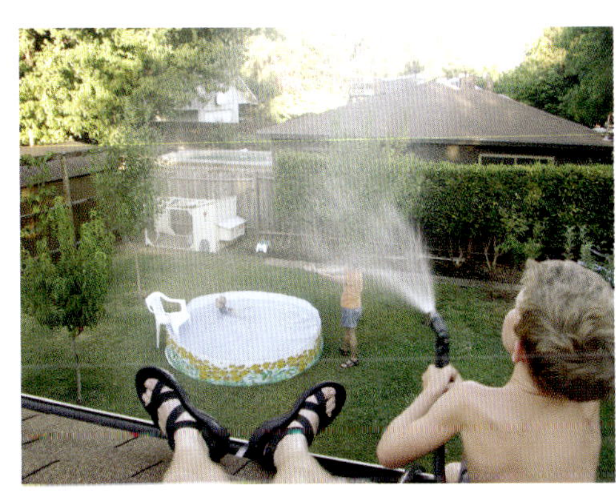

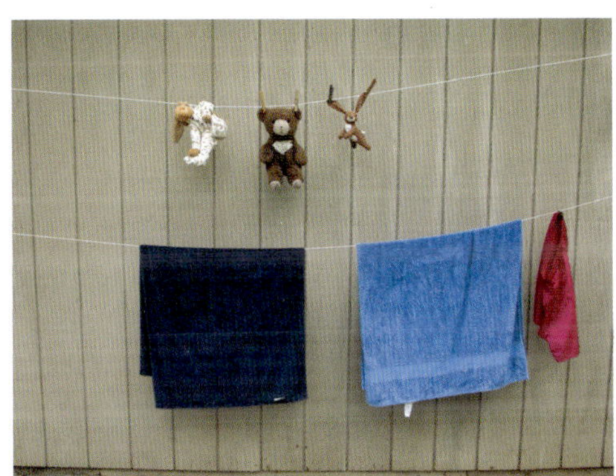

07.11.02

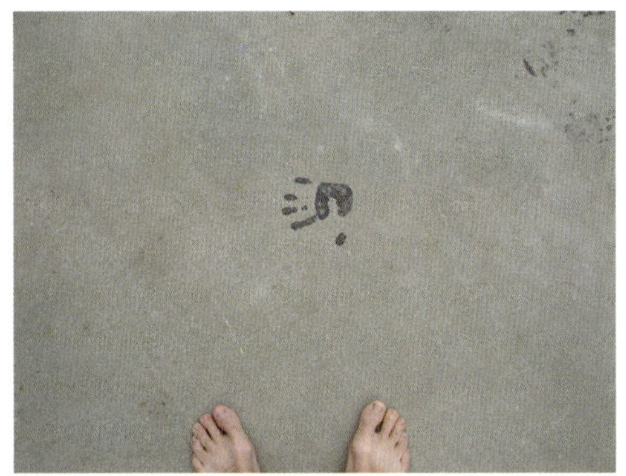

07.12.02

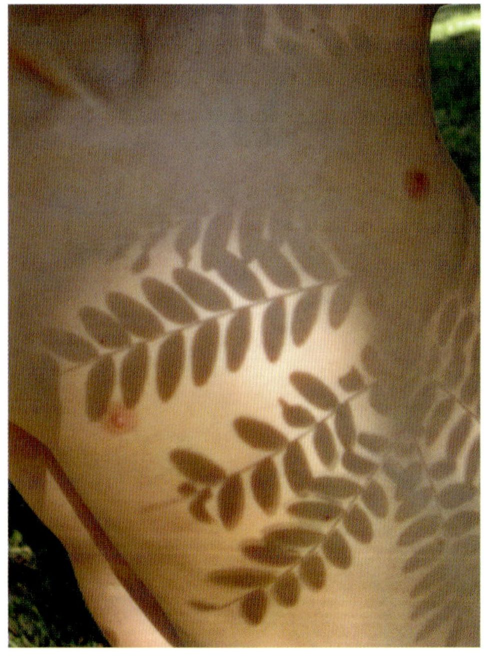

07.13.02

**Morning light,**
**in the shade of the Honey Locust**

07.14.02

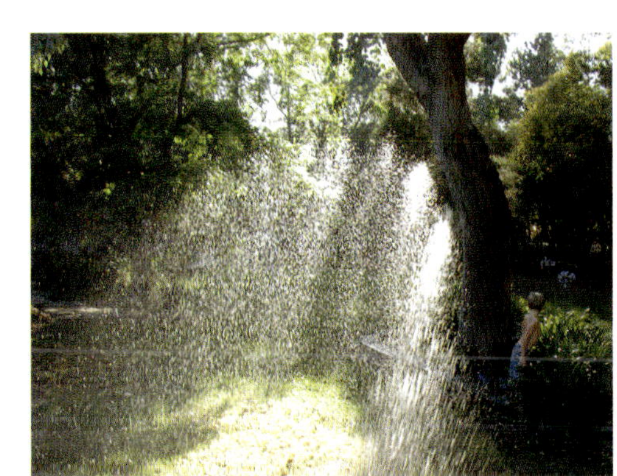

07.15.02

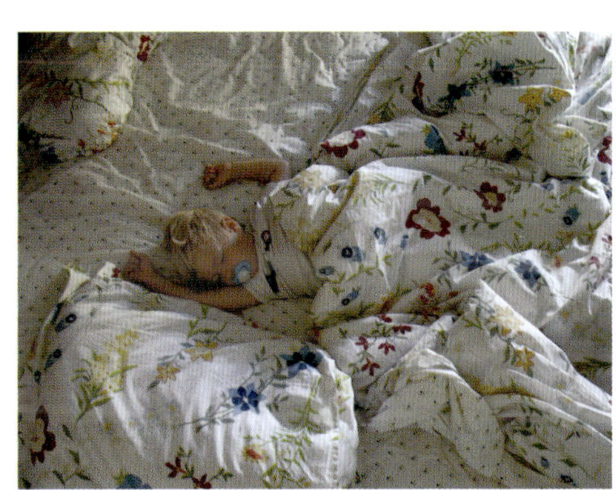

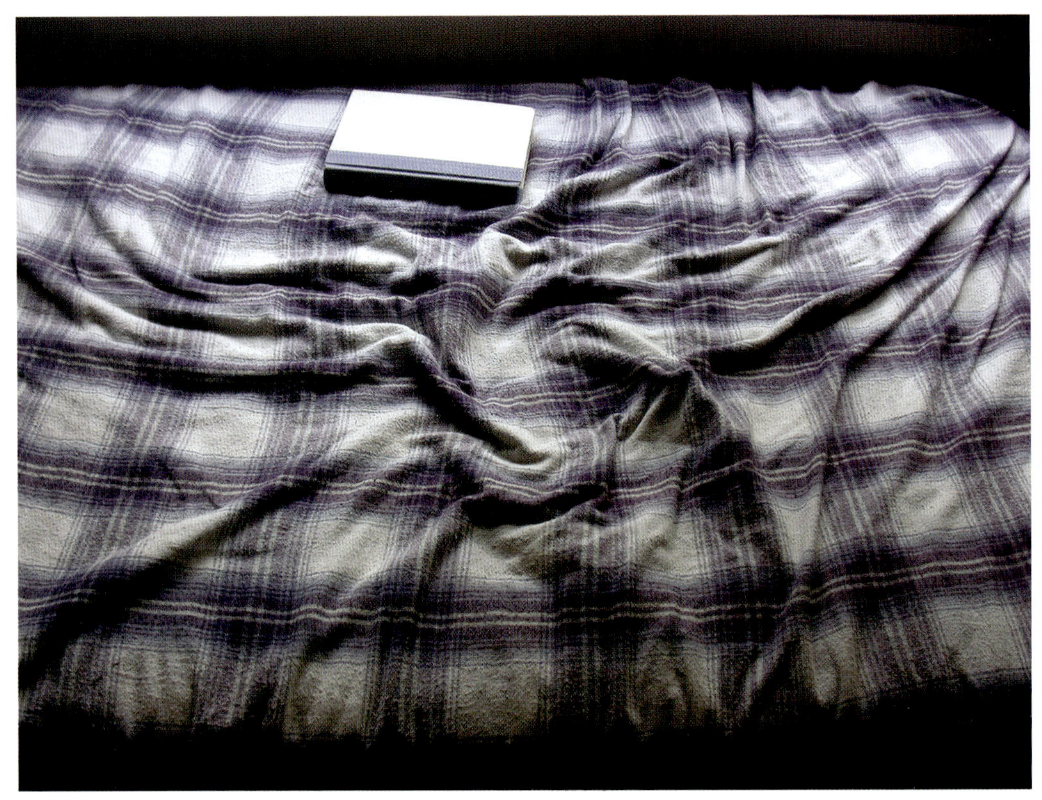

07.16.02

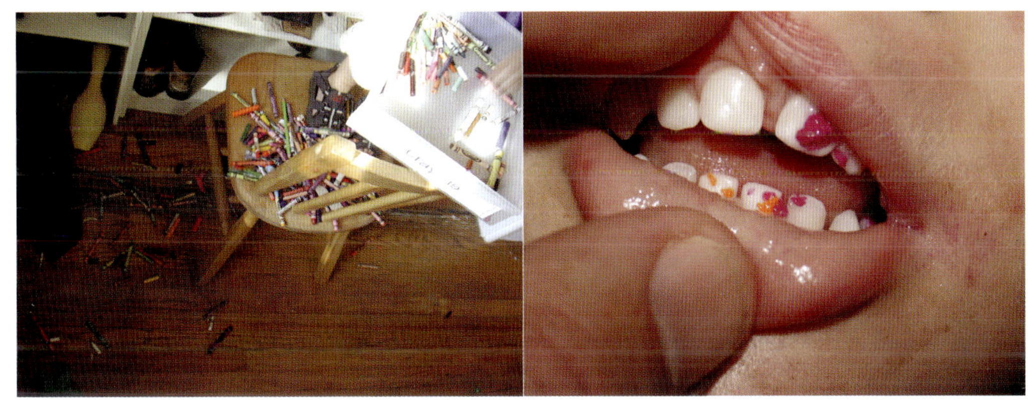

07.17.02

**Crayola snack**

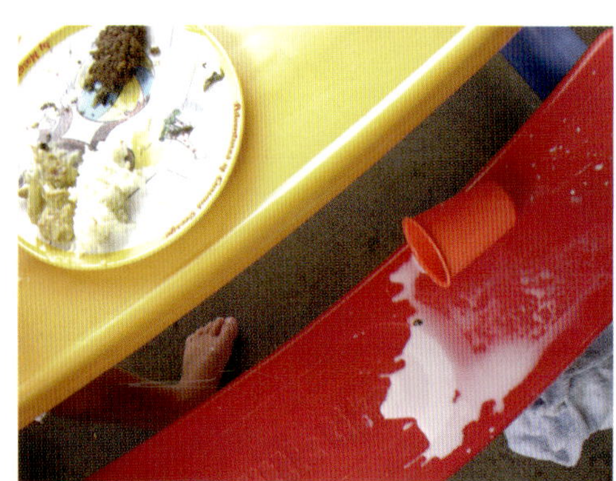

07.18.02

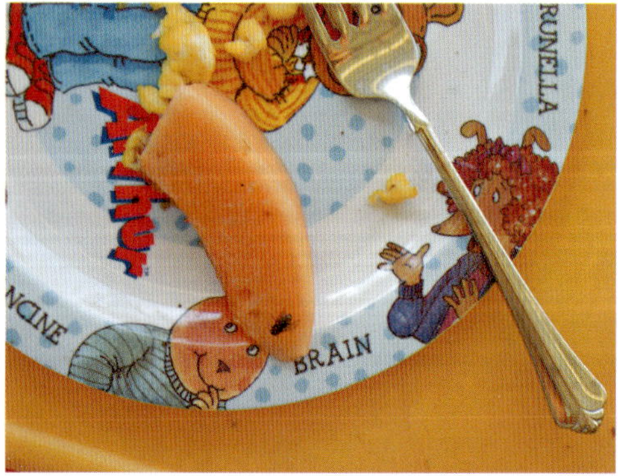


07.19.02

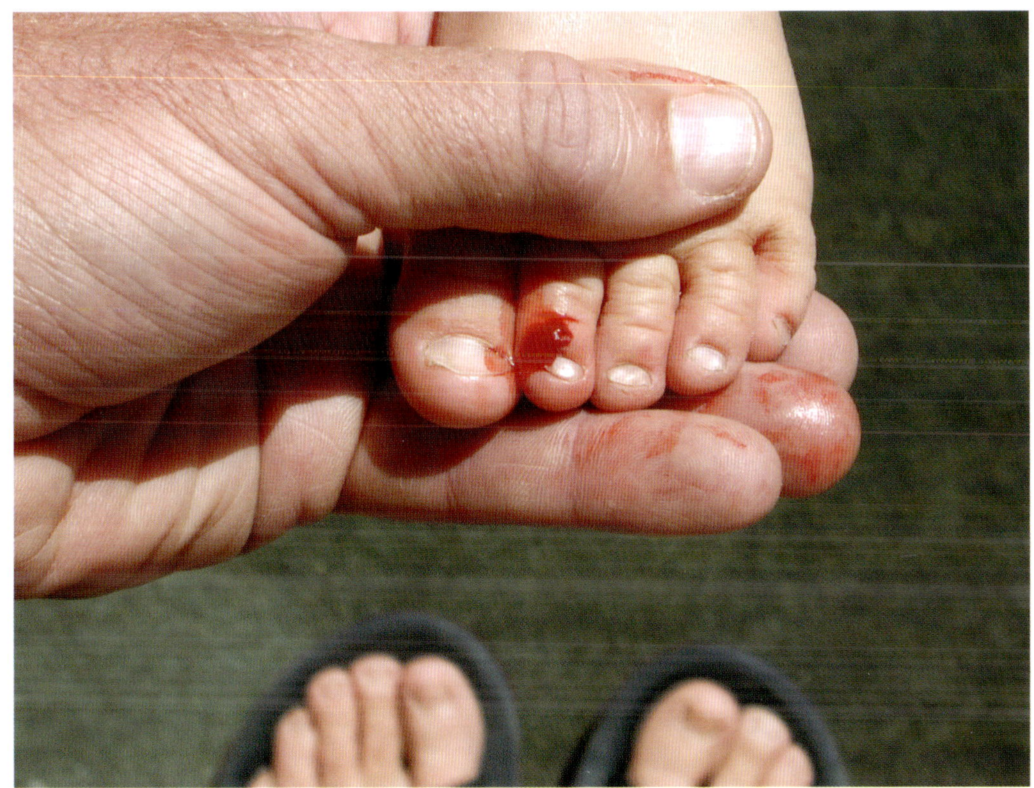

07.20.02

**On our eleventh wedding anniversary**

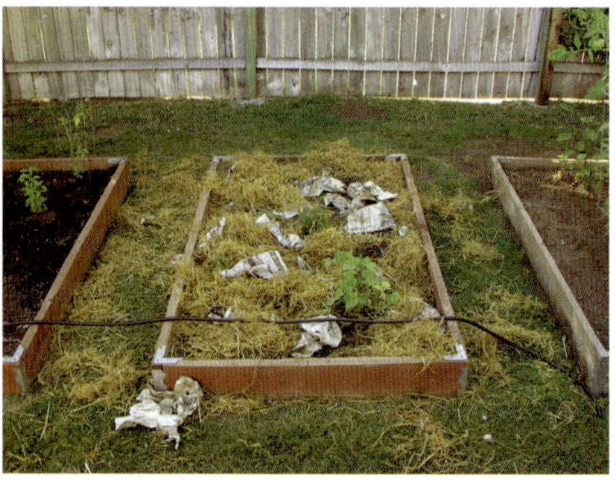

07.21.02

**In the garden:**
**the curse of free-range chickens**

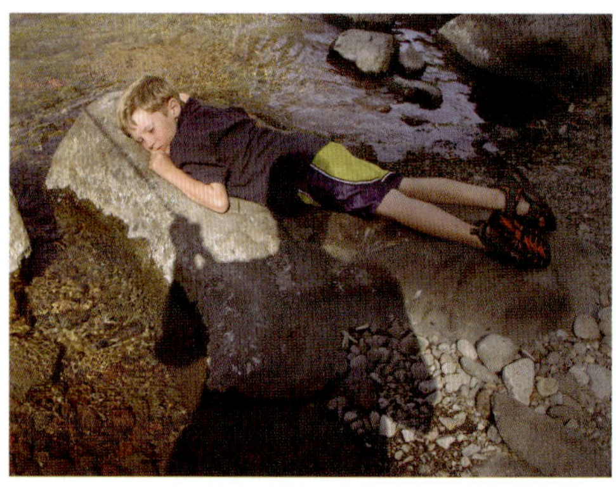

07.22.02

**You pretended to sleep,**
**I pretended to fish**

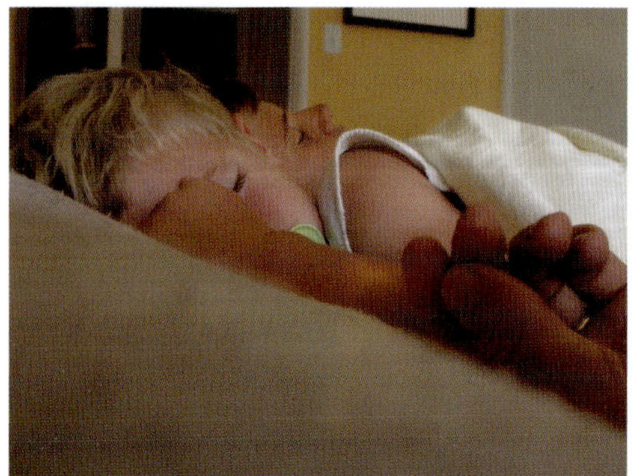

07.23.02

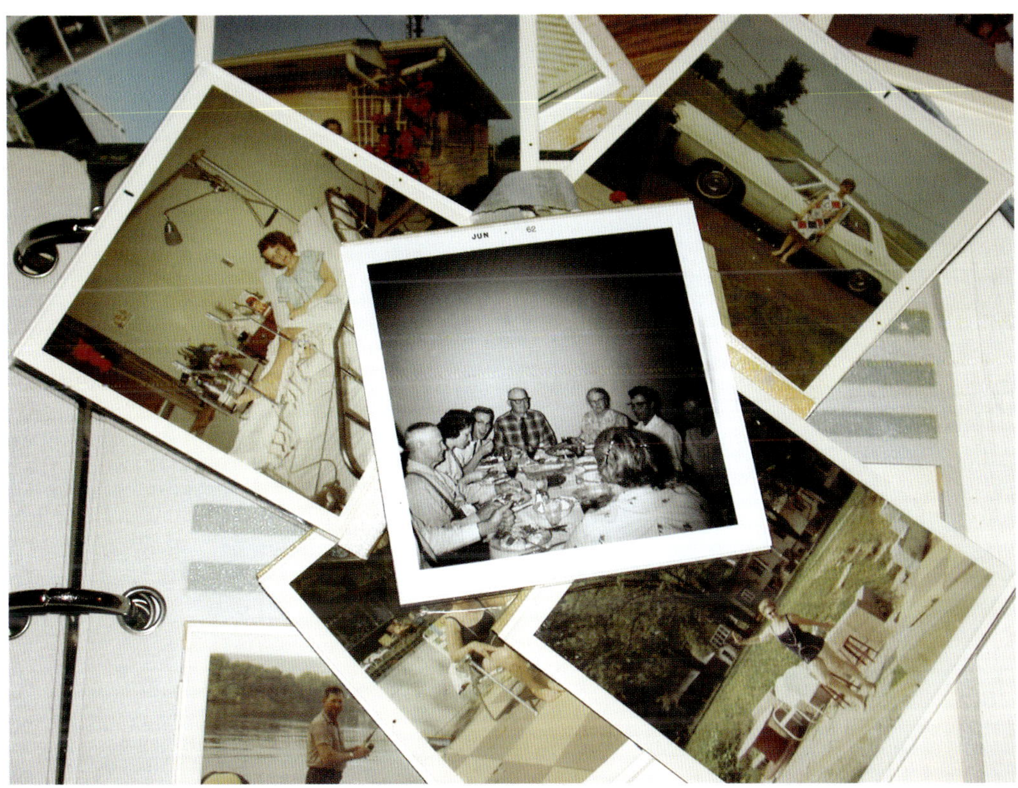


07.24.02

**Photographs of unknown people culled from inherited albums**

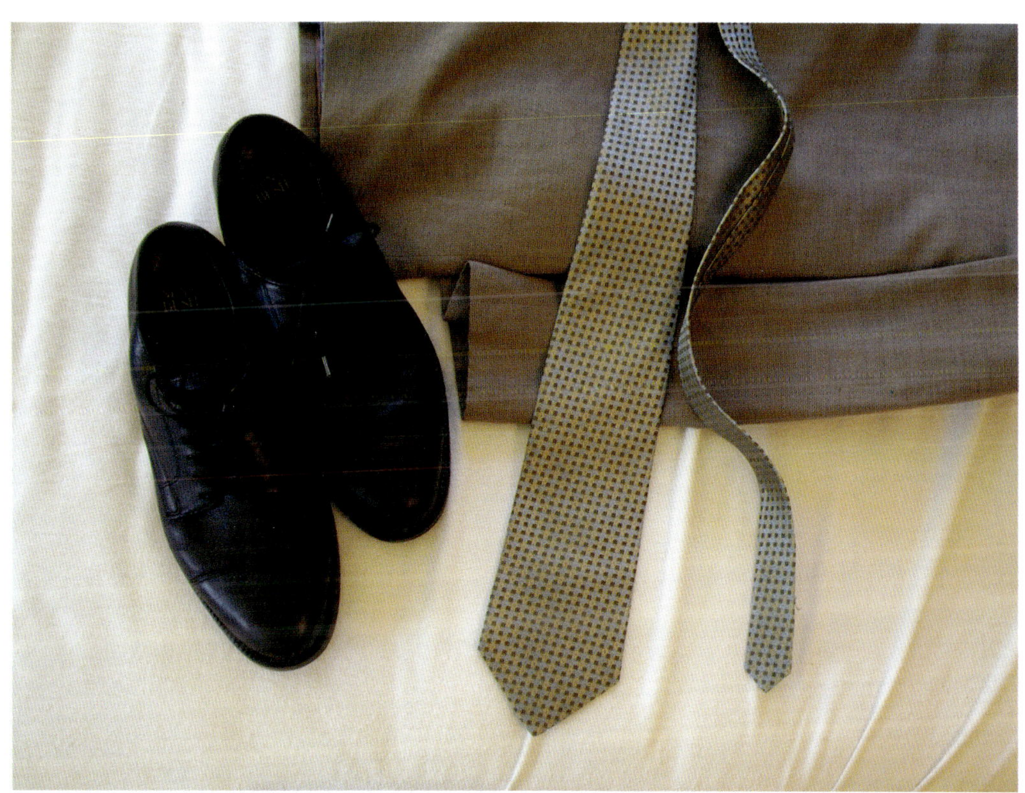

07.25.02

**New tie purchased for a colleague's funeral (cancer)**

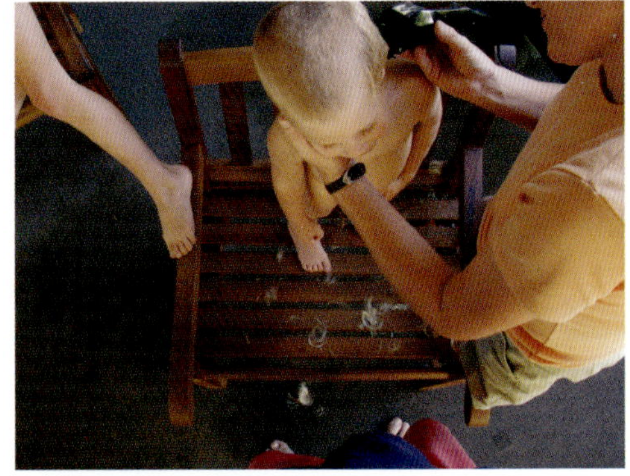

07.26.02

**Summer haircut**

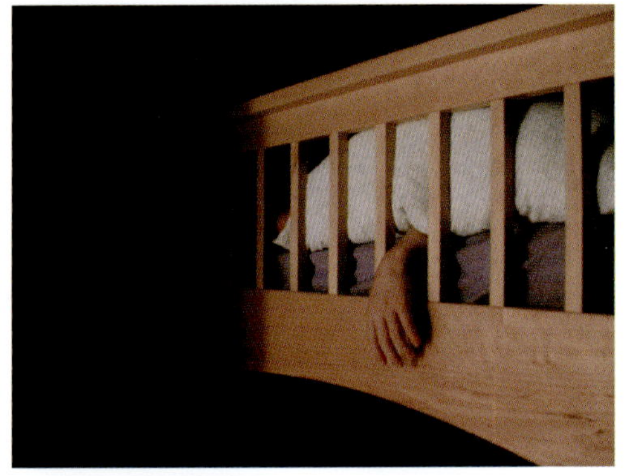

07.27.02

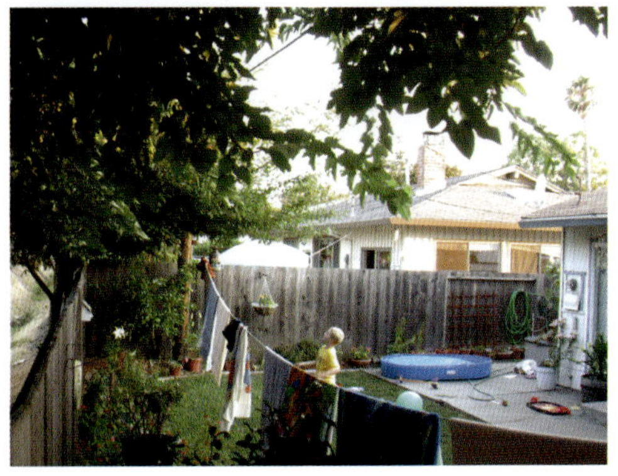

07.28.02

**My brother's backyard**

07.29.02

**On the road**

**near Zamora, CA**

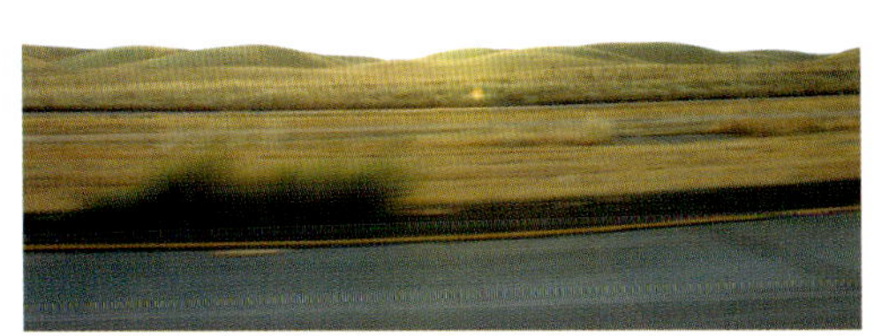

07.30.02

07.31.02

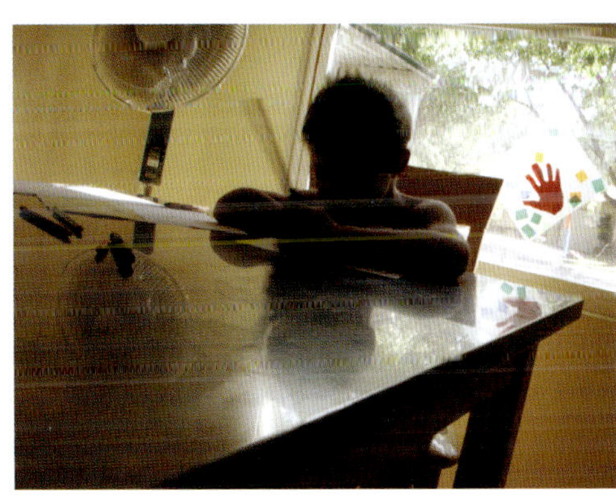

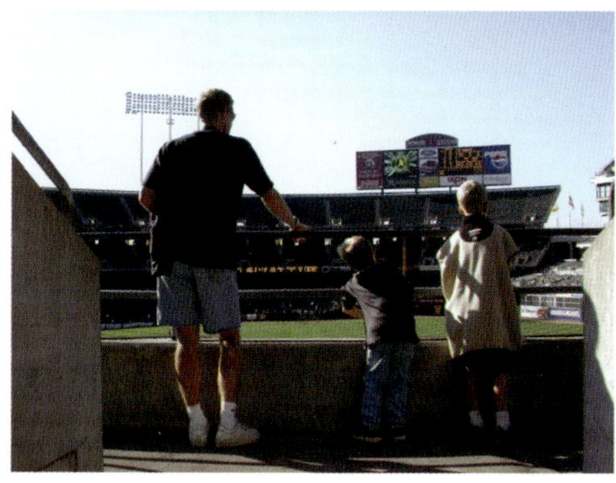

08.01.02

**With my brother and our sons: watching a high school classmate, now in the majors**

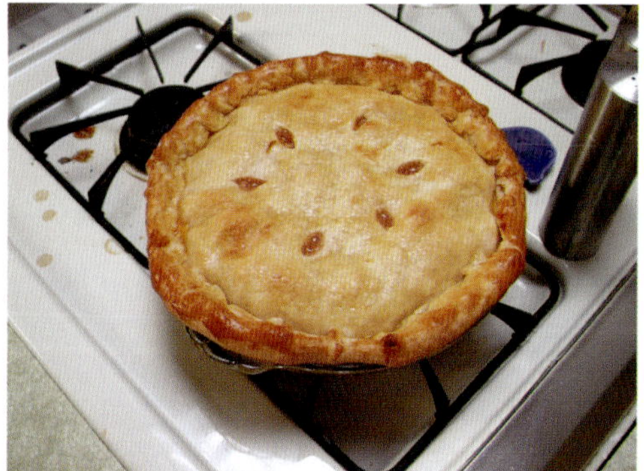

08.02.02

**Peach**

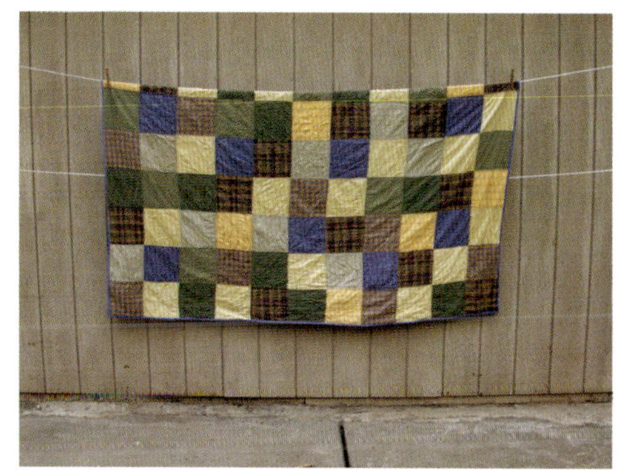

08.03.02

**New summer quilt**

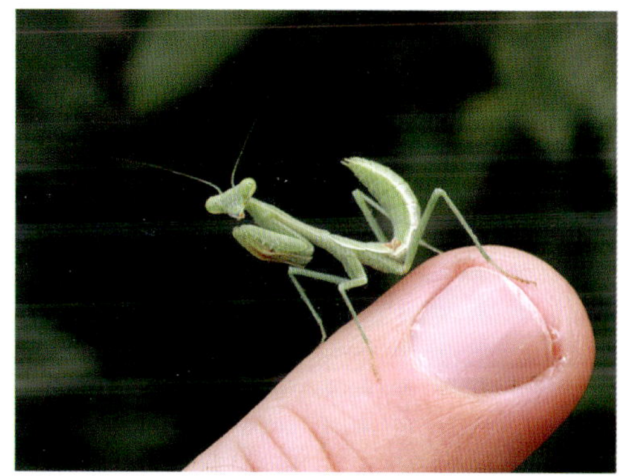

08.04.02

**From the gardenia just outside our bedroom window**

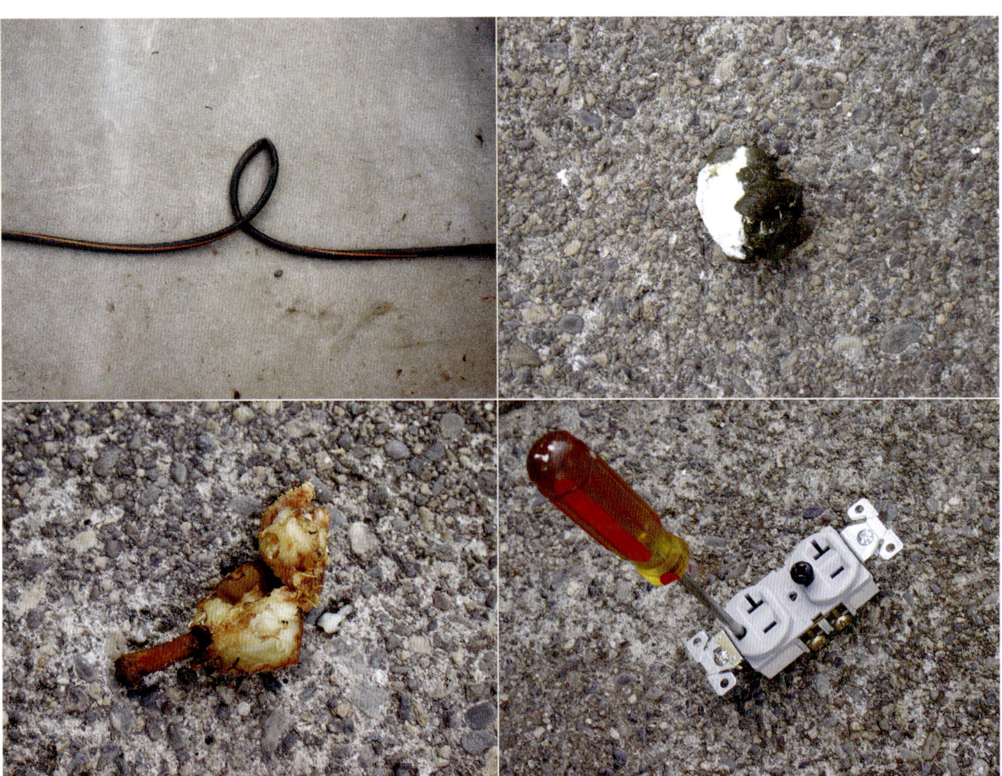

08.05.02

**Backyard sidewalk discoveries: kinked hose, chicken shit, discarded fruit, and child's toy**

08.06.02

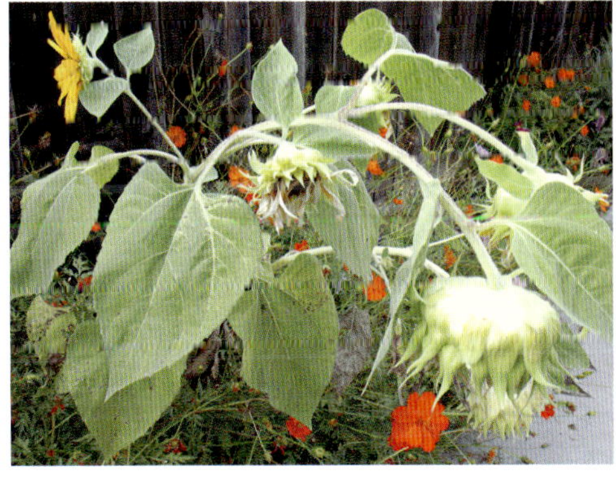

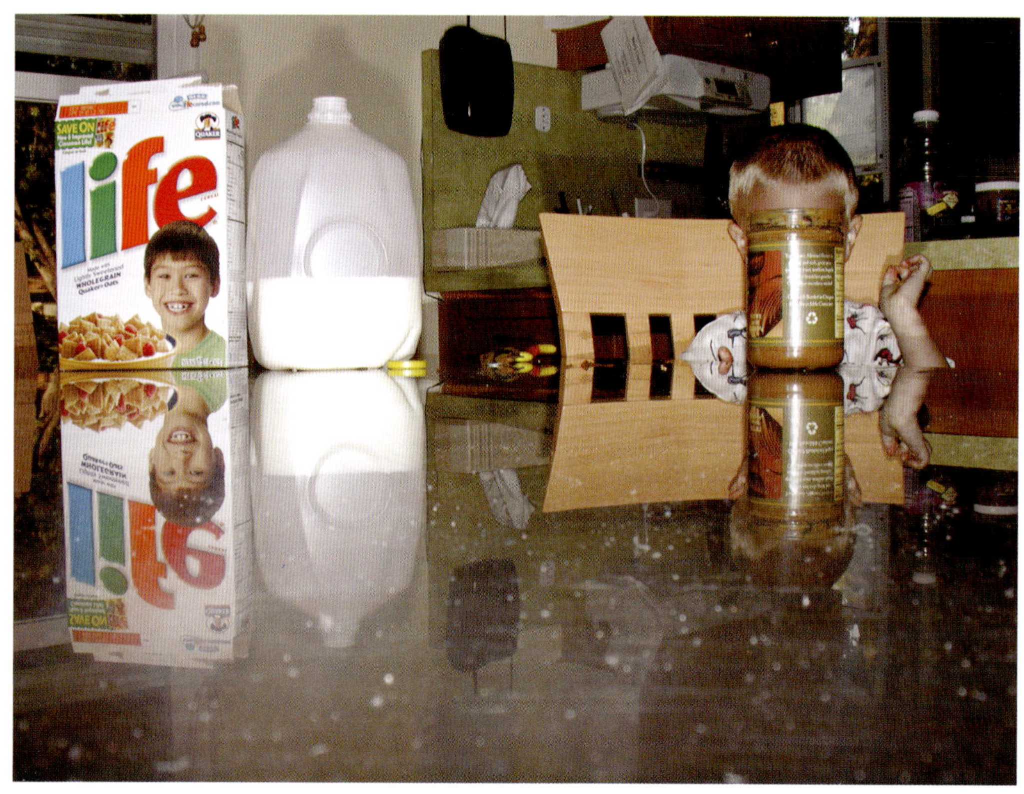


08.07.02

**Life**

08.08.02

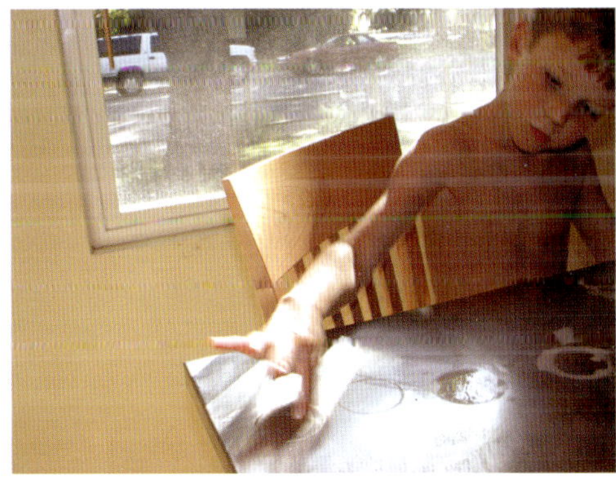

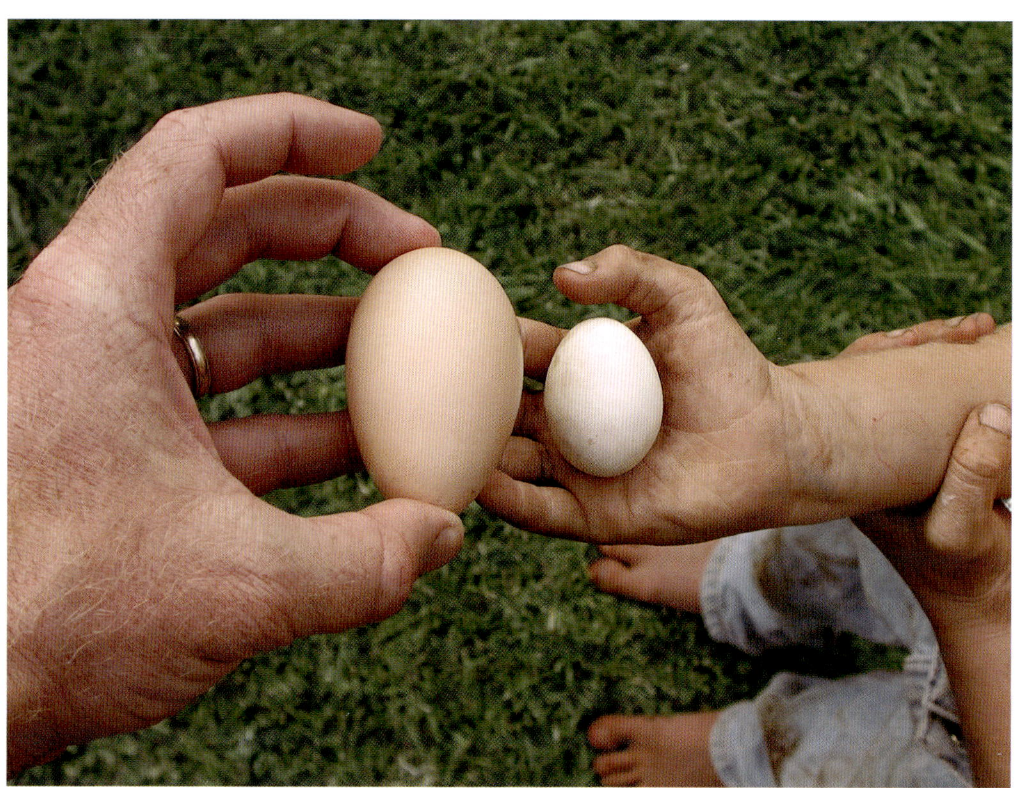

08.09.02

**First and second eggs from our spring chickens**

08.10.02

**Broken camera**

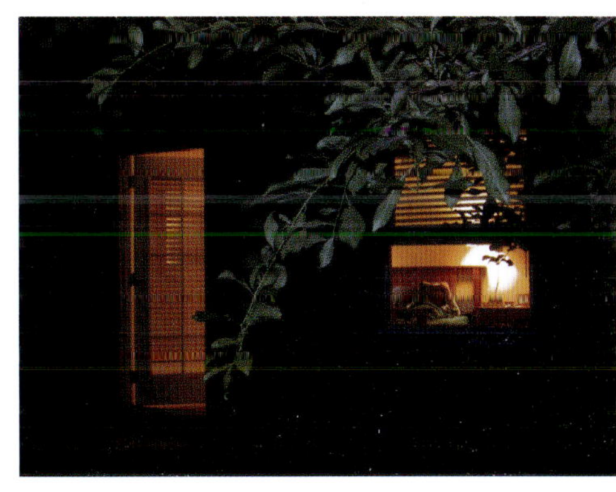

08.11.02

**While you were reading: through the Weeping Santa Rosa Plum**

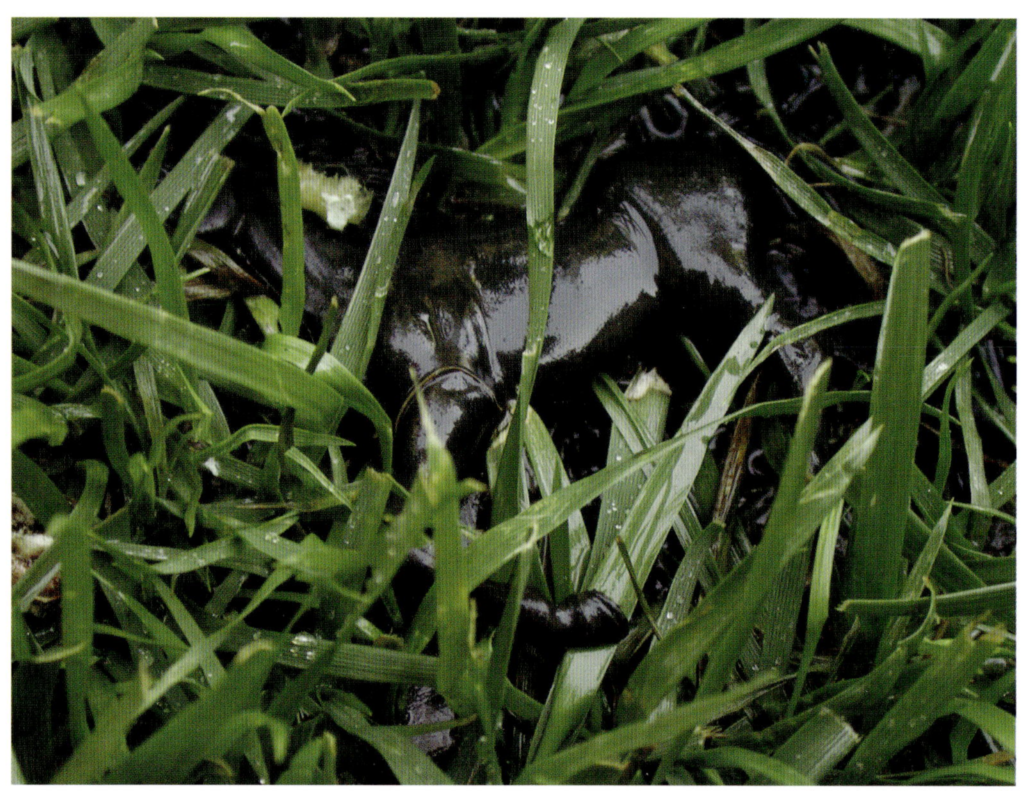

08.12.02

**A black stallion**

08.13.02

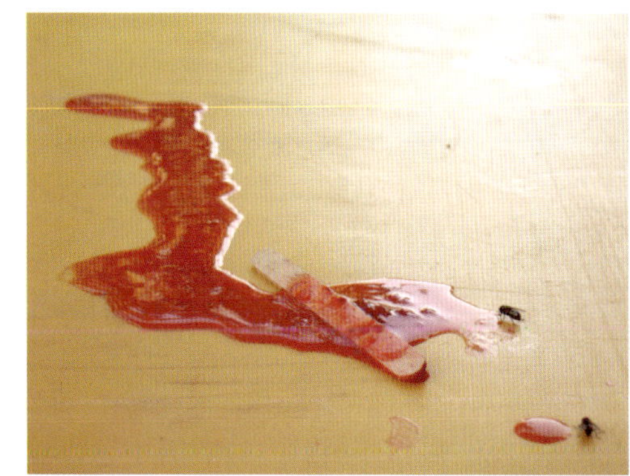

08.14.02

**Their secret stash**

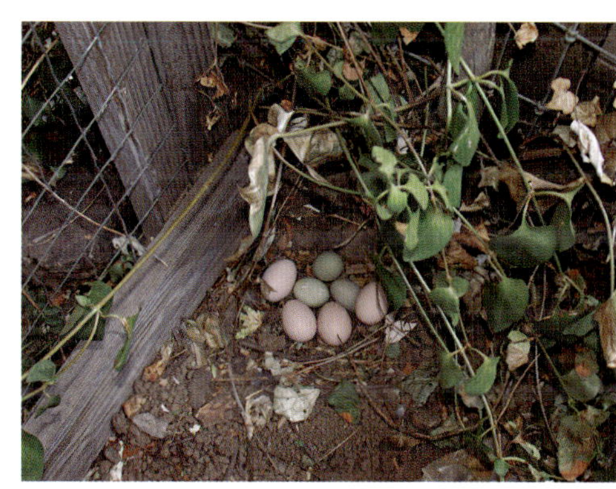

08.15.02

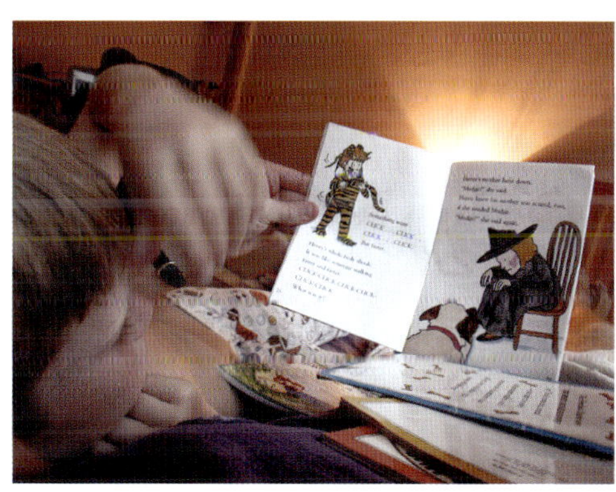

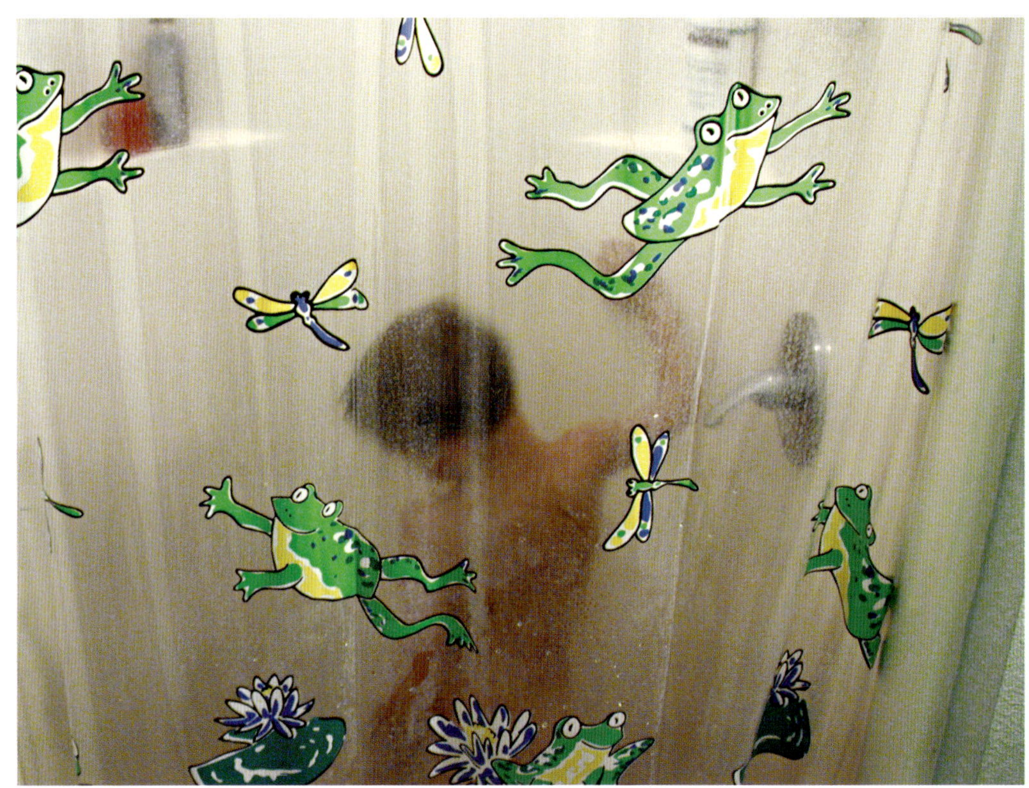

08.16.02

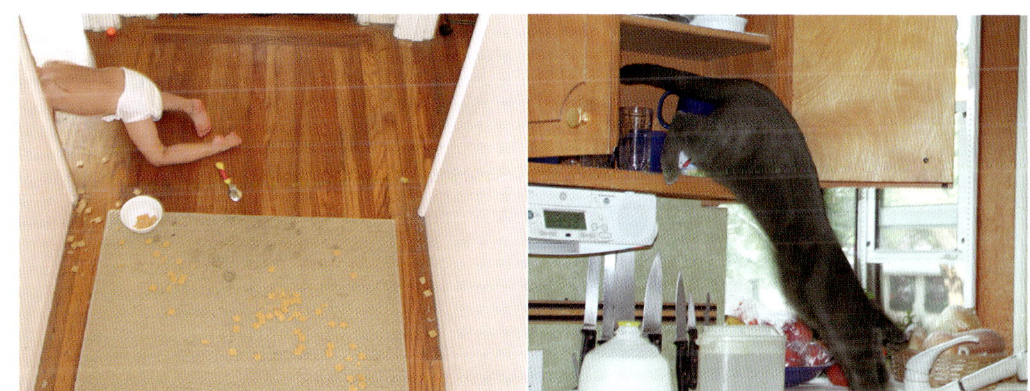

08.17.02

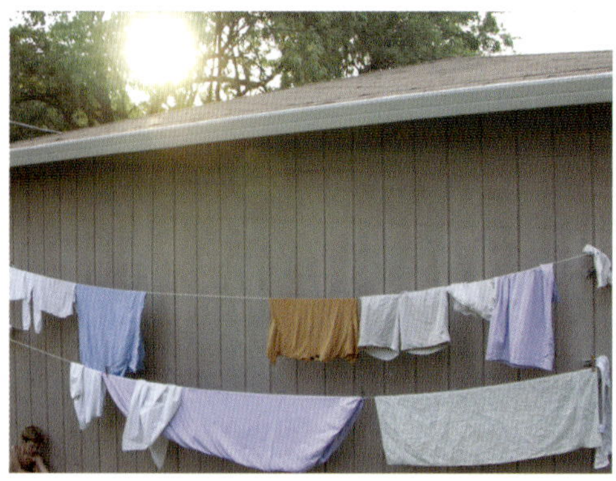

08.18.02

**Sunset, Sunday**

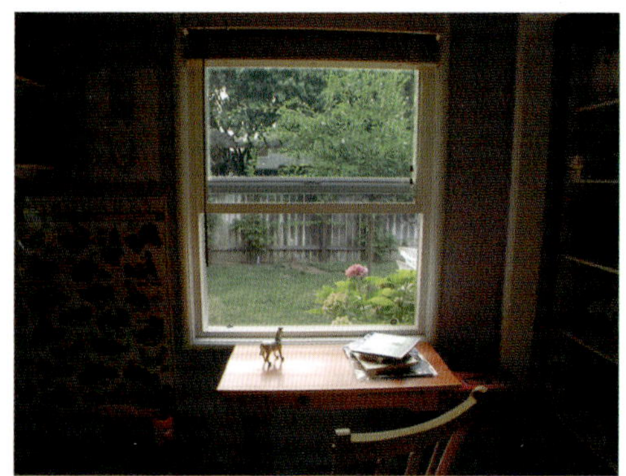

08.19.02

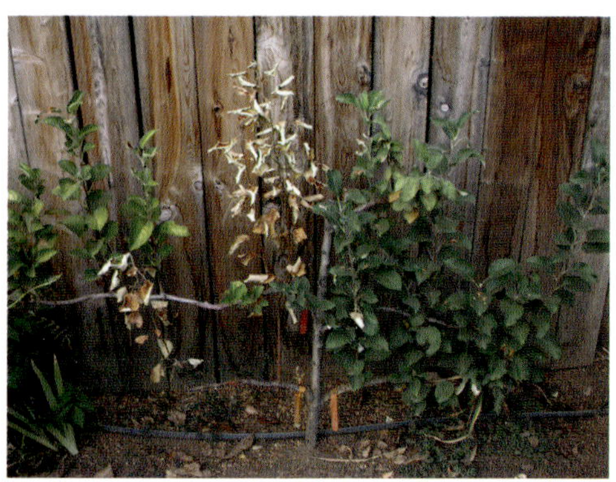

08.20.02

**Our struggling apple tree**

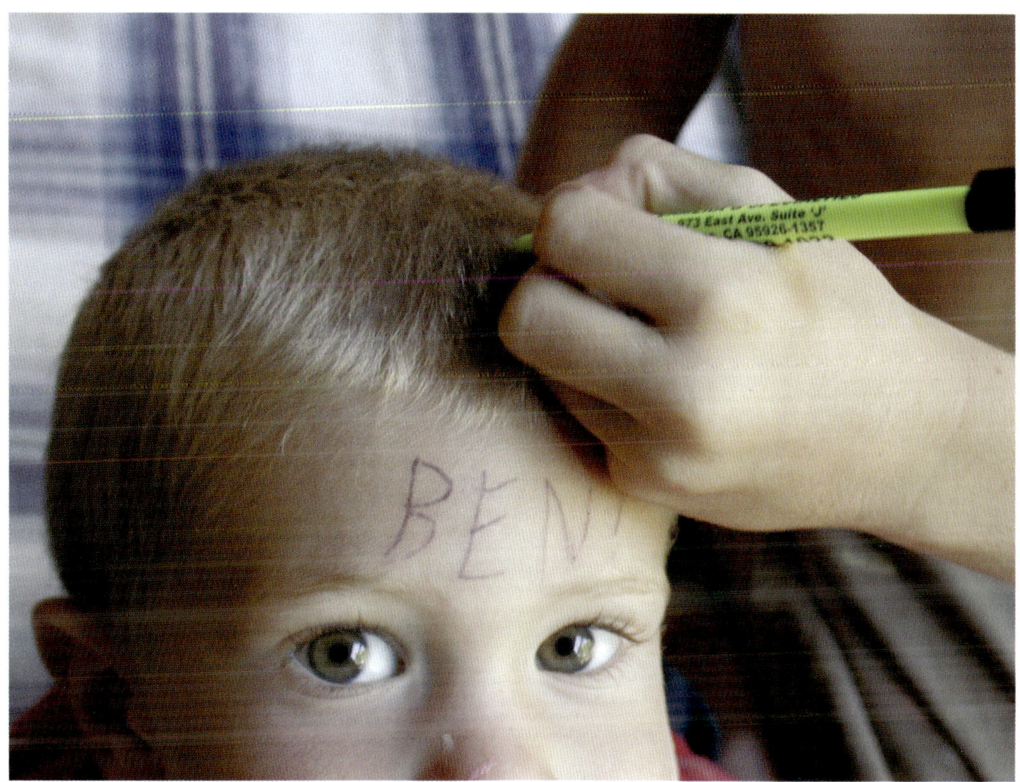


08.21.02

**Ben!**

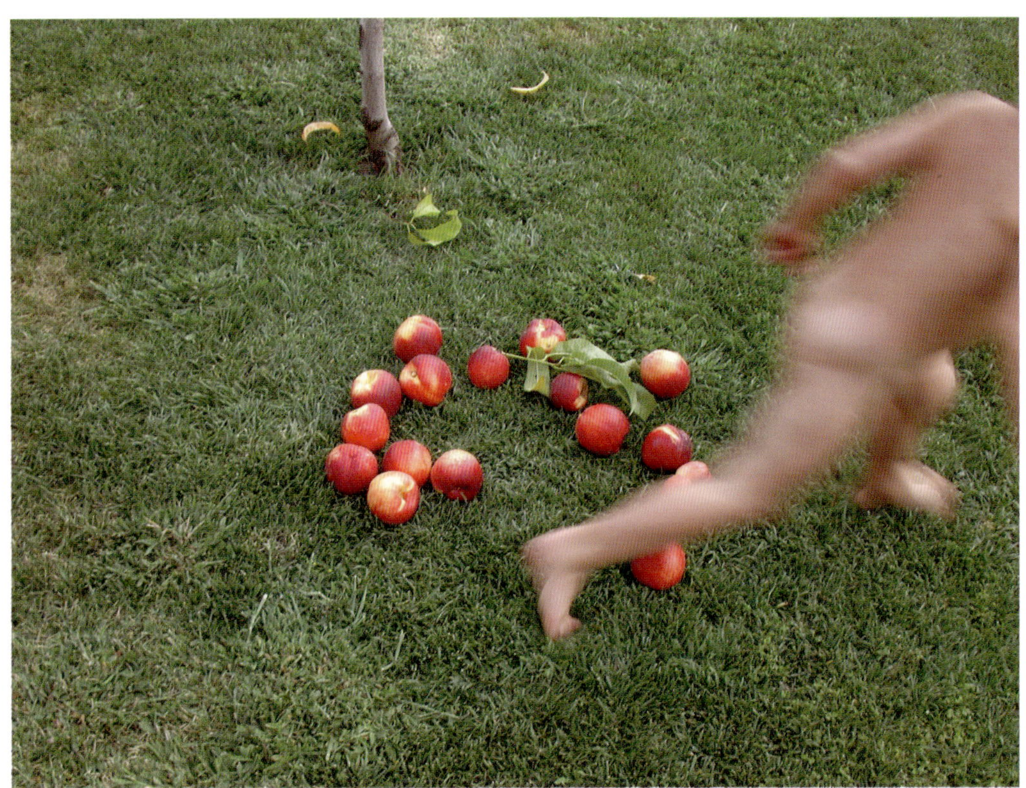

08.22.02

**While contemplating the nectarine harvest**

08.23.02

**Backyard moonrise**

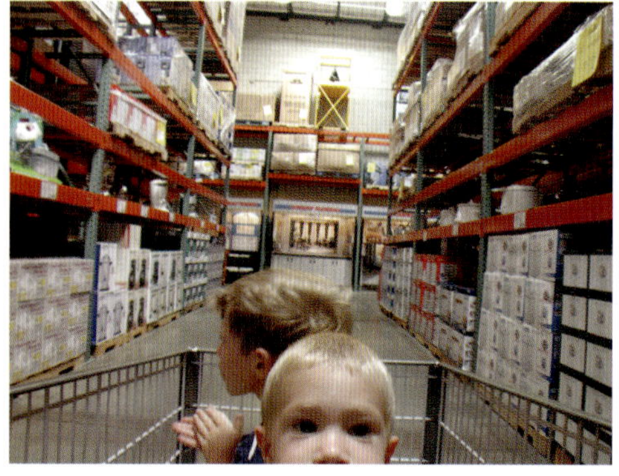

08.24.02

**On a trip to Costco**

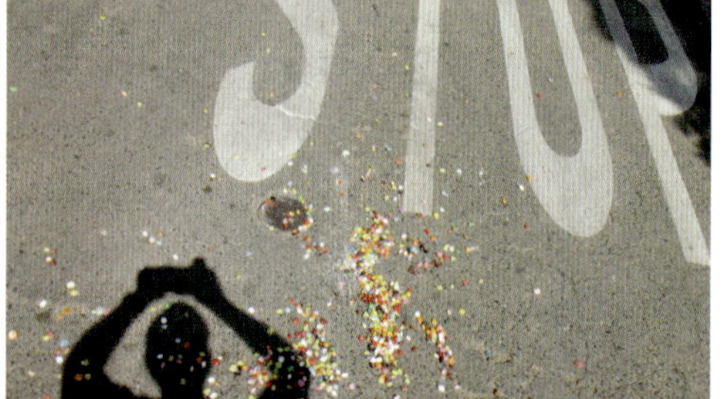

08.25.02

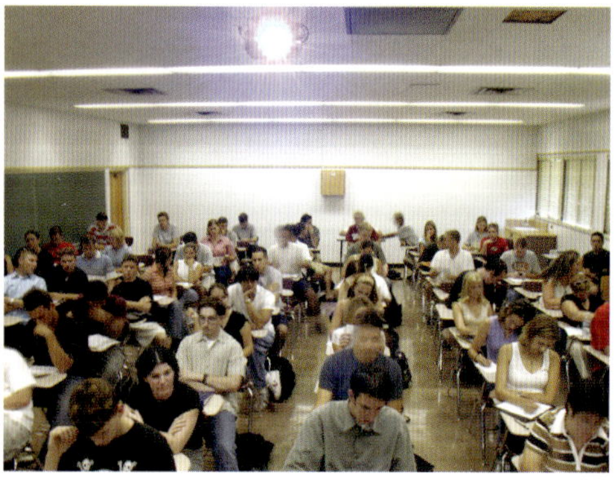

08.26.02

**My day job: first class**

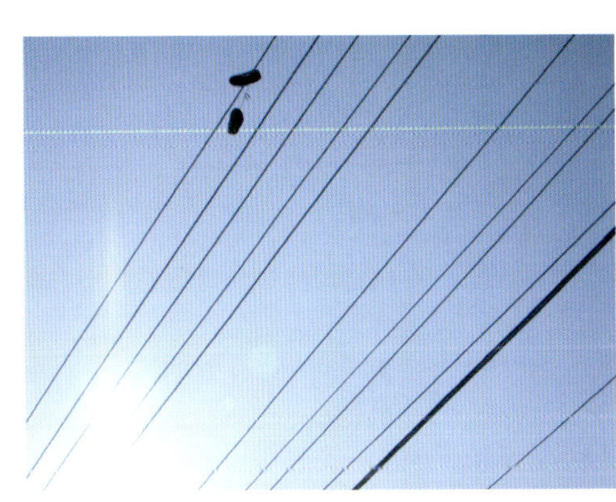
08.27.02

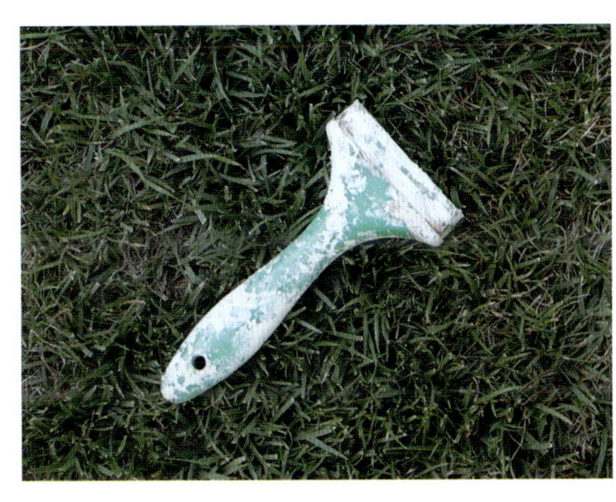
08.28.02

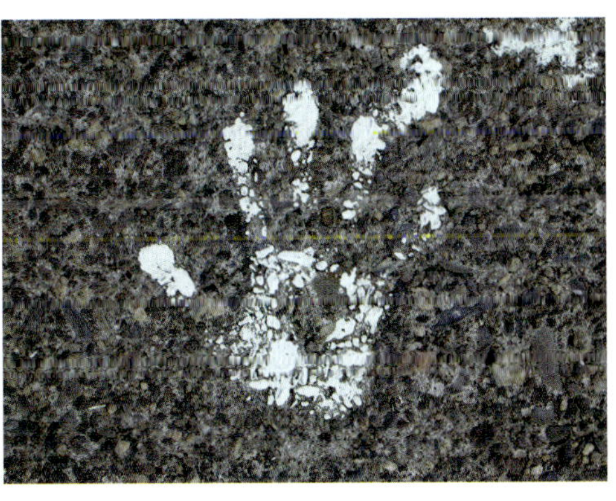
08.29.02

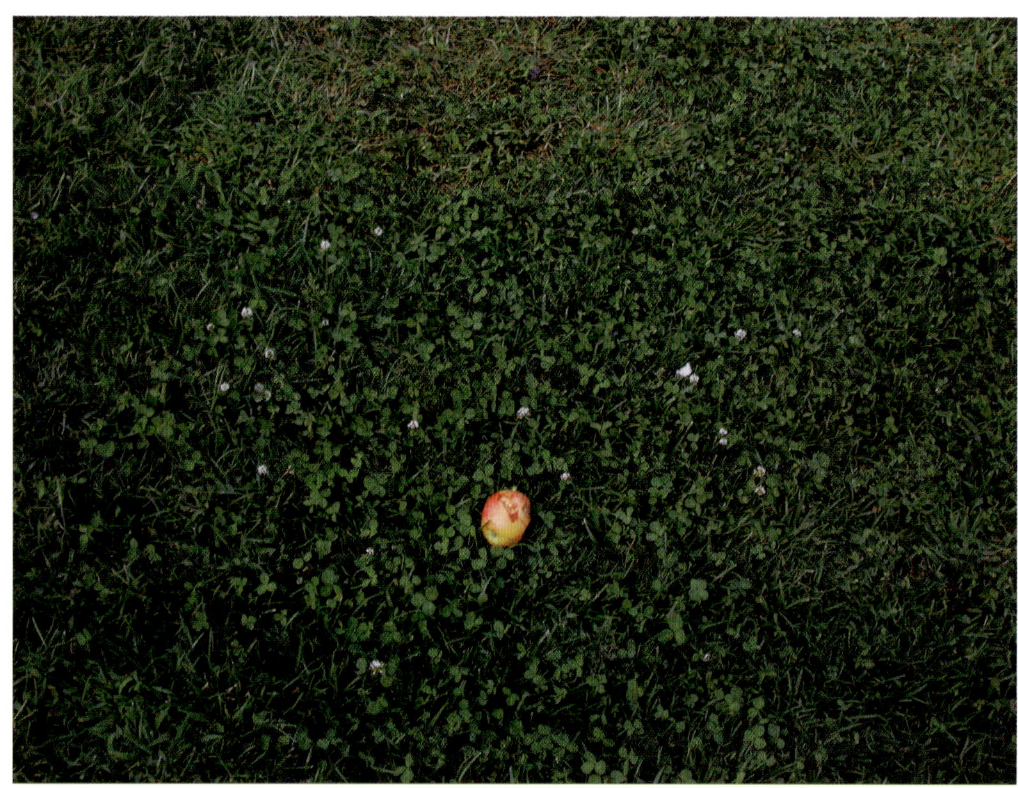

08.30.02

**Our only apple of the season, picked early, then cast aside**

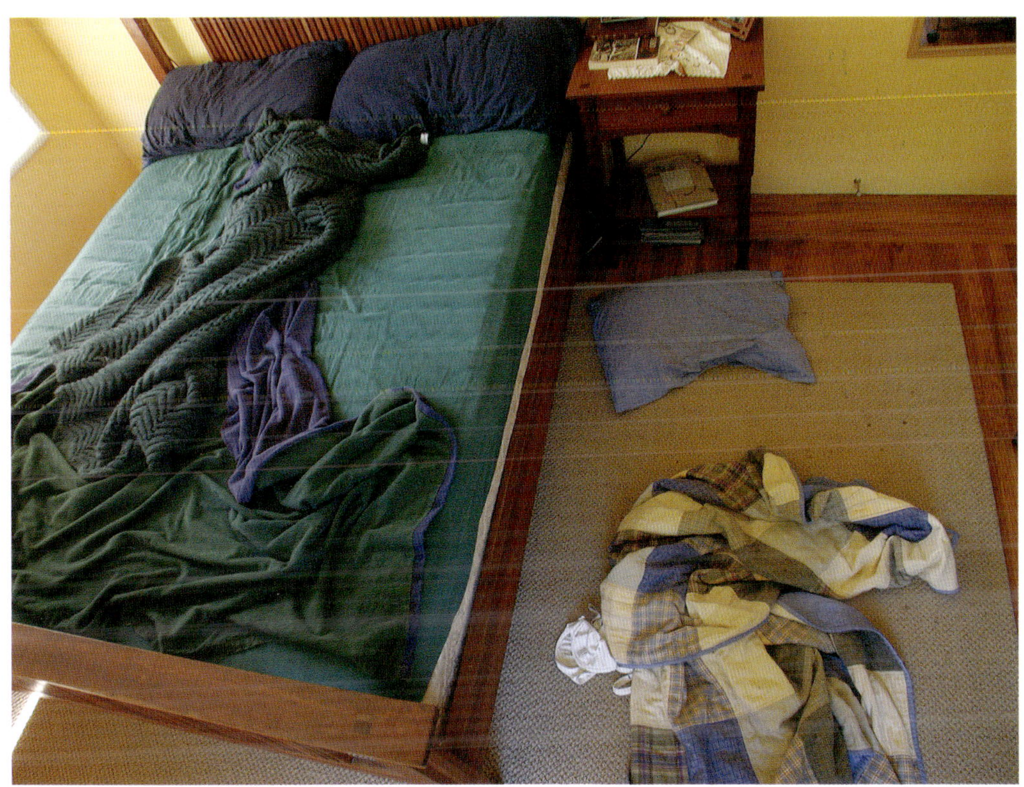

08.31.02

**A fear of dinosaurs**

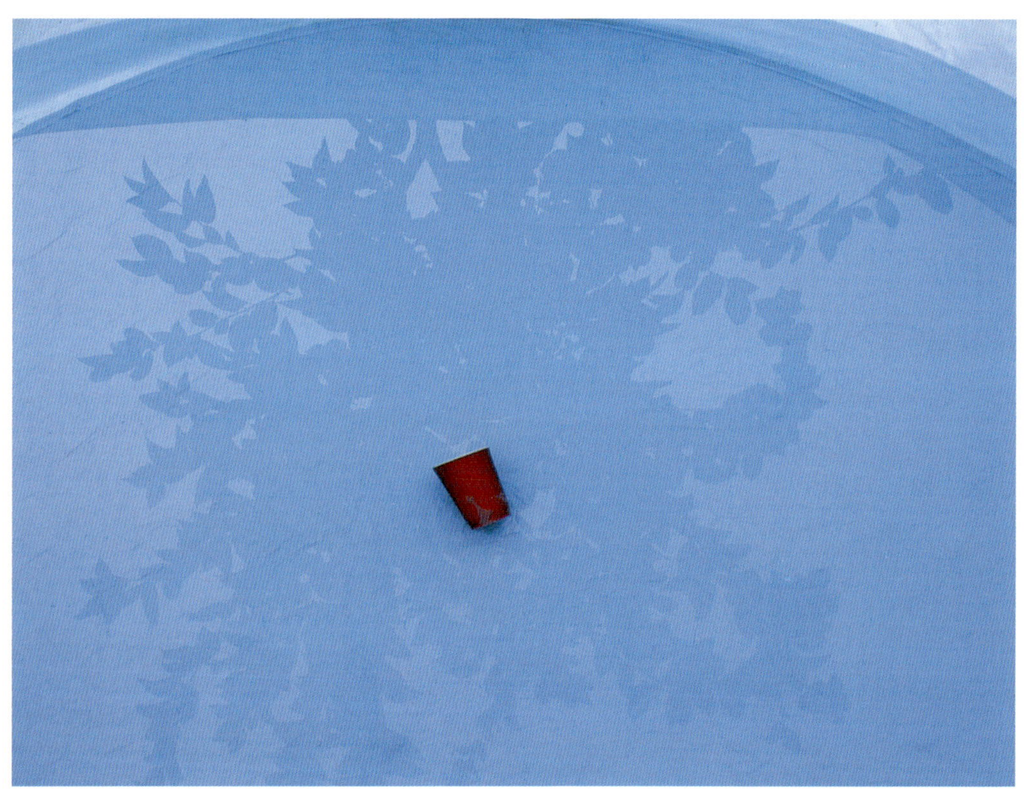

09.01.02

**Persimmon tree in pool at sunrise**

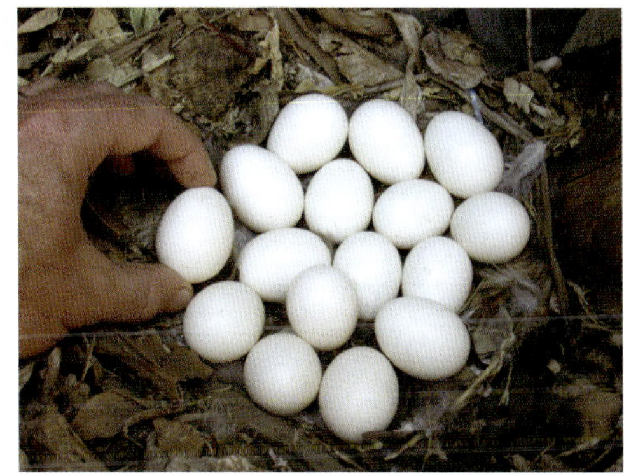

09.02.02

**Another secret stash, more than two weeks old**

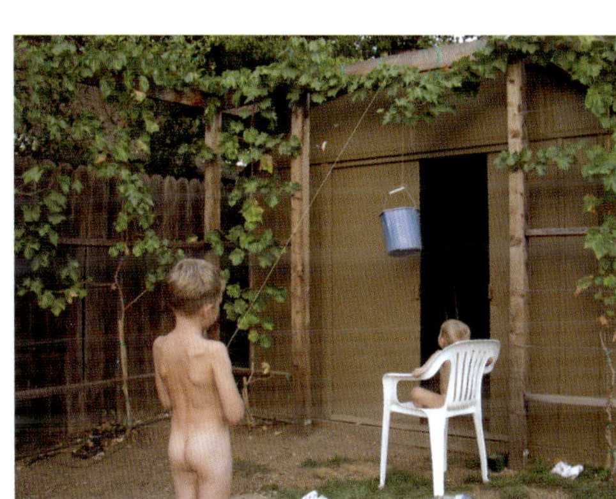

09.03.02

**A curious contraption**

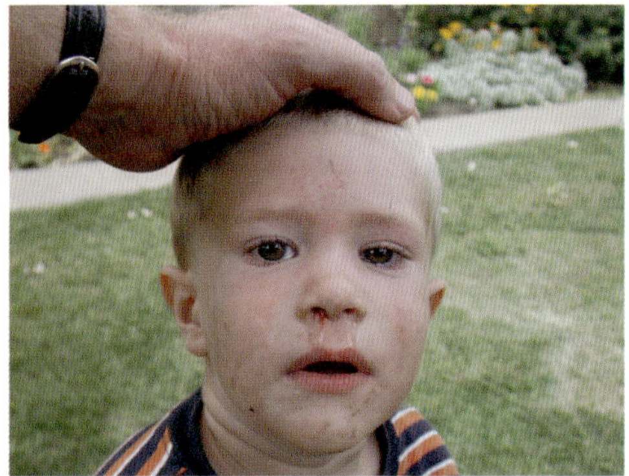

09.04.02

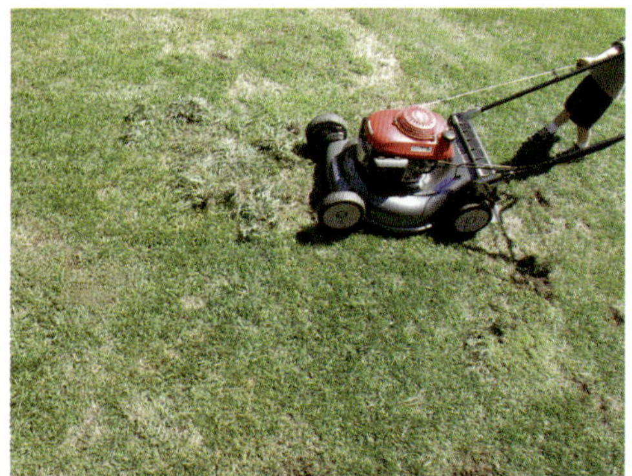

09.05.02

**Brand new mower,**
**same old crappy lawn**

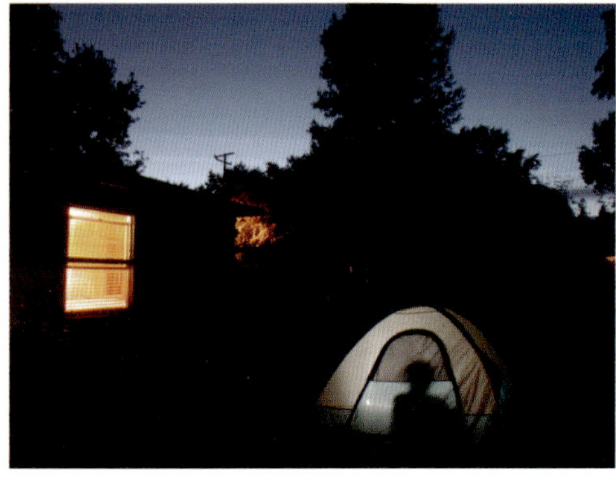

09.06.02

**Friday night,**
**backyard camp**

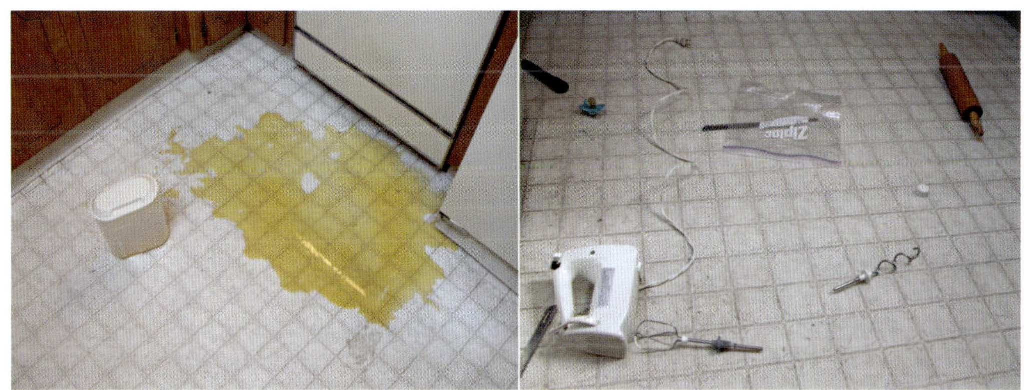

09.07.02

**The kitchen floor at 9:49 AM**

**Same place, same day, an hour and fifteen minutes later**

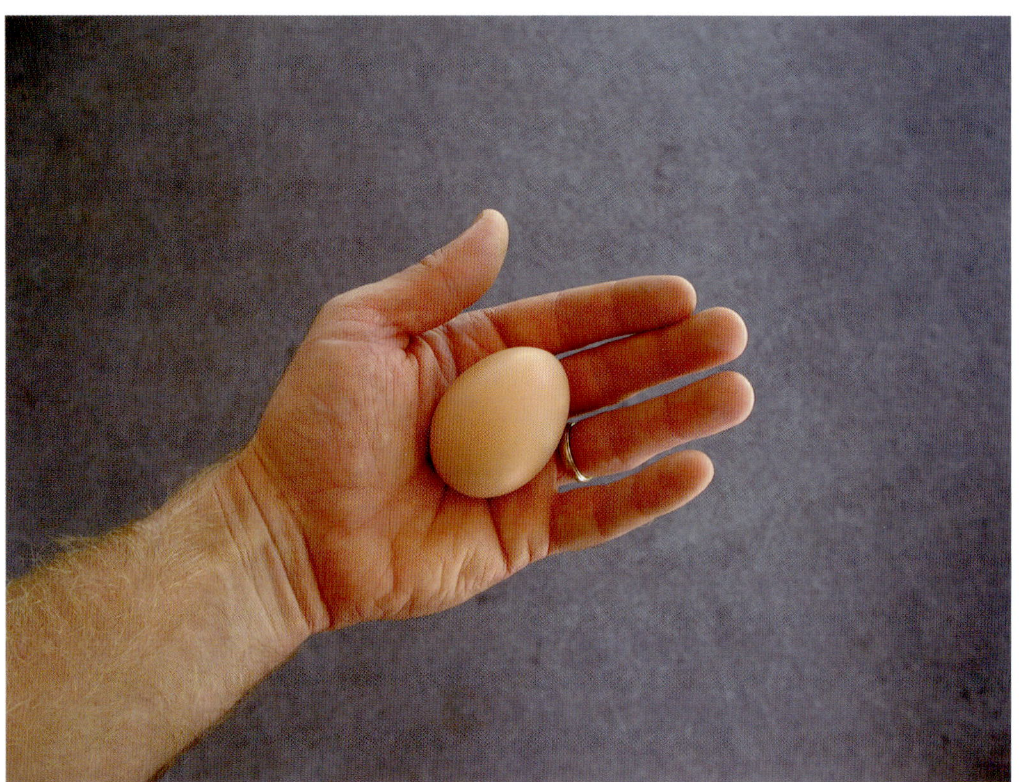

09.08.02

**From "Yellow," our most faithful hen**

09.09.02

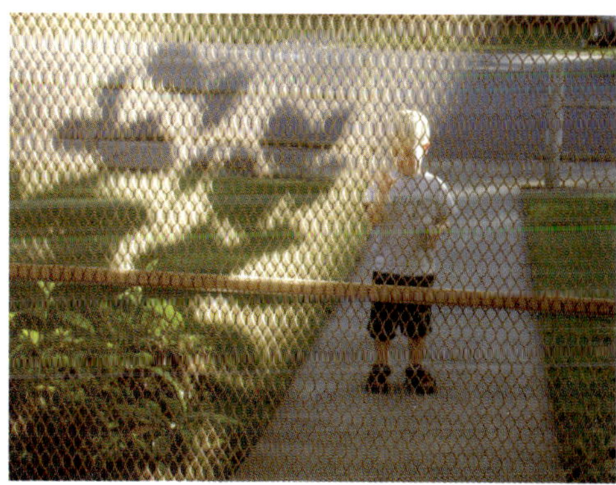

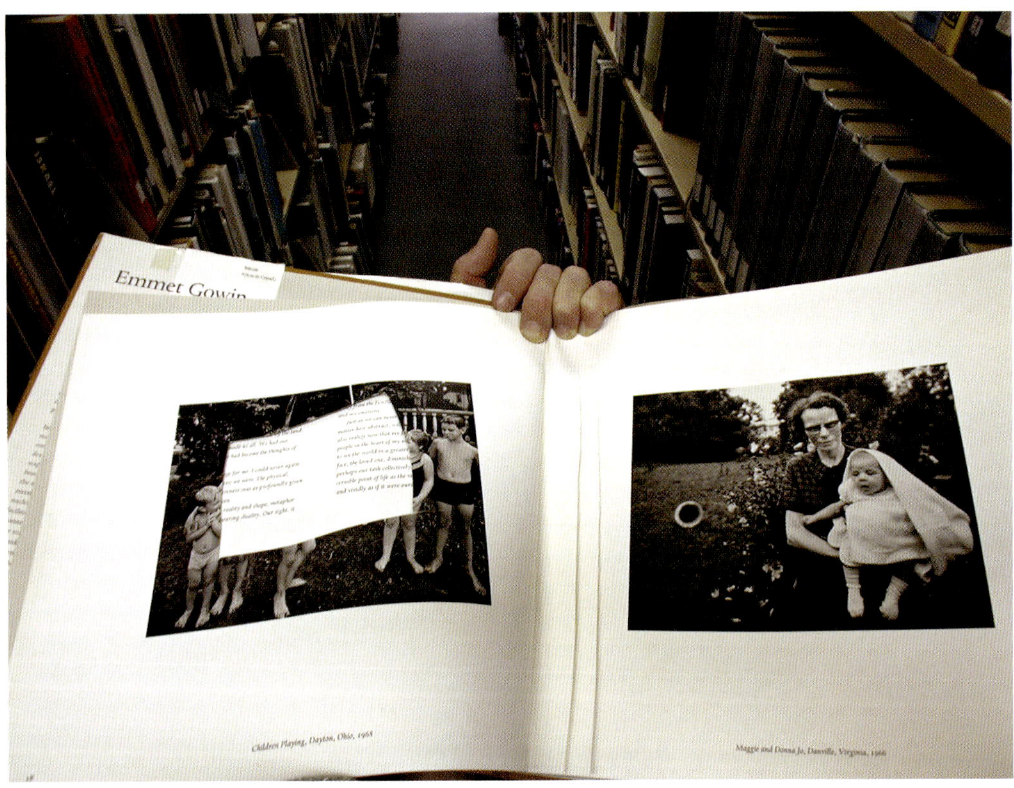


09.10.02

**On a trip to the library: looking for pictures of Emmet Gowin's family**

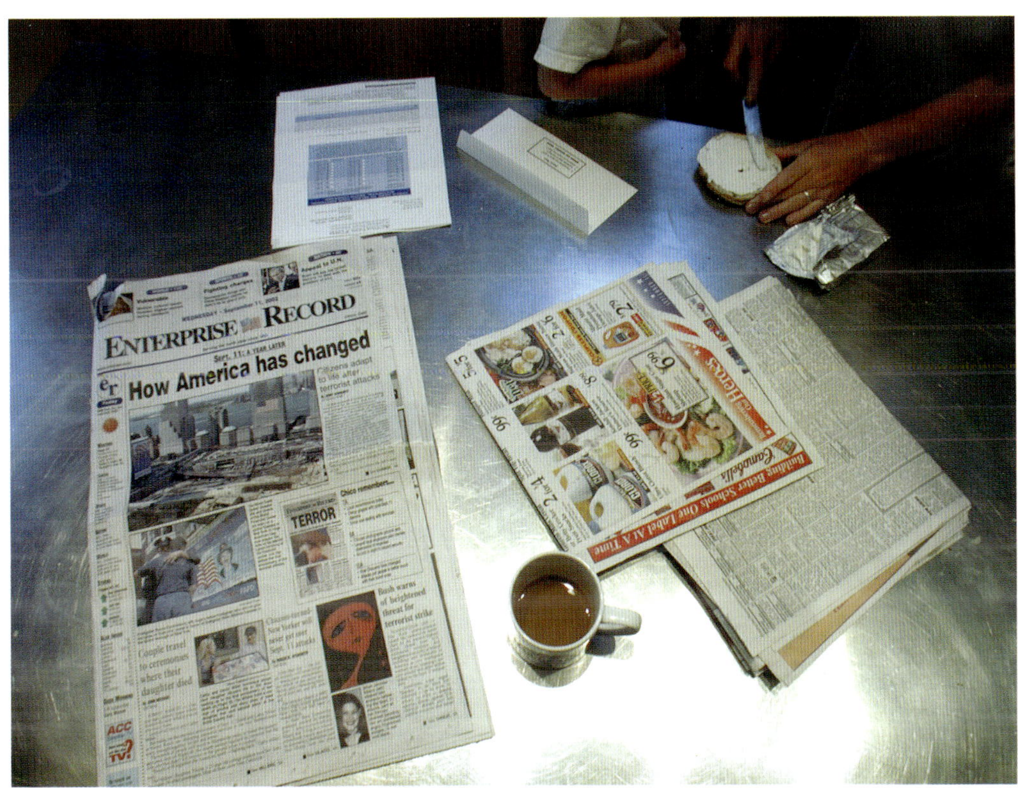


09.11.02

**Contemplating the missing: an ordinary morning exactly one year later (September 11, 2002)**

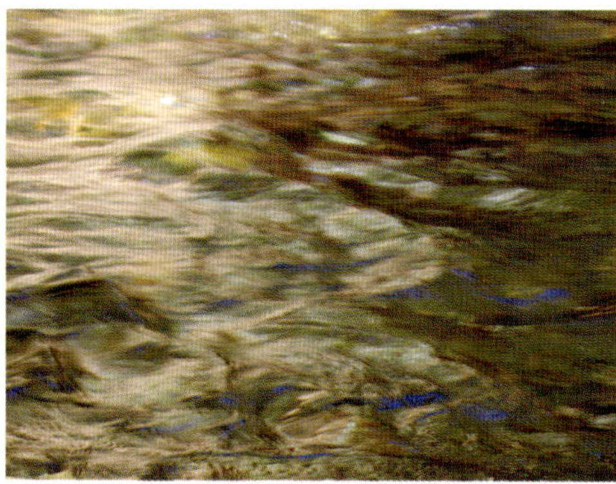

09.12.02
**Chico Creek at noon, reflecting on the events of the year**

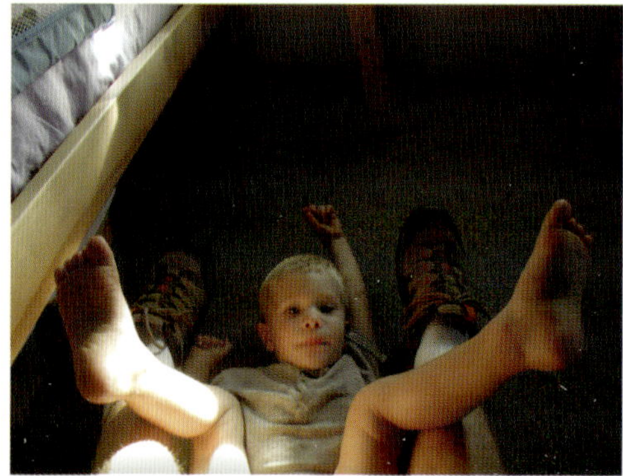

09.13.02
**Diaper change**

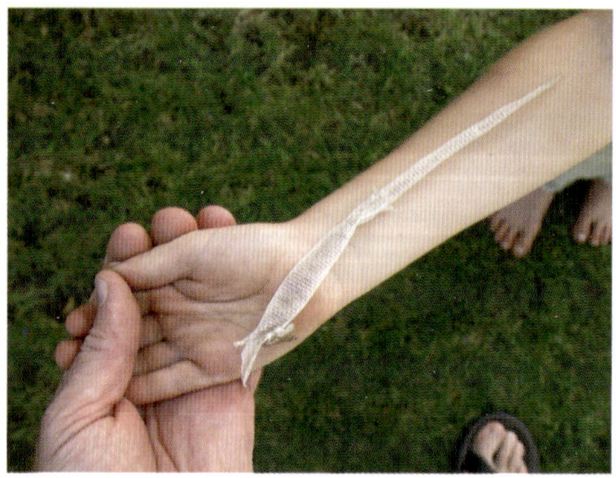

09.14.02
**A perfect lizard skin**

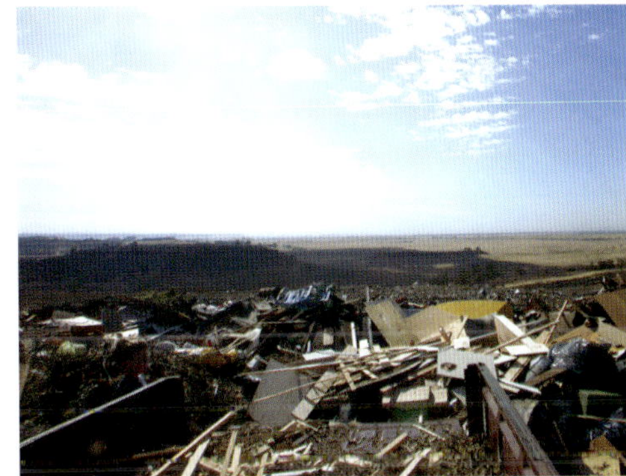

09.15.02

**Our trip to the dump**

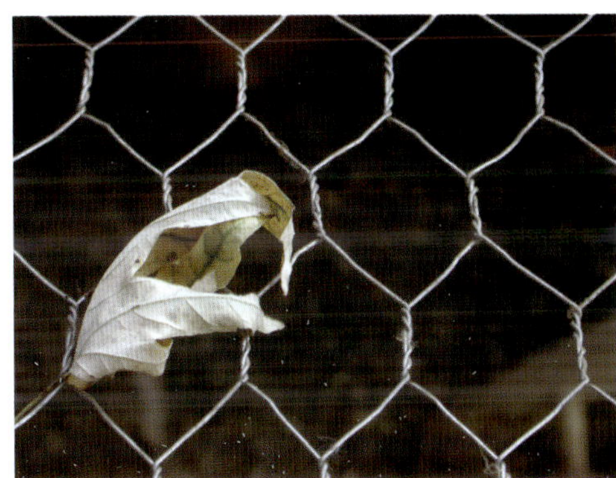

09.16.02

**Autumn comes to the chicken coop**

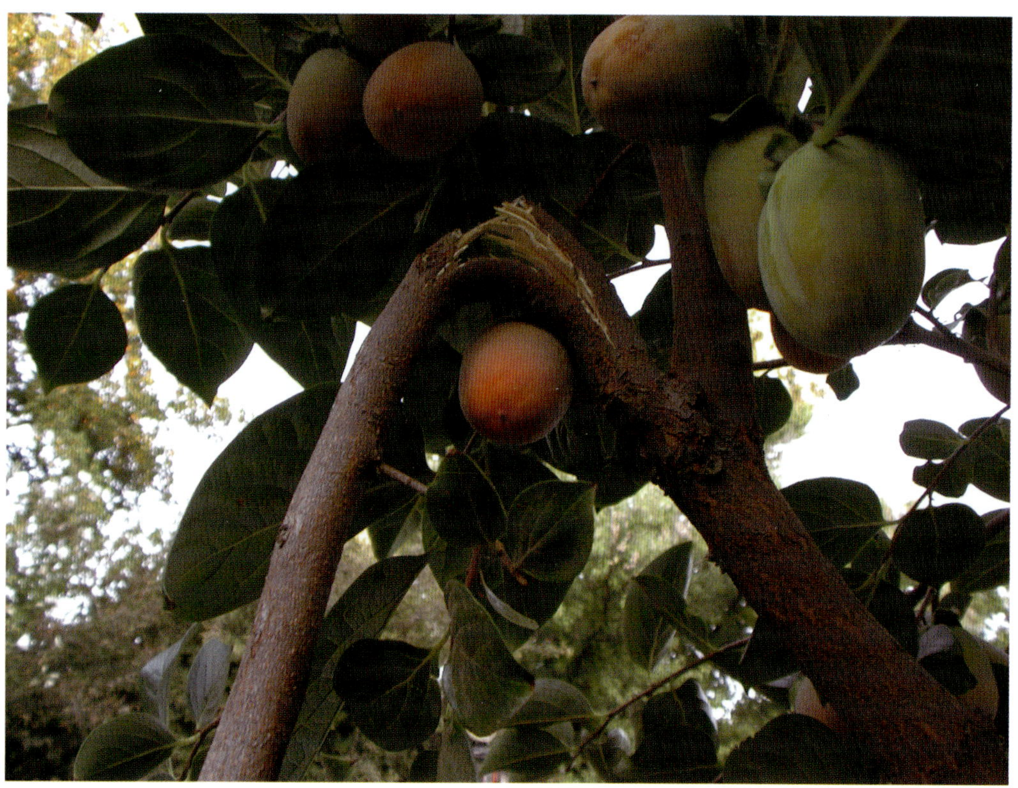

09.17.02

**Too much fruit**

09.18.02
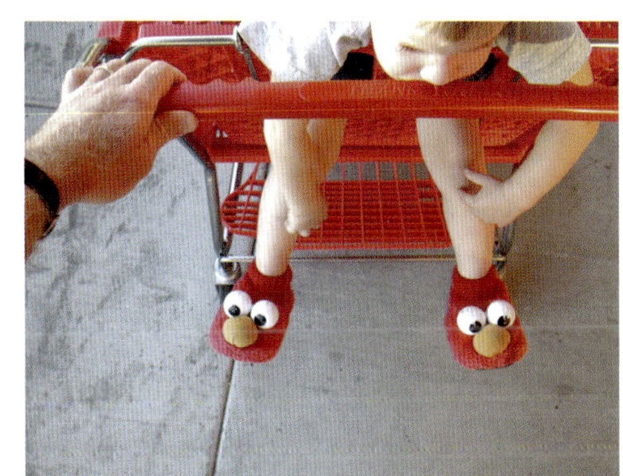

09.19.02
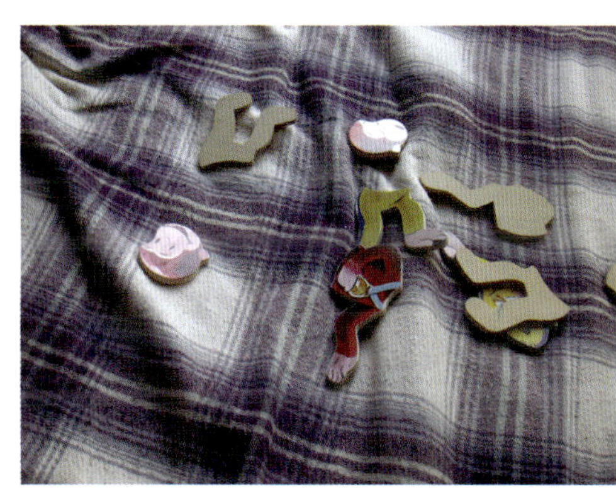

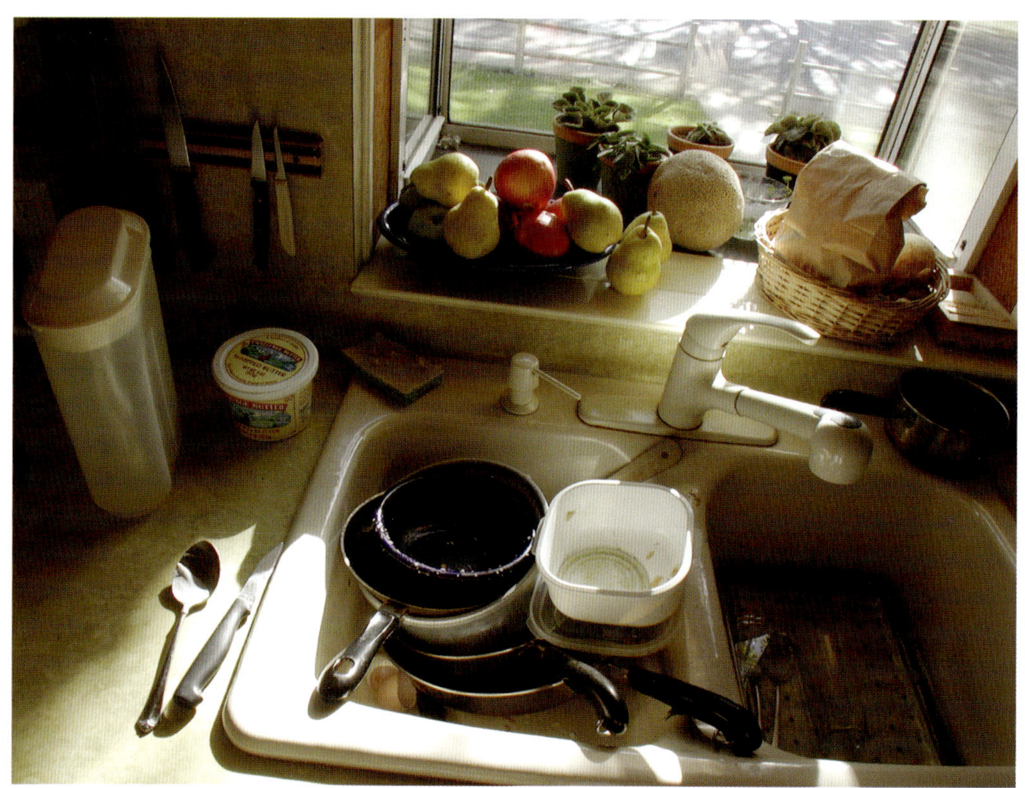

09.20.02

**Still life with fruit**

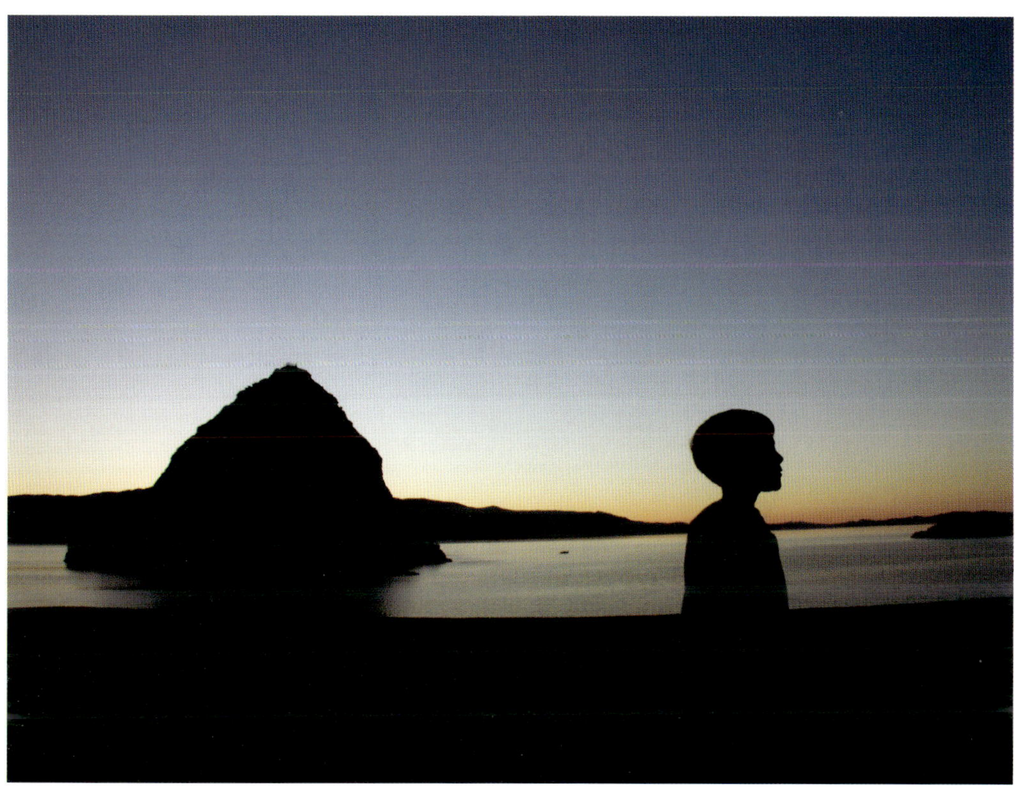

09.21.02

**Last light of the summer: Pyramid Lake, Nevada**

# autumn

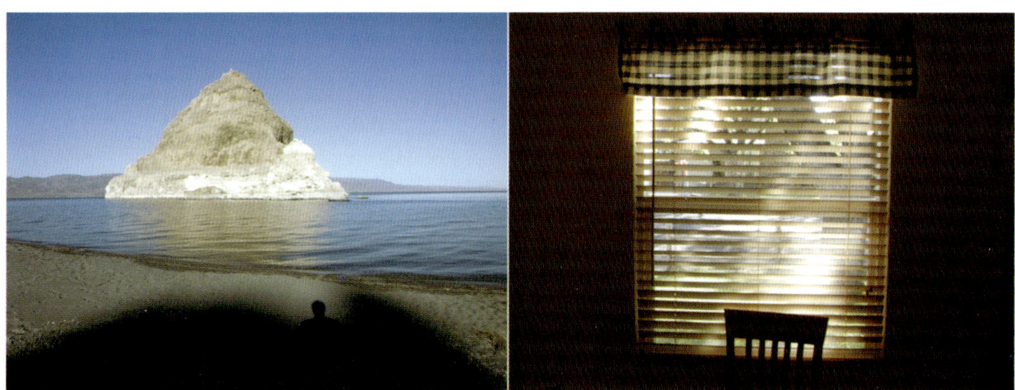

09.22.02

**Autumnal equinox at Pyramid Lake, then back home in Chico**

09.23.02

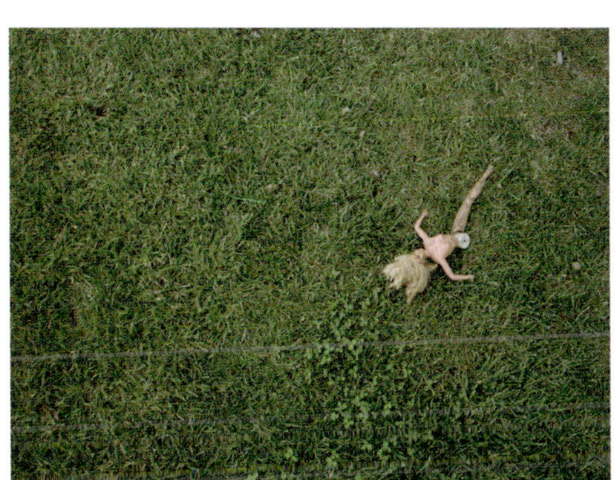

09.24.02

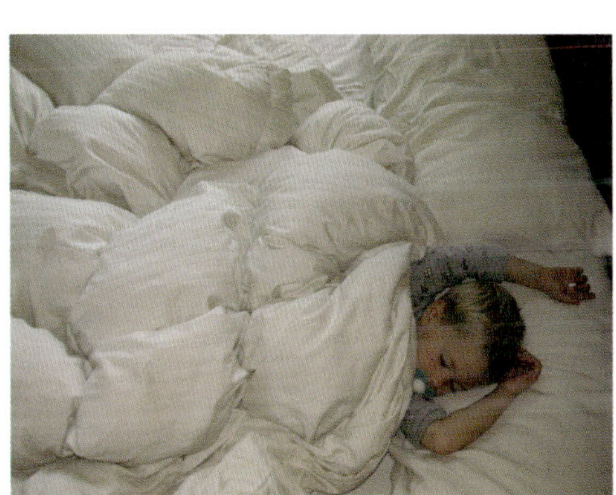

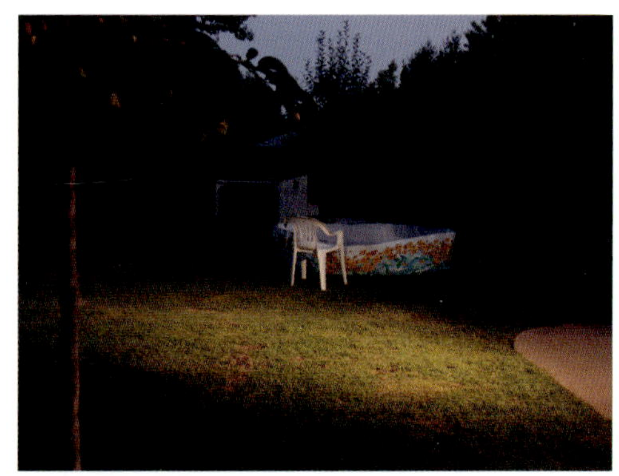

09.25.02

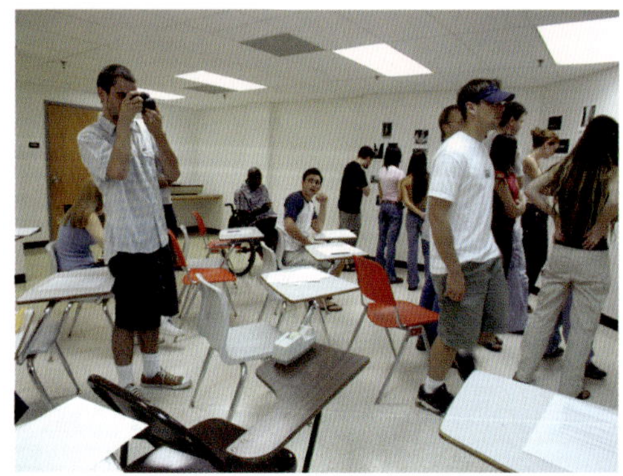

09.26.02

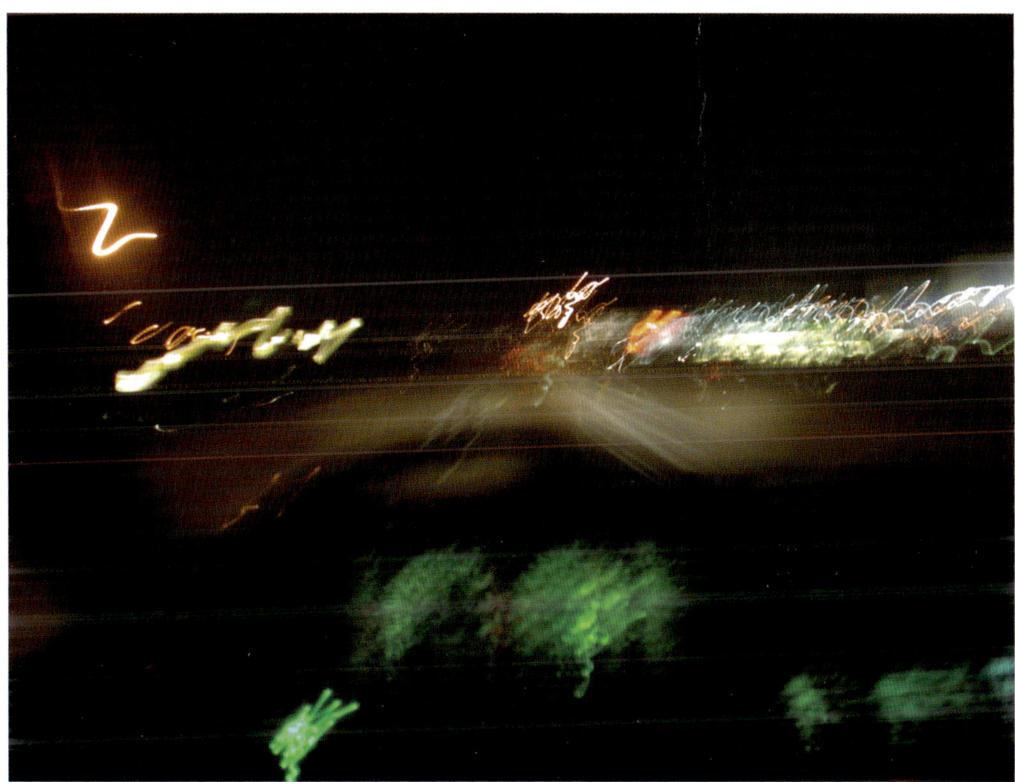

09.27.02

**Late on a Friday, driving myself home from work**

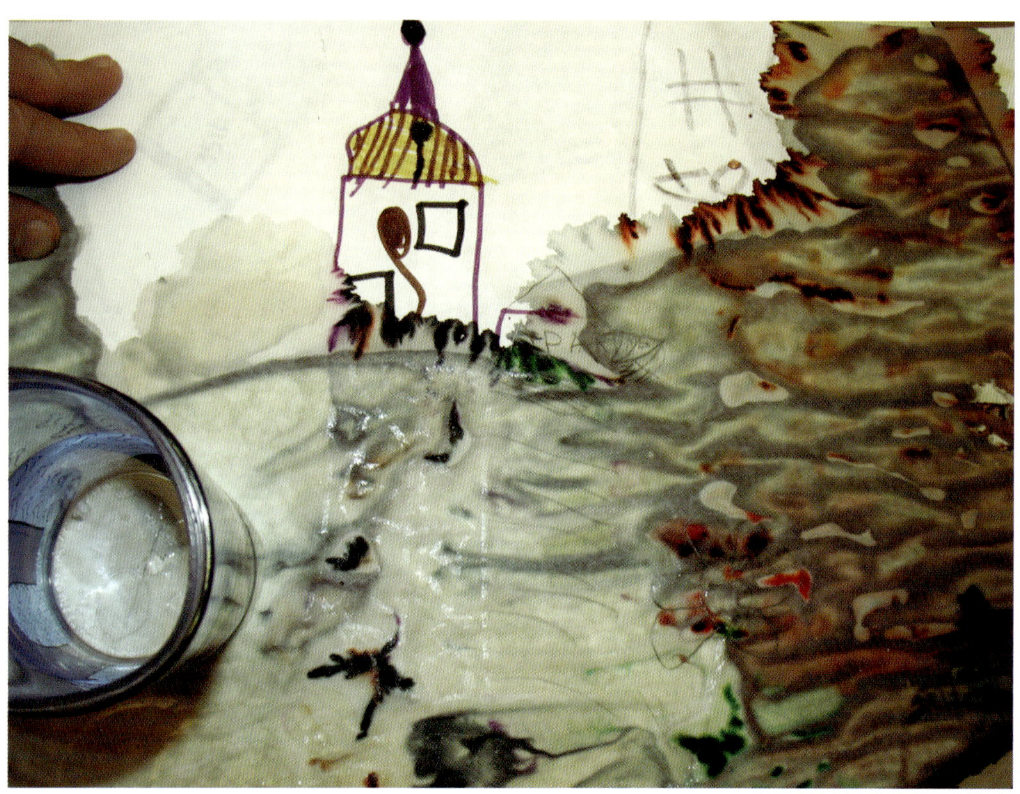

09.28.02

**Another city in ruins**

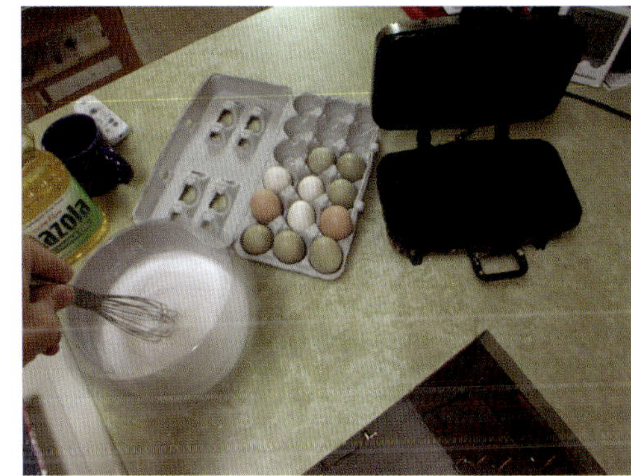

09.29.02

**Free-range waffles**

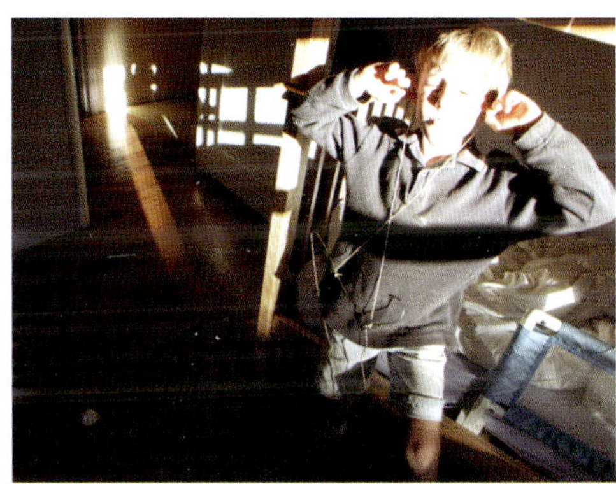

09.30.02

**Curious contraption #2:**
**clothes-hanger as tuning fork**

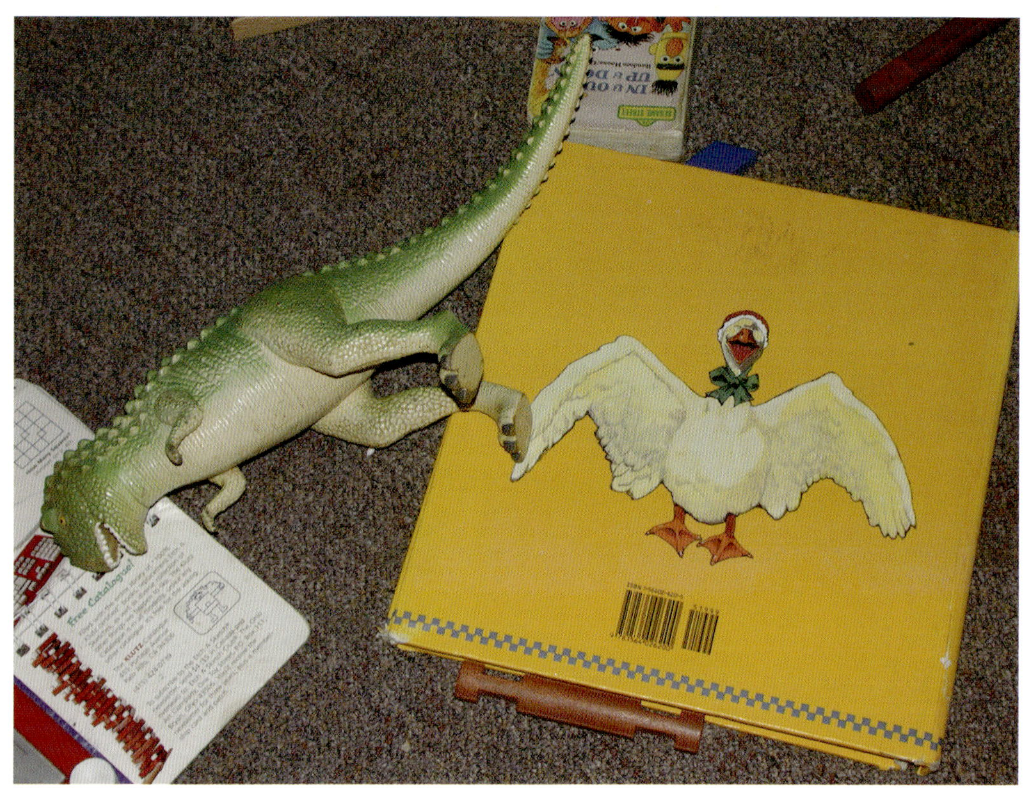

10.01.02

**Happy animals**

10.02.02

**Morning commute**

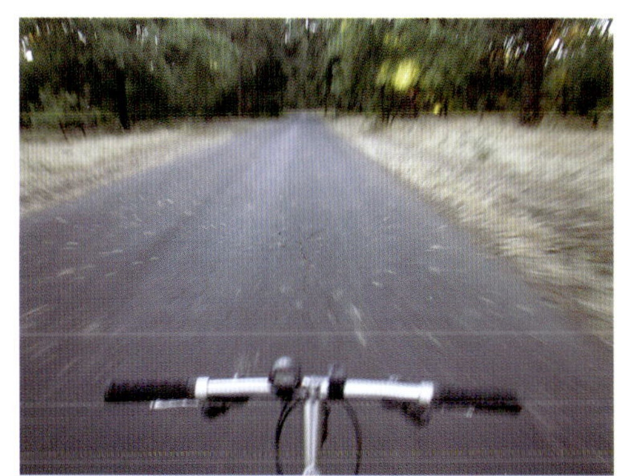

10.03.02

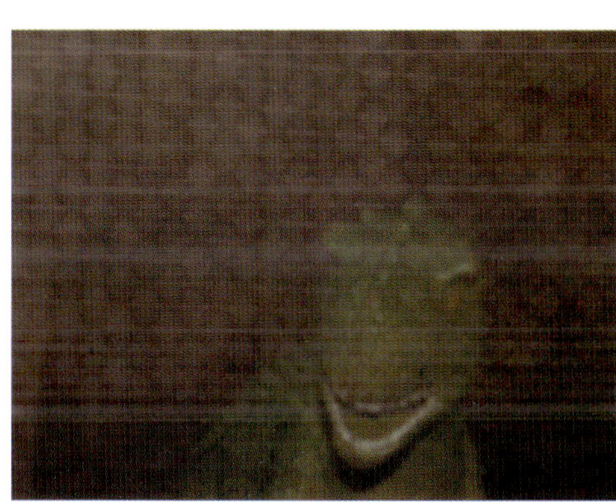

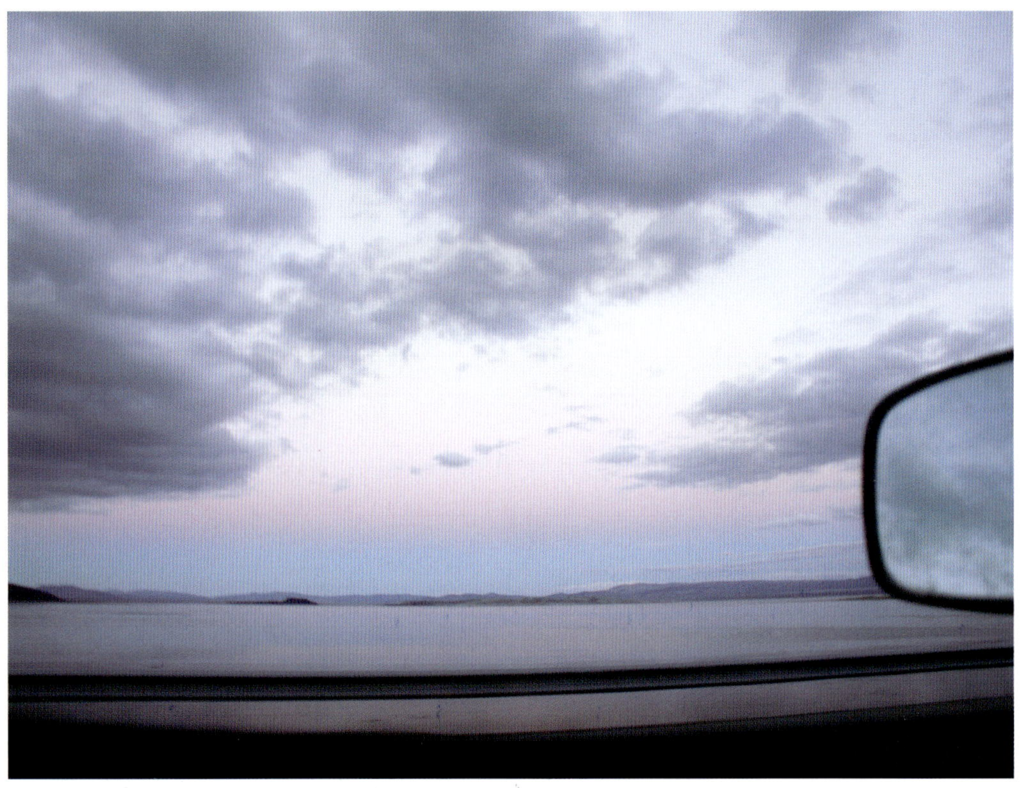

10.04.02

**On a trip to Yosemite: Mono Lake at sunset**

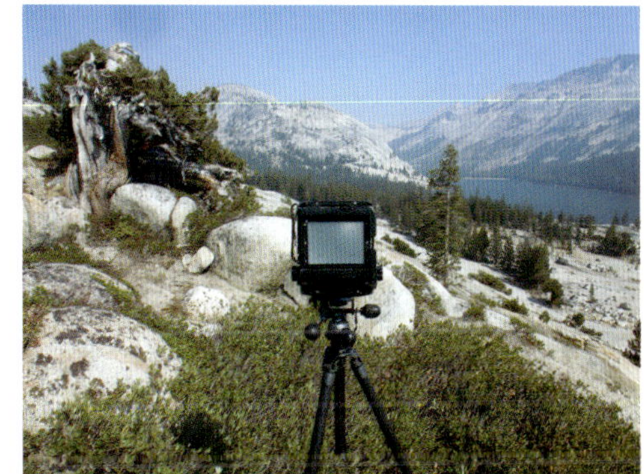

10.05.02
**Rephotographing Edward Weston's Juniper above Lake Tenaya, Yosemite**

10.06.02
**Leaving Glacier Point, Yosemite**

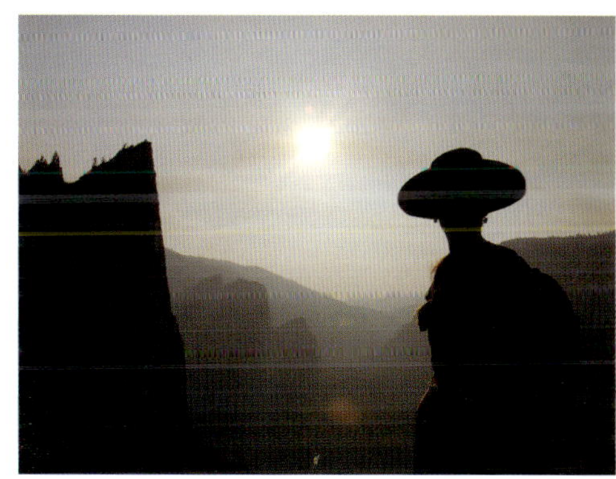

10.07.02
**Valley of the Yosemite from Union Point**

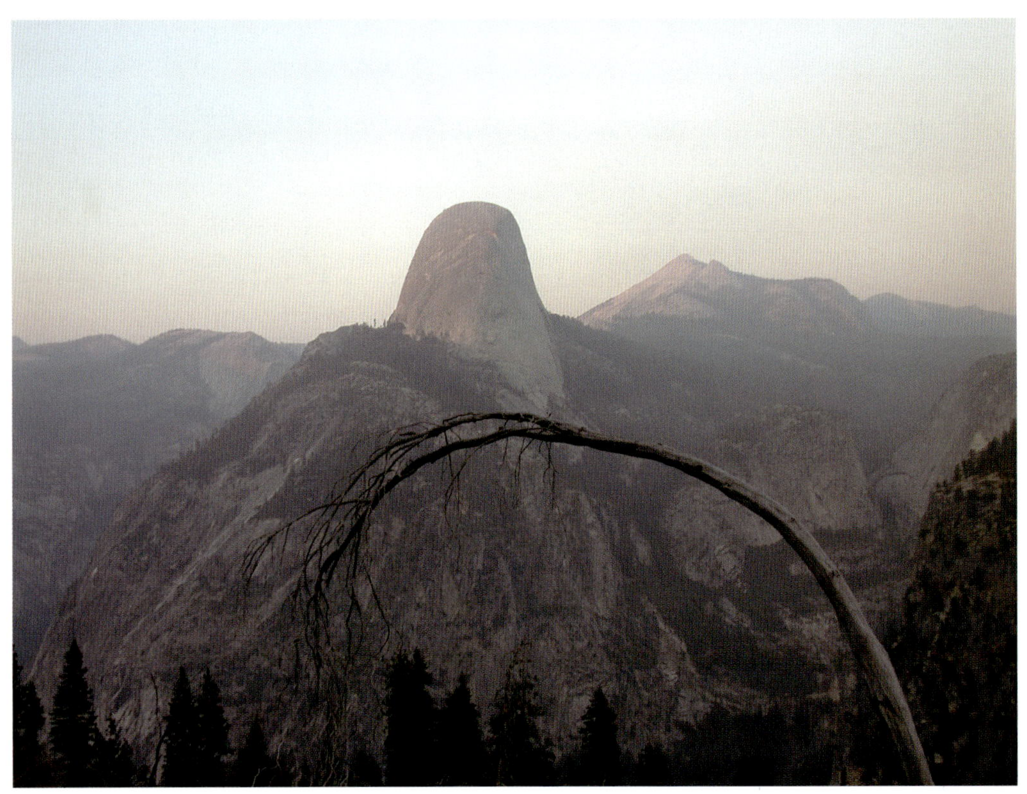

10.08.02

**Half Dome from the Four Mile Trail, Yosemite**

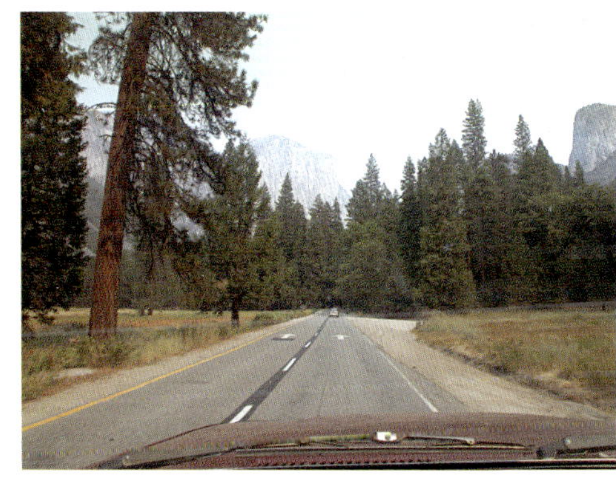

10.09.02
**Driving through the Valley**

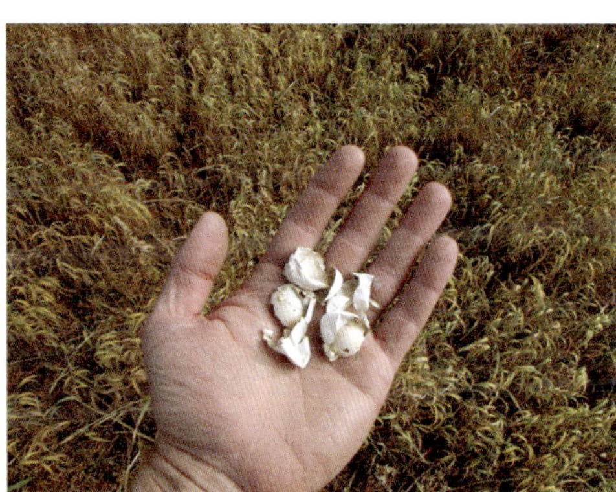

10.10.02
**More eggs,
this time in a Yosemite meadow**

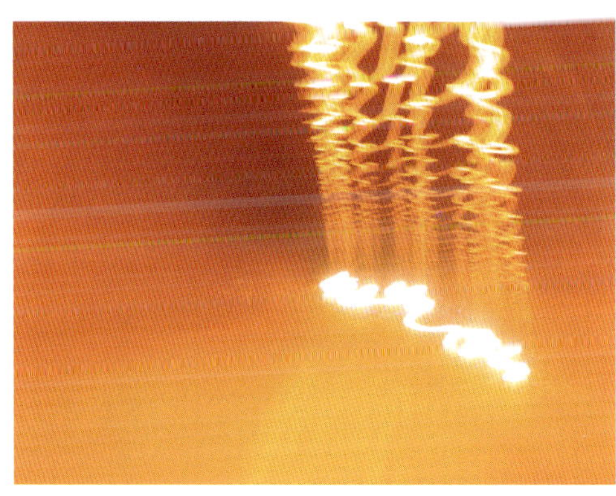

10.11.02
**Late-night driving,
somewhere in Nevada**

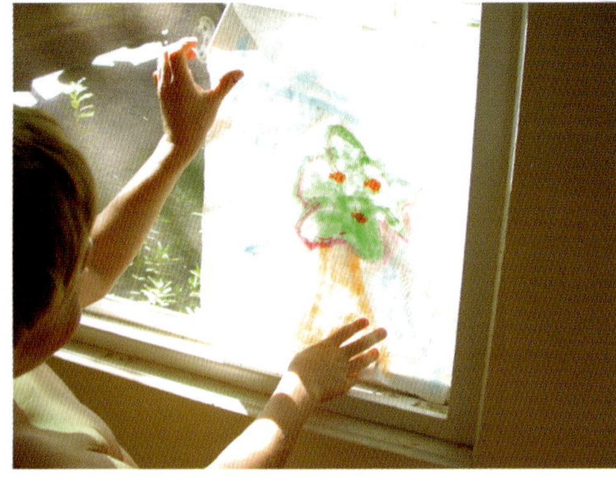

10.12.02

**Back home in Chico**

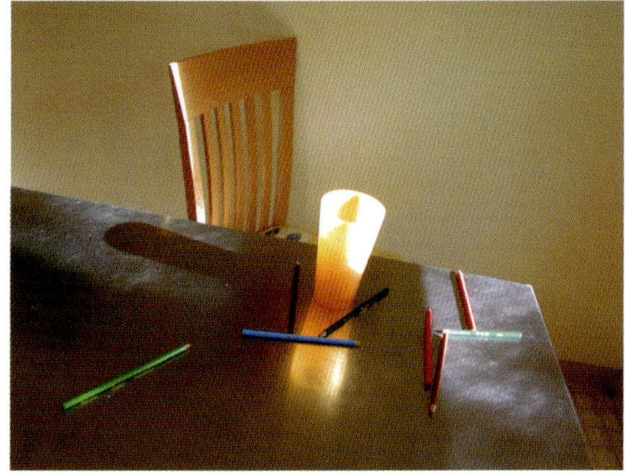

10.13.02

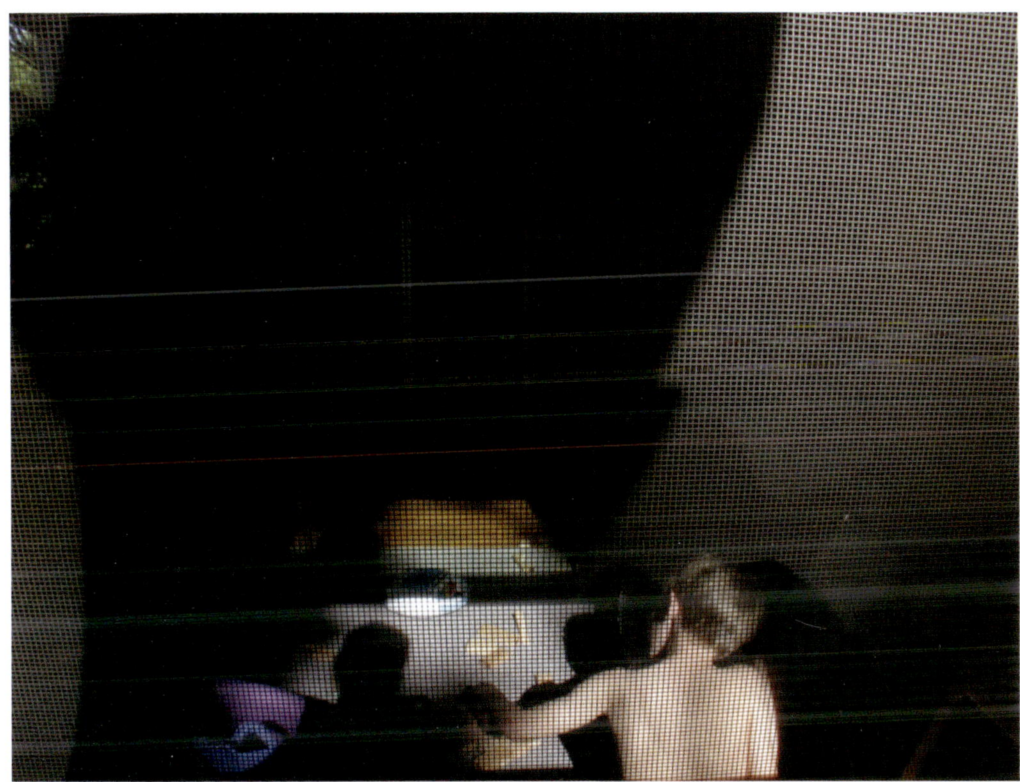

10.14.02

**Outside, looking in**

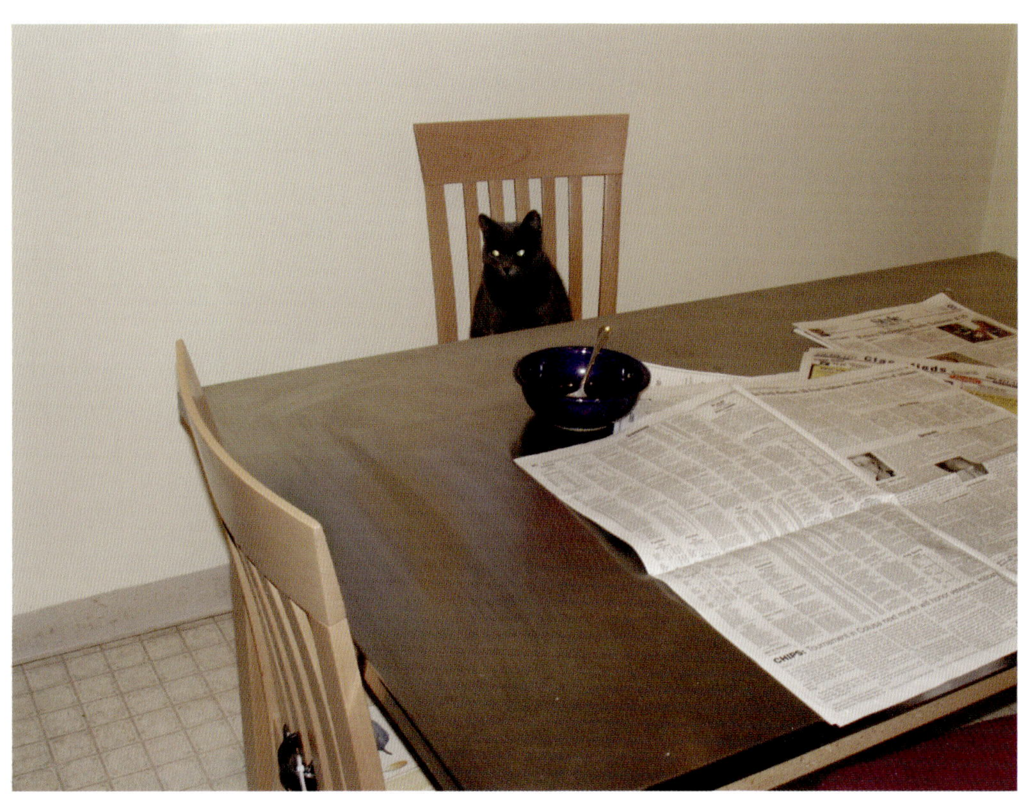


10.15.02

**Breakfast, 6:00 AM**

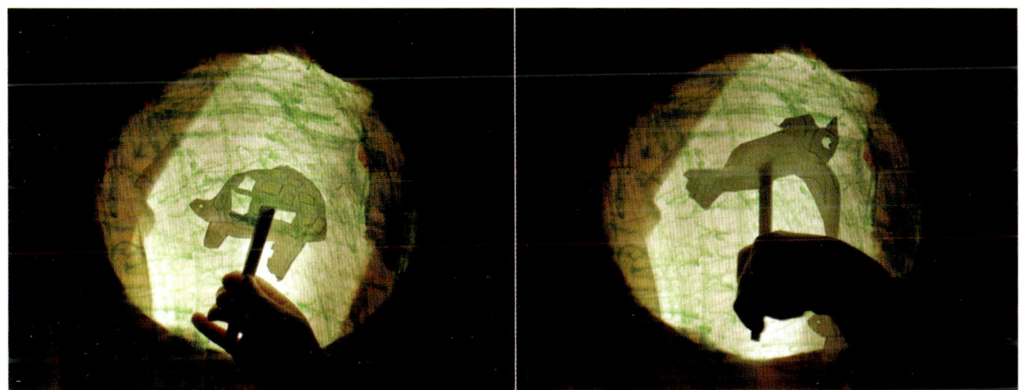

10.16.02

**Domestic drama: scenes from "The Turtle Who Wouldn't Pay Attention," a shadow-puppet play in two acts**

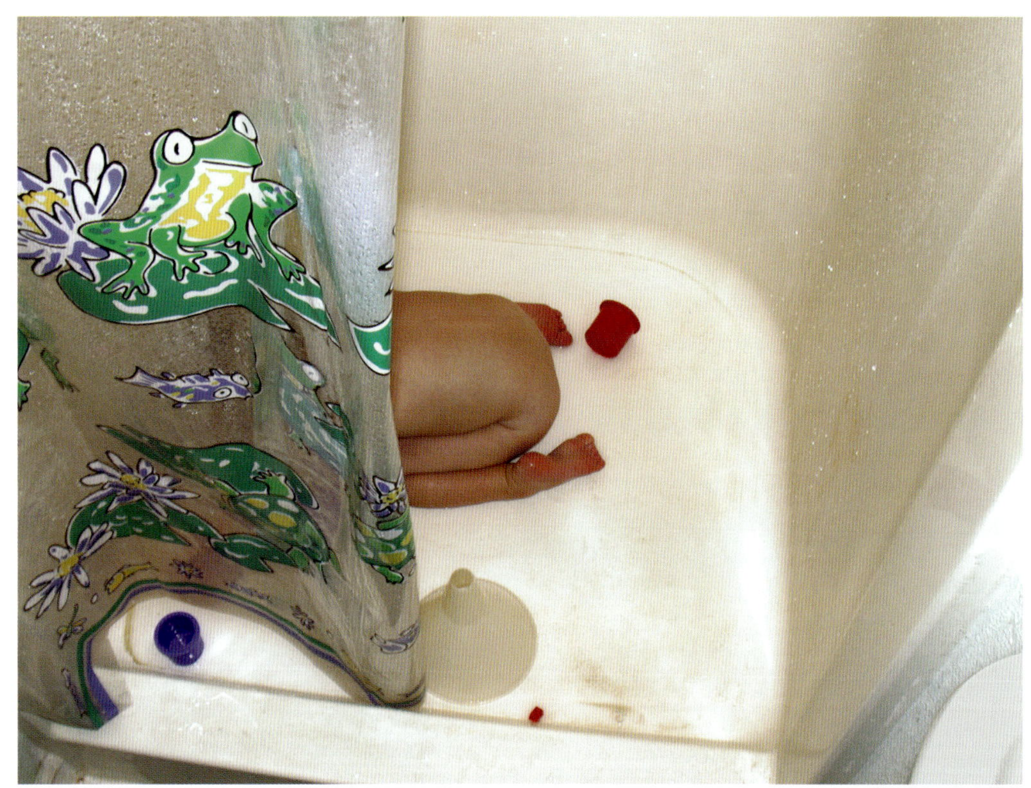

10.17.02

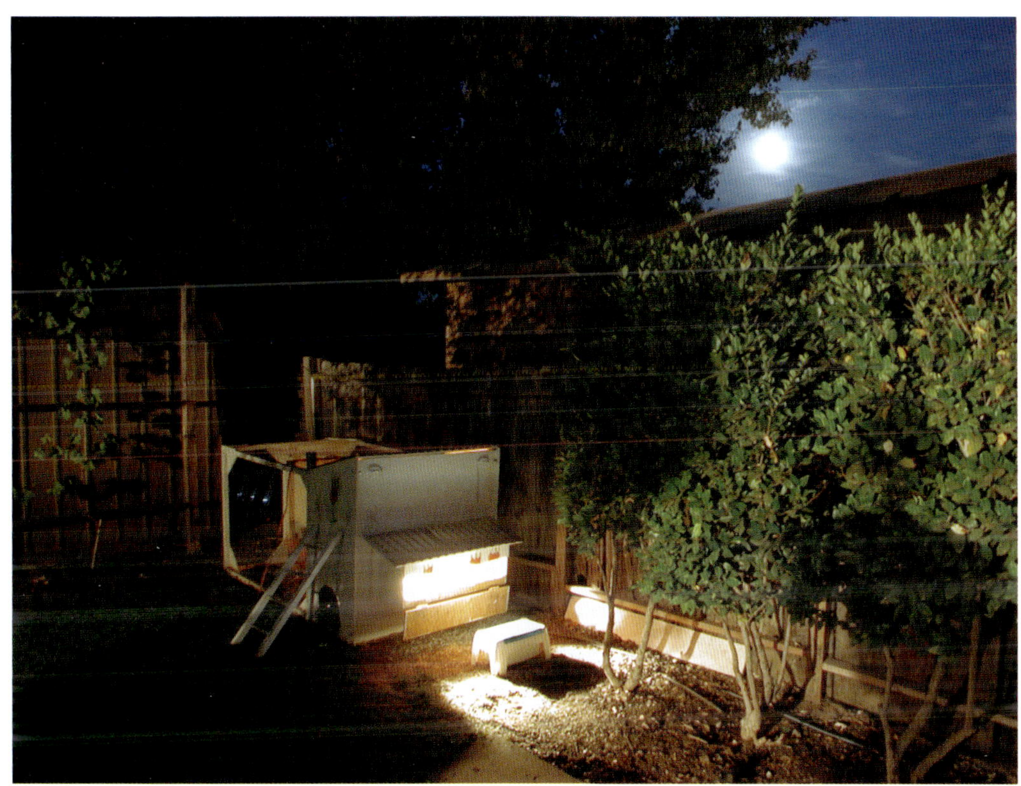

10.18.02

**Moonrise over chicken coop**

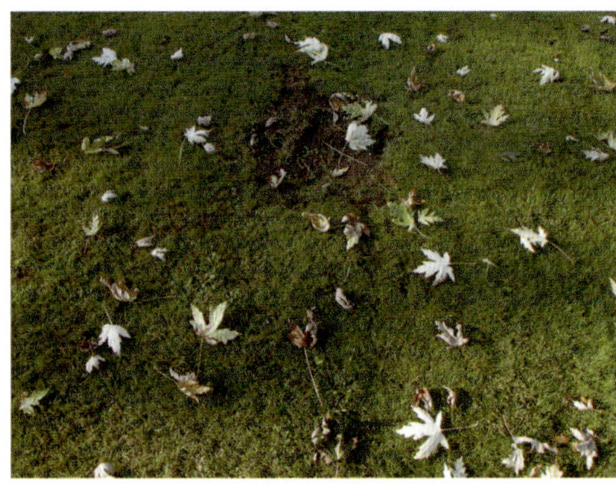

10.19.02

**Site of the transplanted maple, long since trampled**

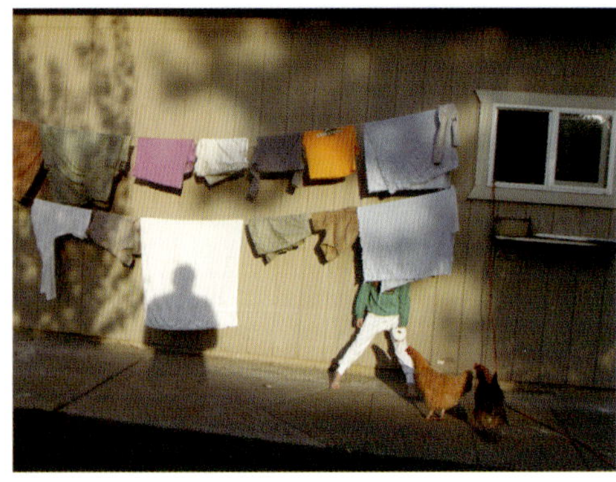

10.20.02

**Sunday morning**

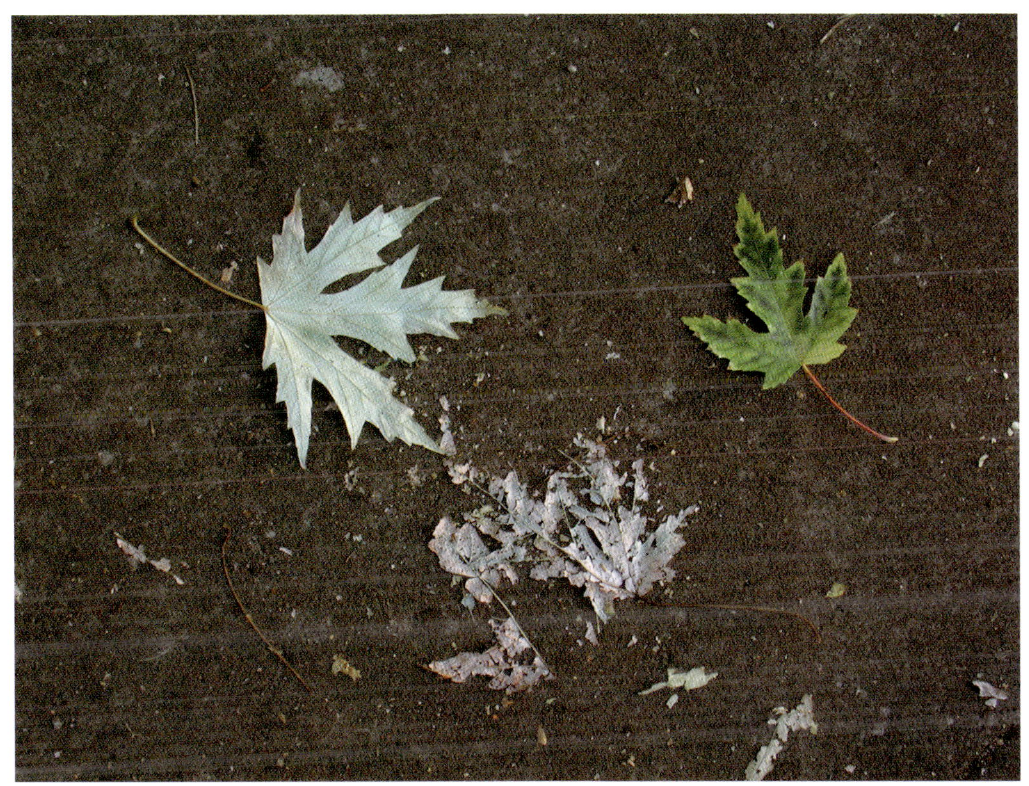

10.21.02

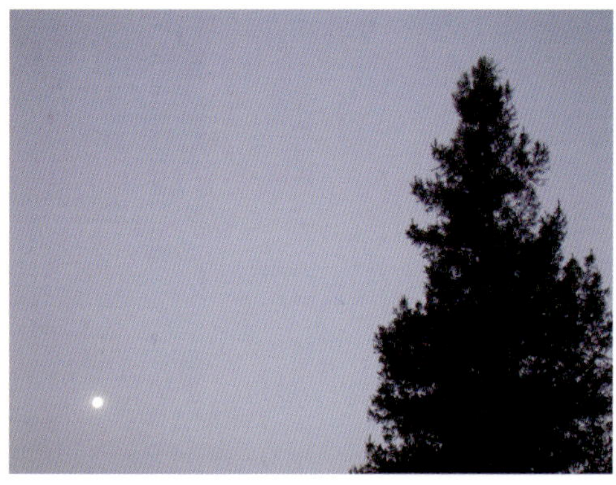

10.22.02

**Descending moon at dawn**

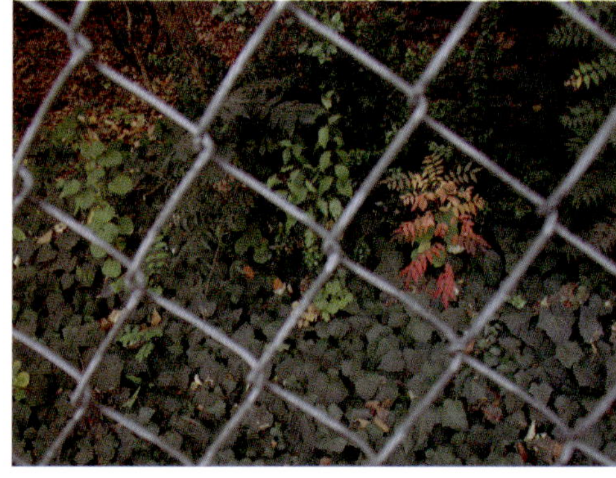

10.23.02

**Wilderness scene,
roadside embankment,
Highway 99**

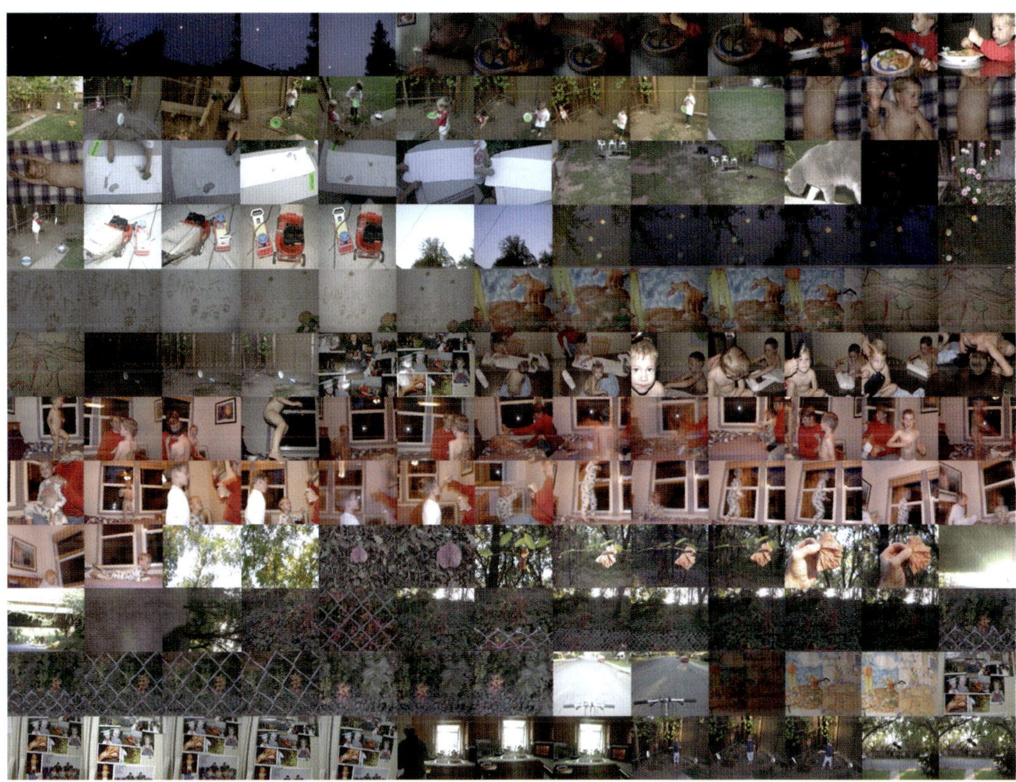

10.24.02

**All 156 disappointing pictures from the last 24 hours**

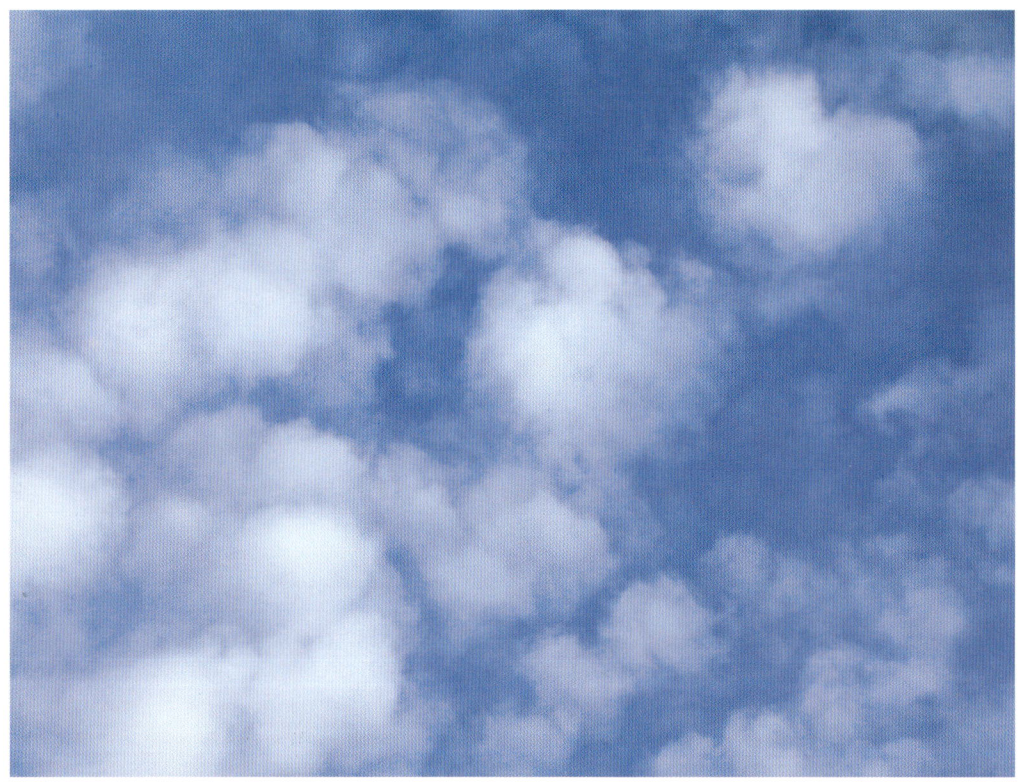

10.25.02

**After an endless day of grading student photographs of pets, skateboarders, small children—and more pets**

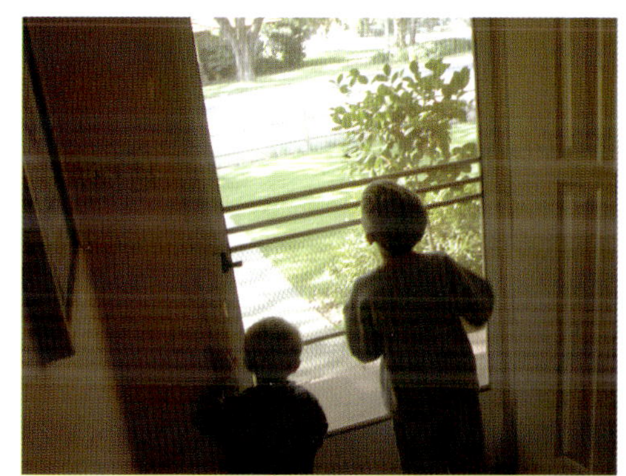

10.26.02

**As the Jehovah's Witnesses depart**

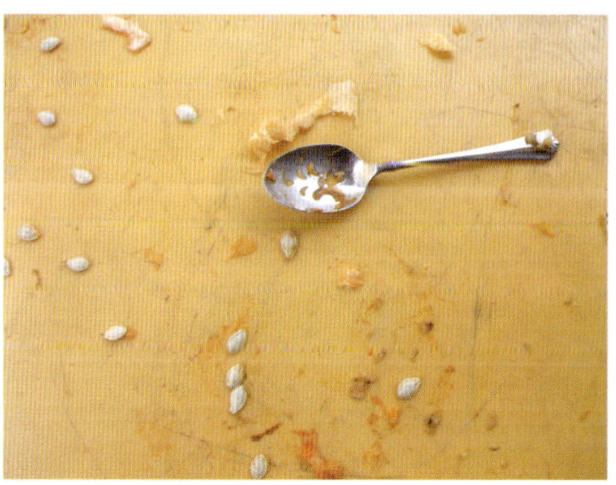

10.27.02

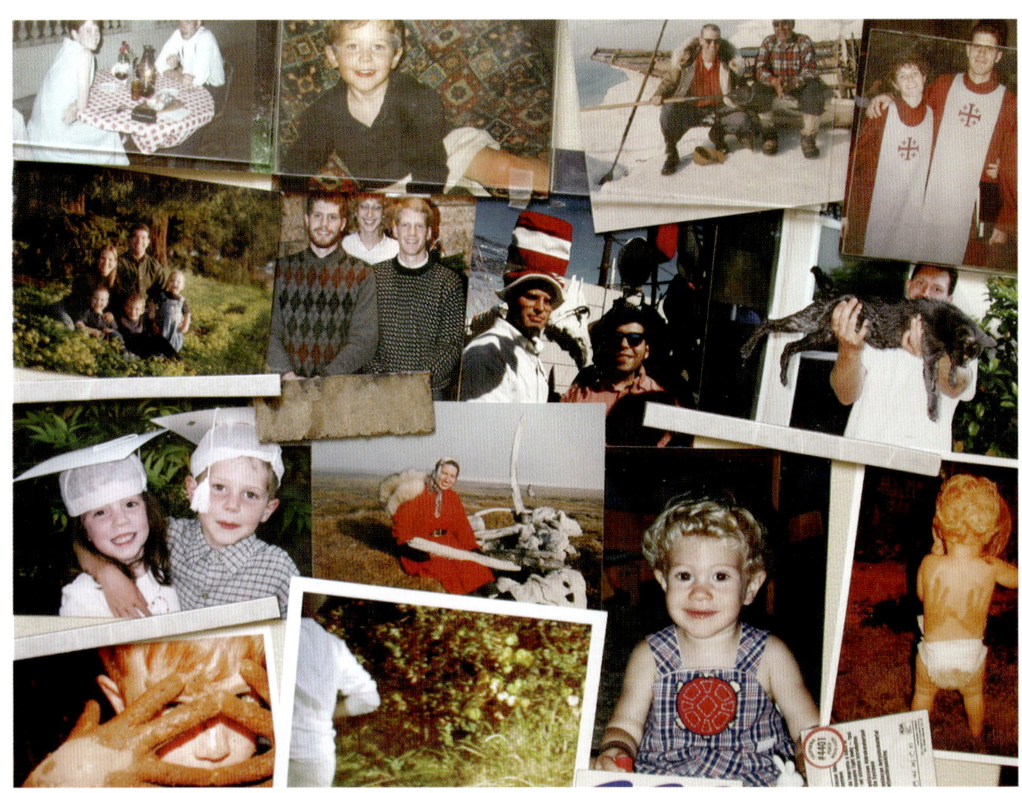

10.28.02

**Refrigerator photos**

10.29.02

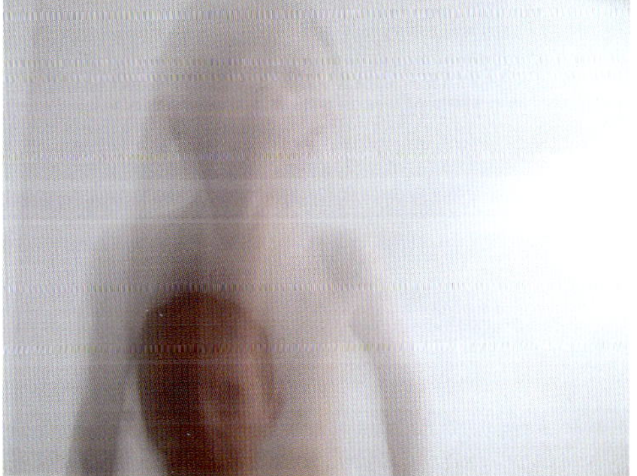

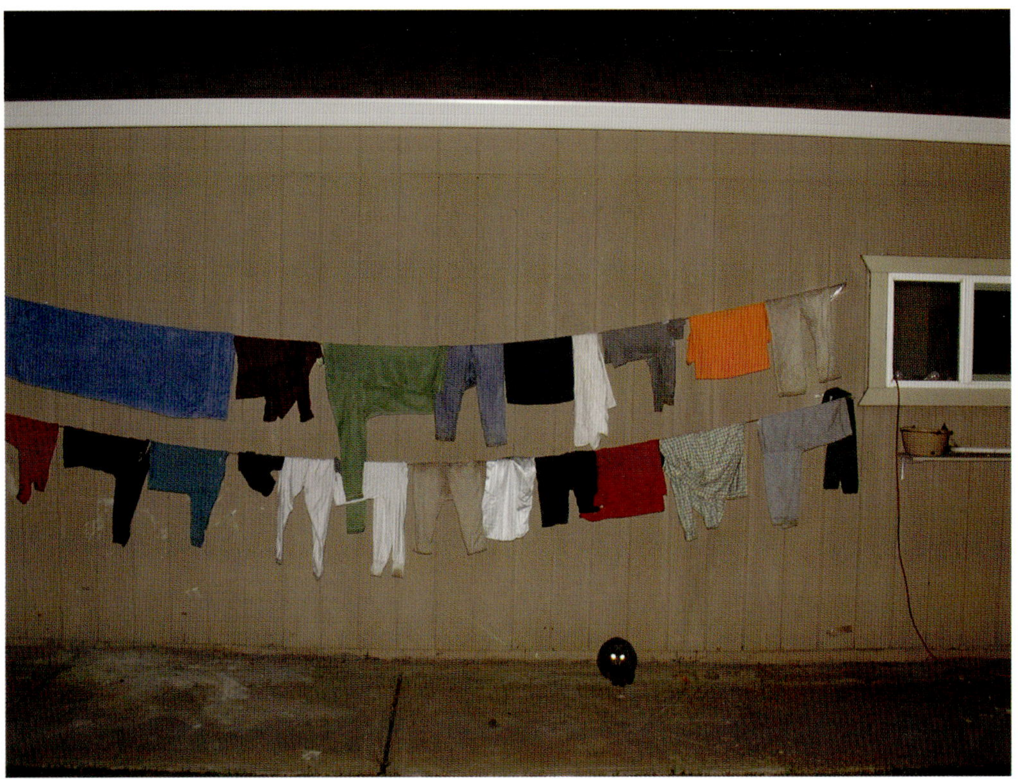

10.30.02

**Two-eyed cat**

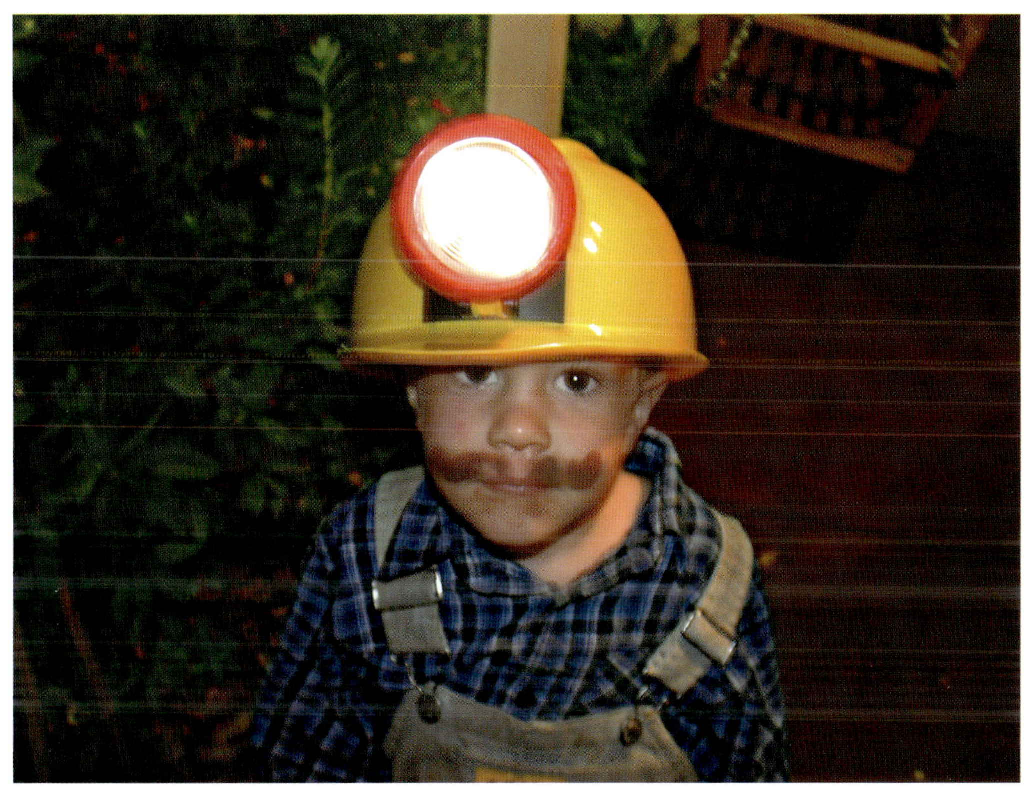

10.31.02

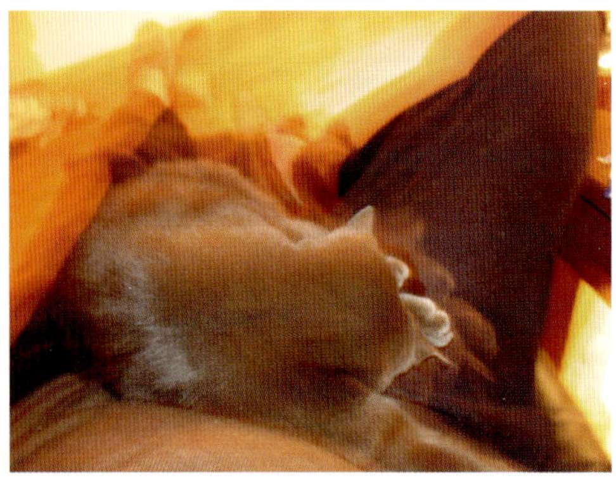

11.01.02

**Fireside, cat in lap**

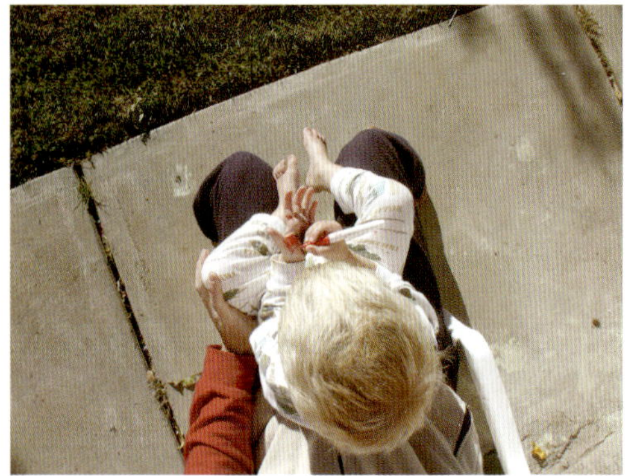

11.02.02

**Sunrise, child in lap**

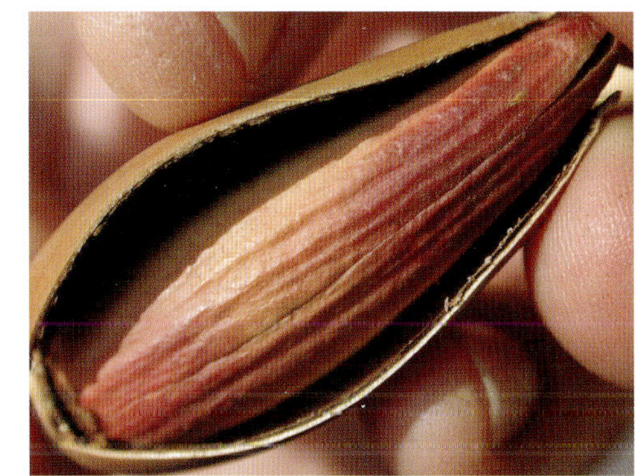

11.03.02

**On a walk**
**beneath the Valley Oaks**

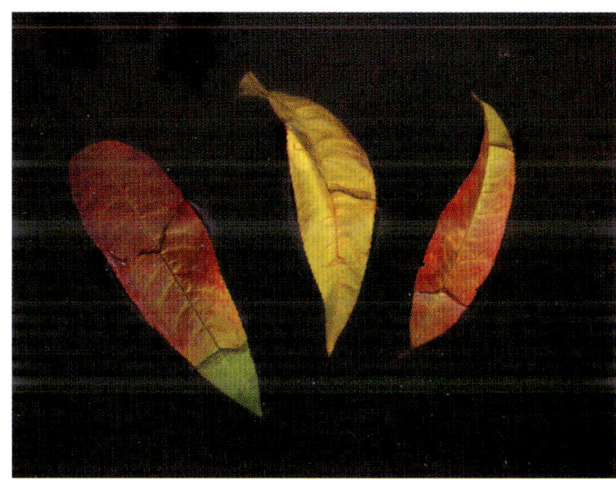

11.04.02

**From our White Lady Peach**

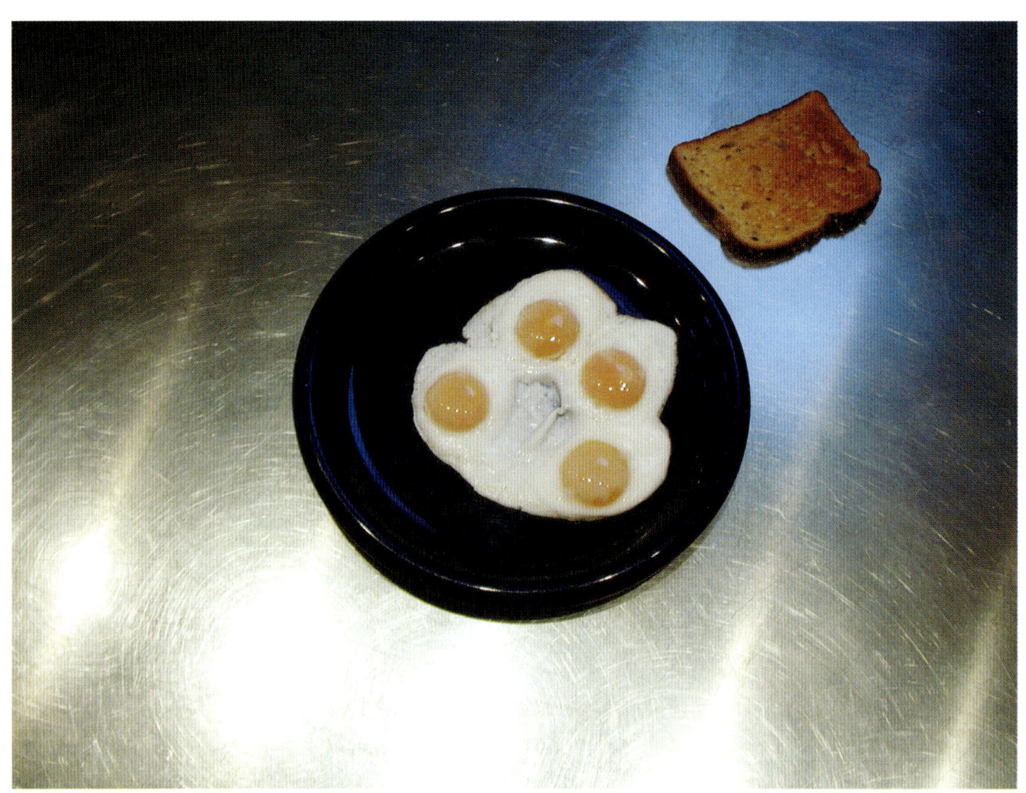

11.05.02

**Chicken bounty**

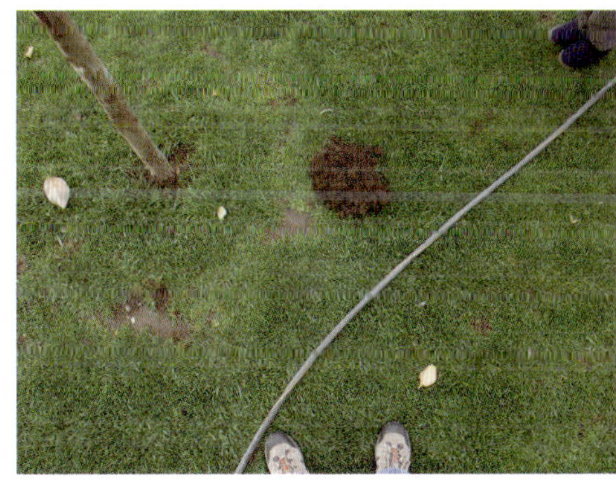

11.06.02

**Gopher!**

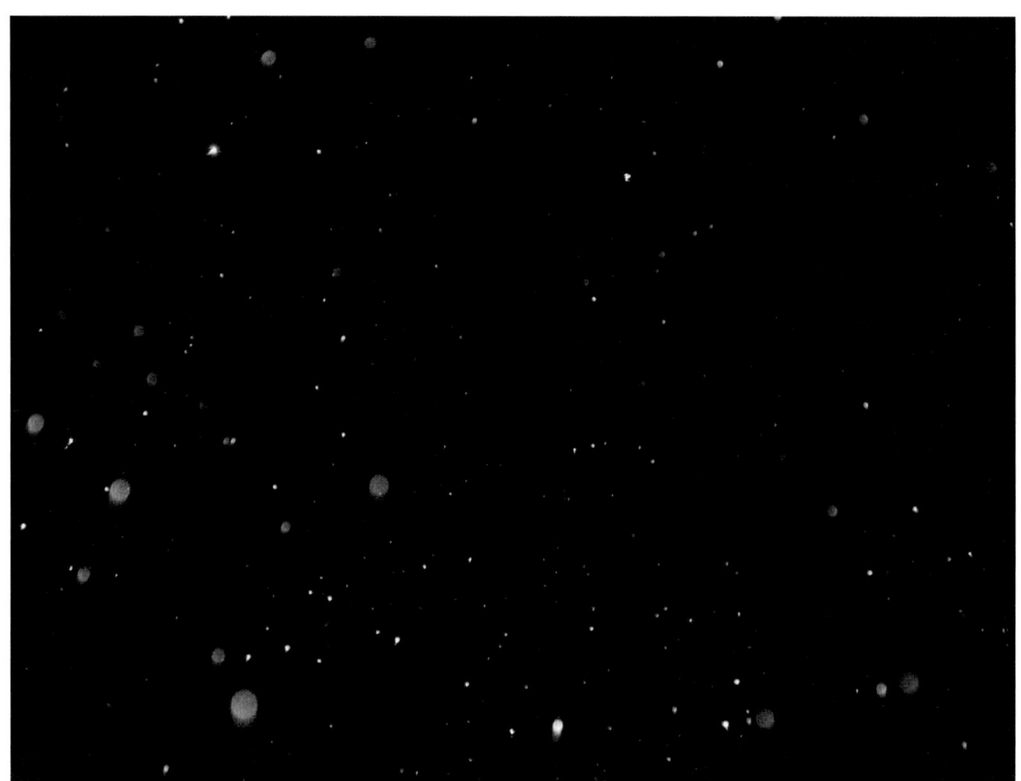

11.07.02

**Looking up into the first autumn storm**

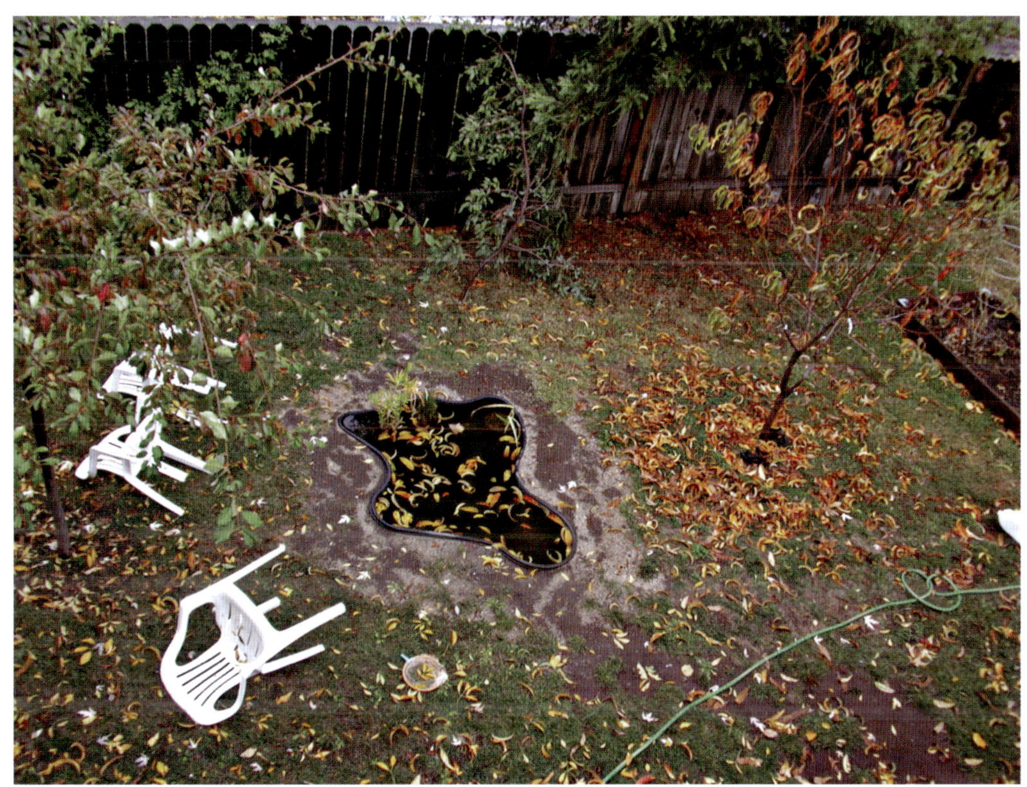

11.08.02

**After the storm**

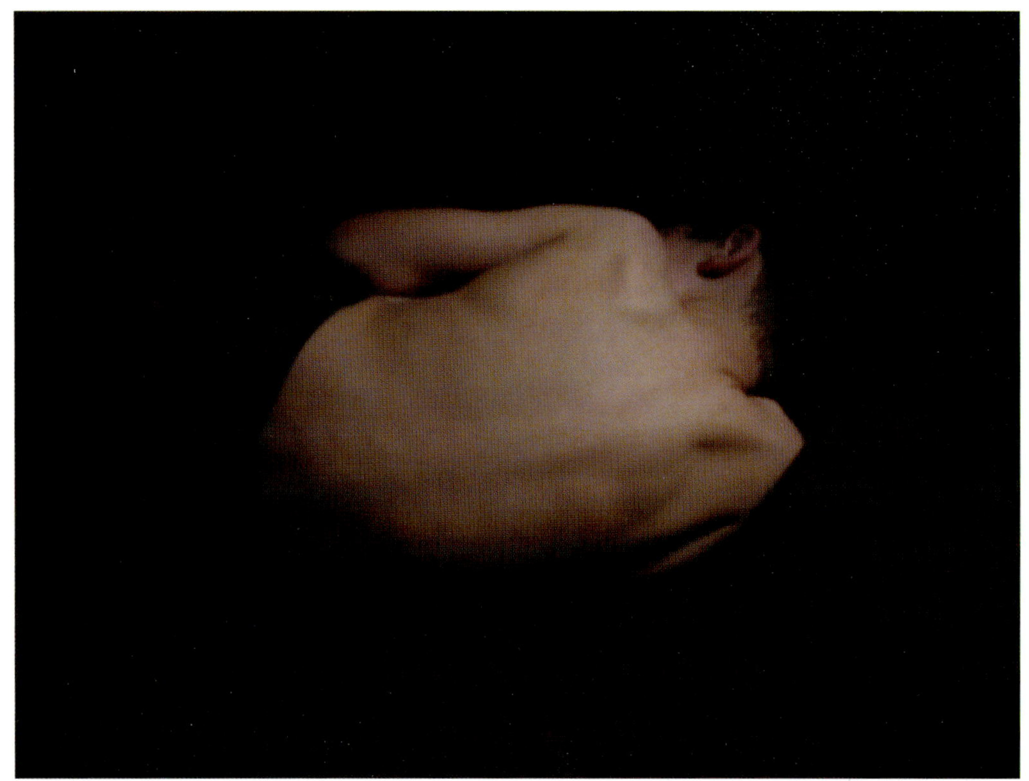

11.09.02

11.10.02

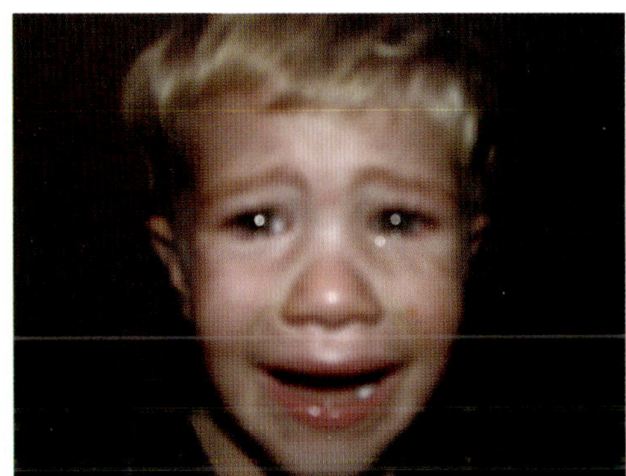

11.11.02

**The compost pile**

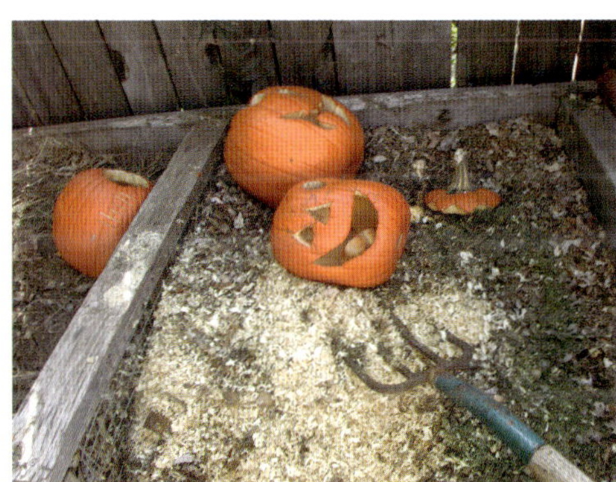

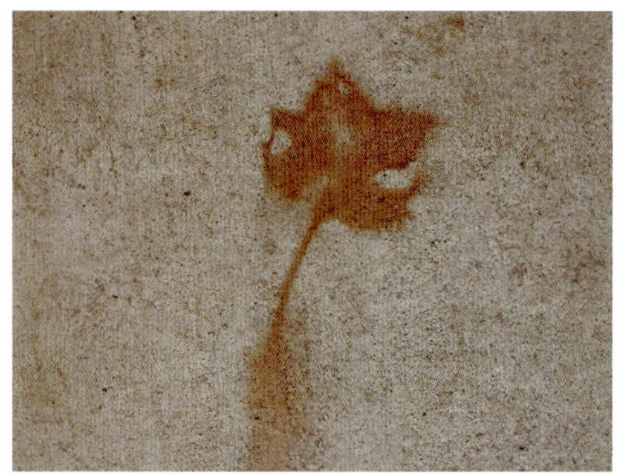

11.12.02

**Tulip Poplar**

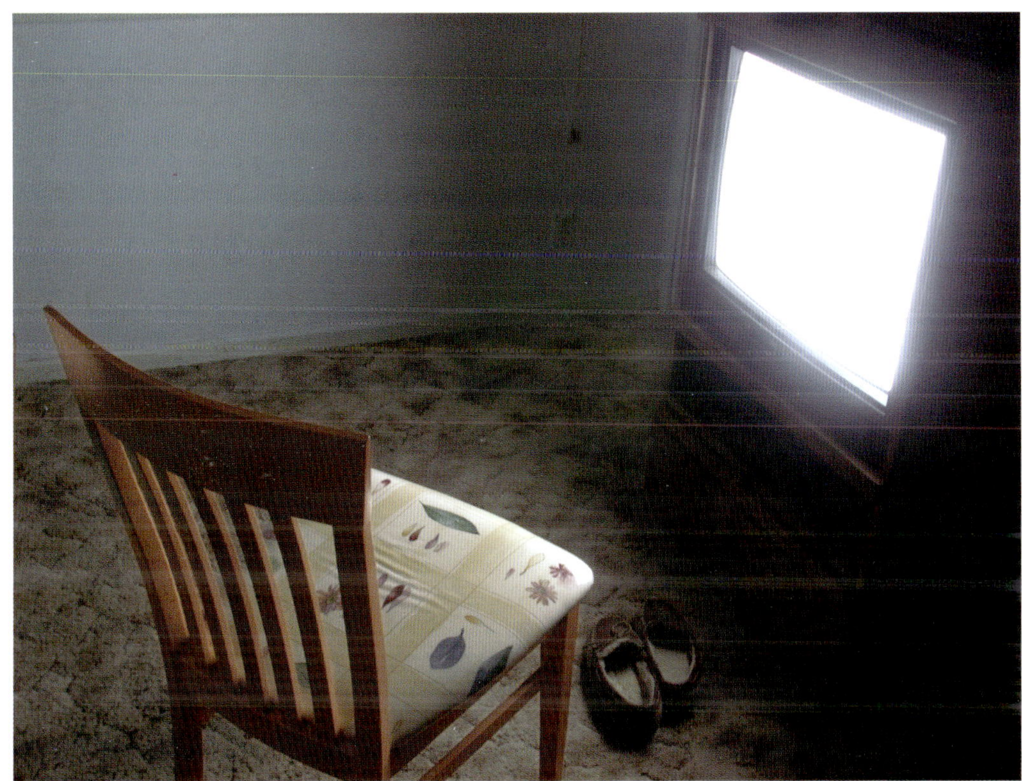

11.13.02

**Insomnia**

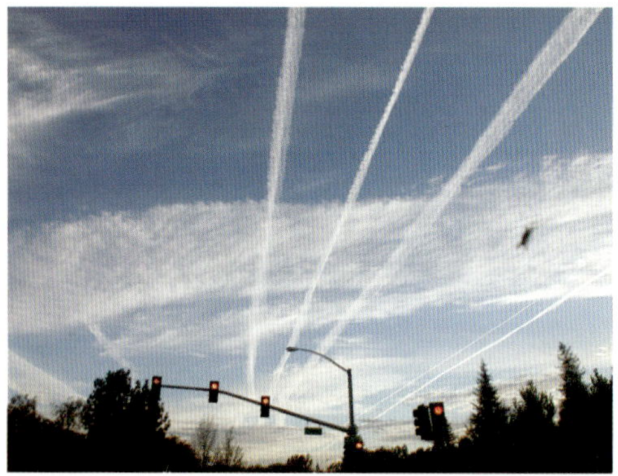

11.14.02

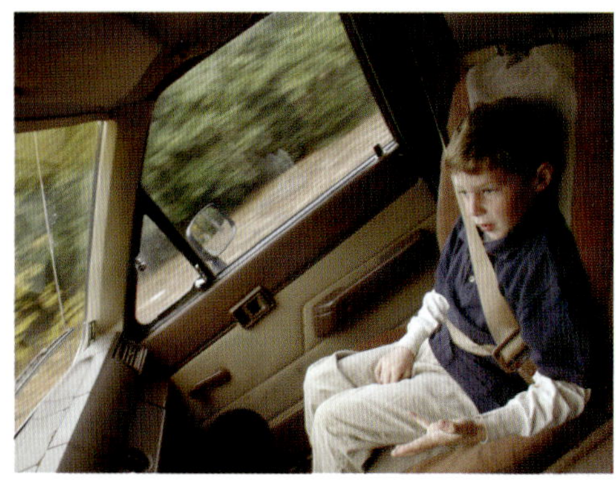

11.15.02

**Driving my son to school**

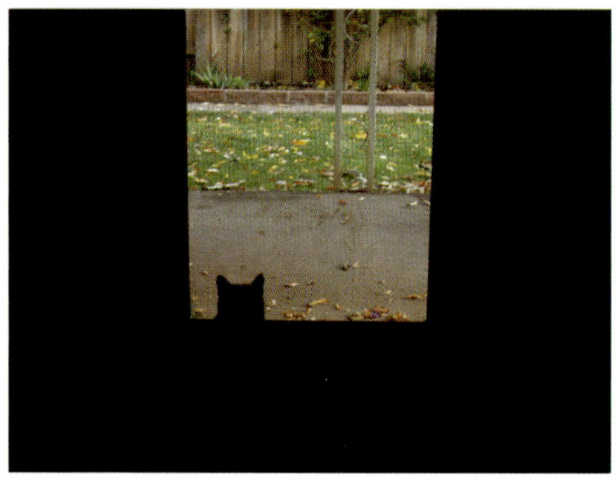

11.16.02

**Indecisive cat**

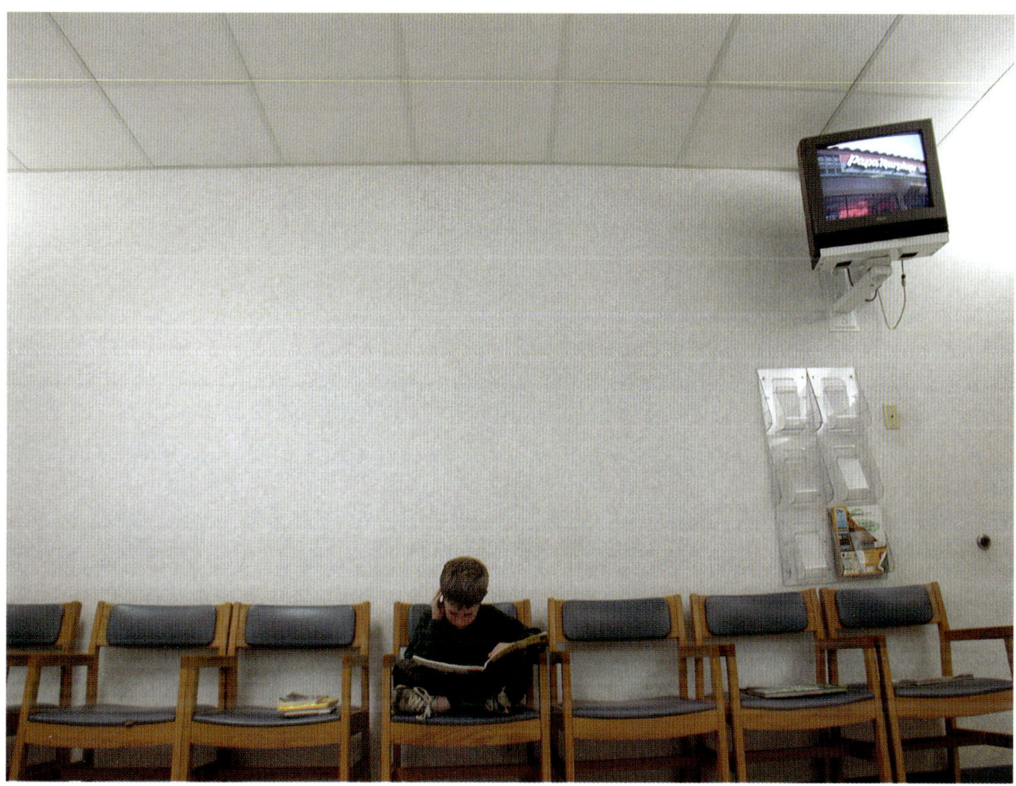

11.17.02

**Nighttime visit to the emergency room (bar soap smushed into ear canal)**

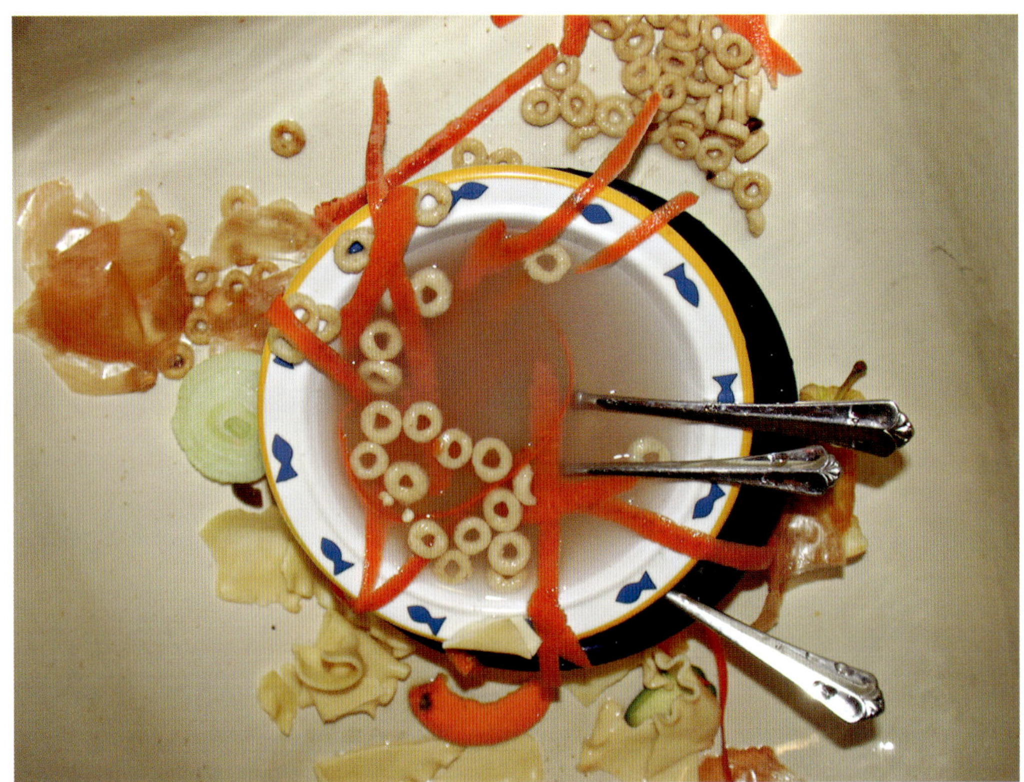

11.18.02

**Arrangement in orange, yellow, and blue**

11.19.02

**Moonrise among the traffic lights**

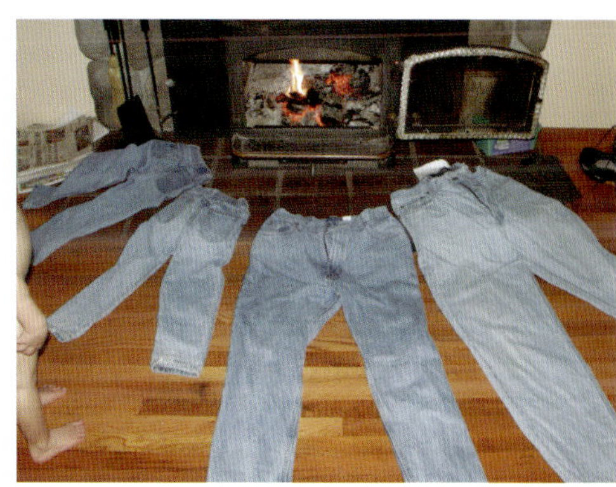

11.20.02

**Drying the family laundry**

11.21.02

**On the drive home**

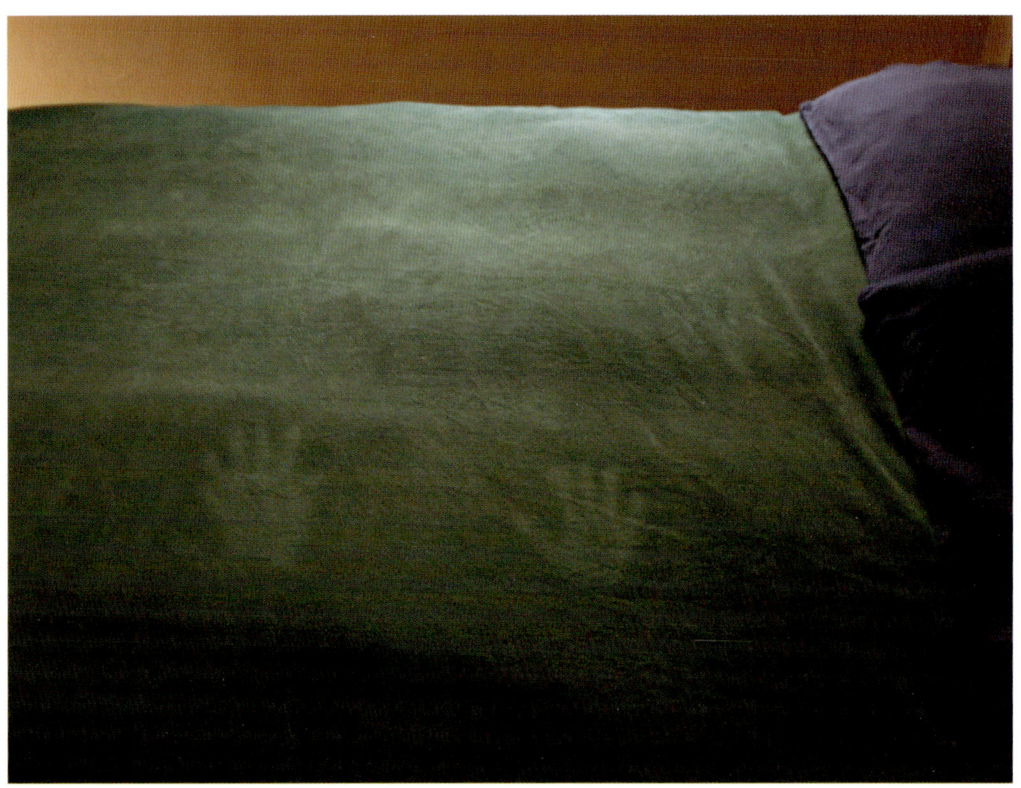

11.22.02

**A little like those ancient cave paintings in France (look carefully)**

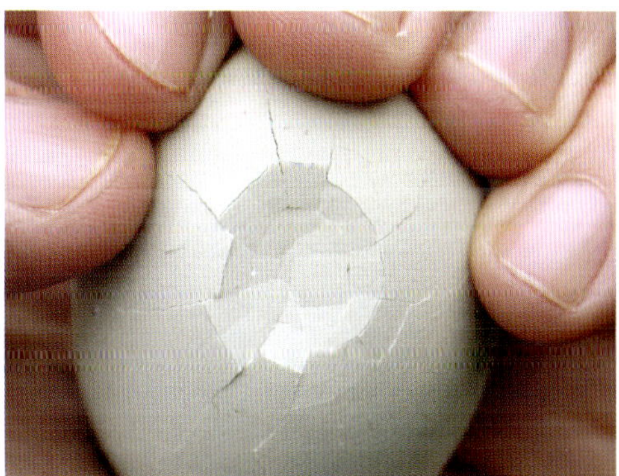

11.23.02

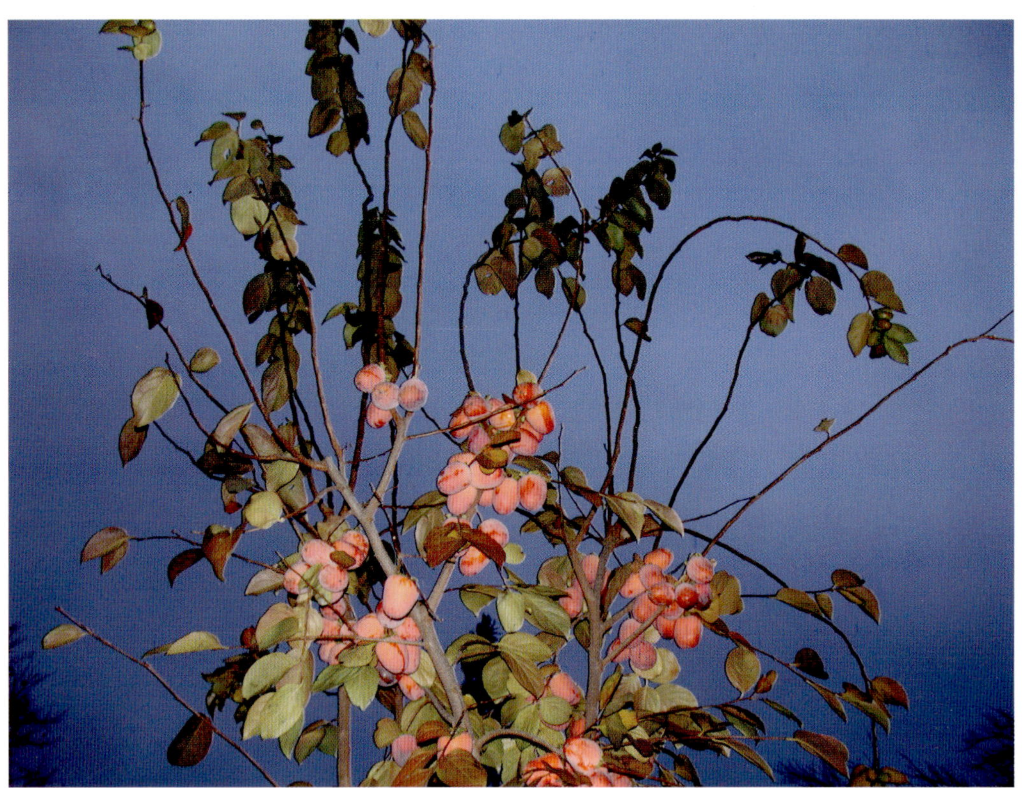

11.24.02

**Chocolate Persimmons at dusk**

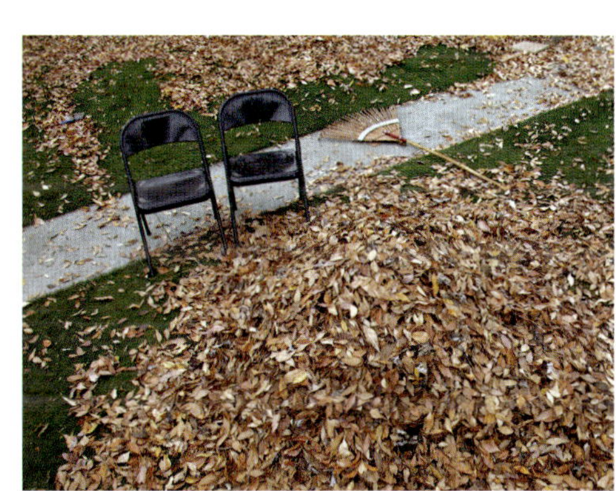
11.25.02

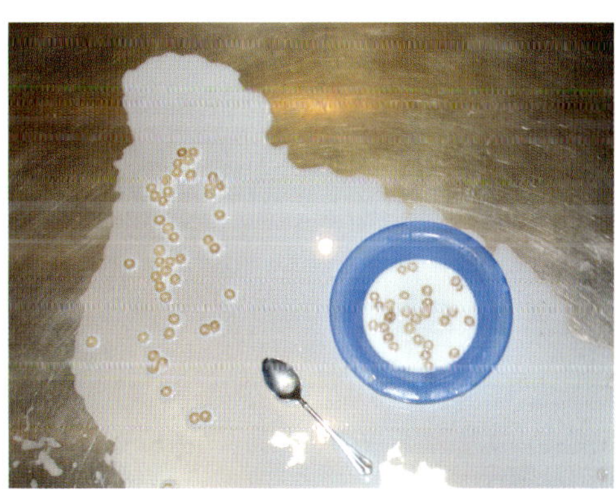
11.26.02

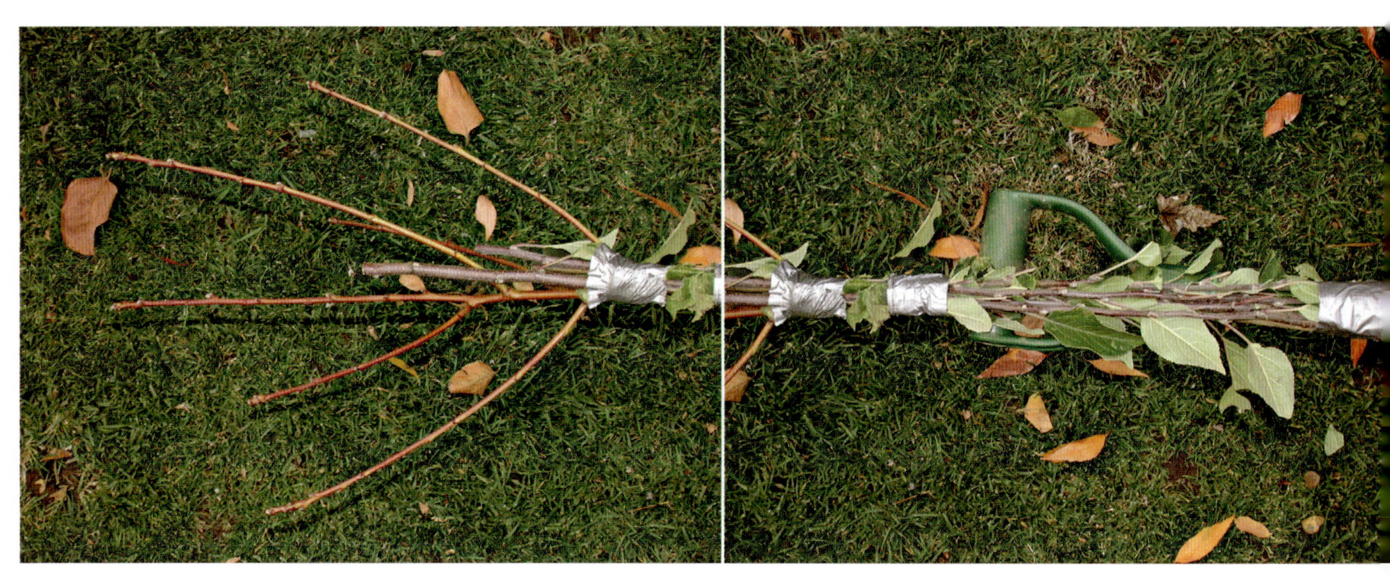

11.27.02

**Found object sculpture with camping shovel, fruit tree cuttings, duct tape, basketball, plastic picnic table, and note: "DO NOT TOCH BORD" (do not touch bird)**

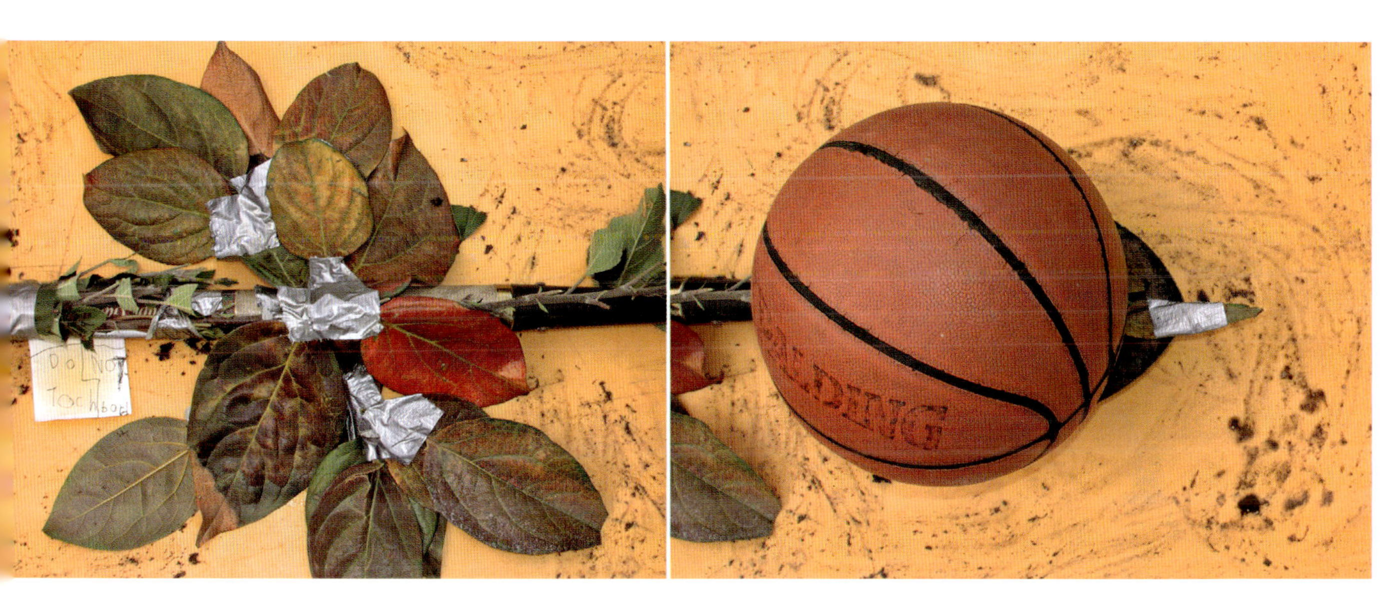
Do Not!
Tochbord
LDING

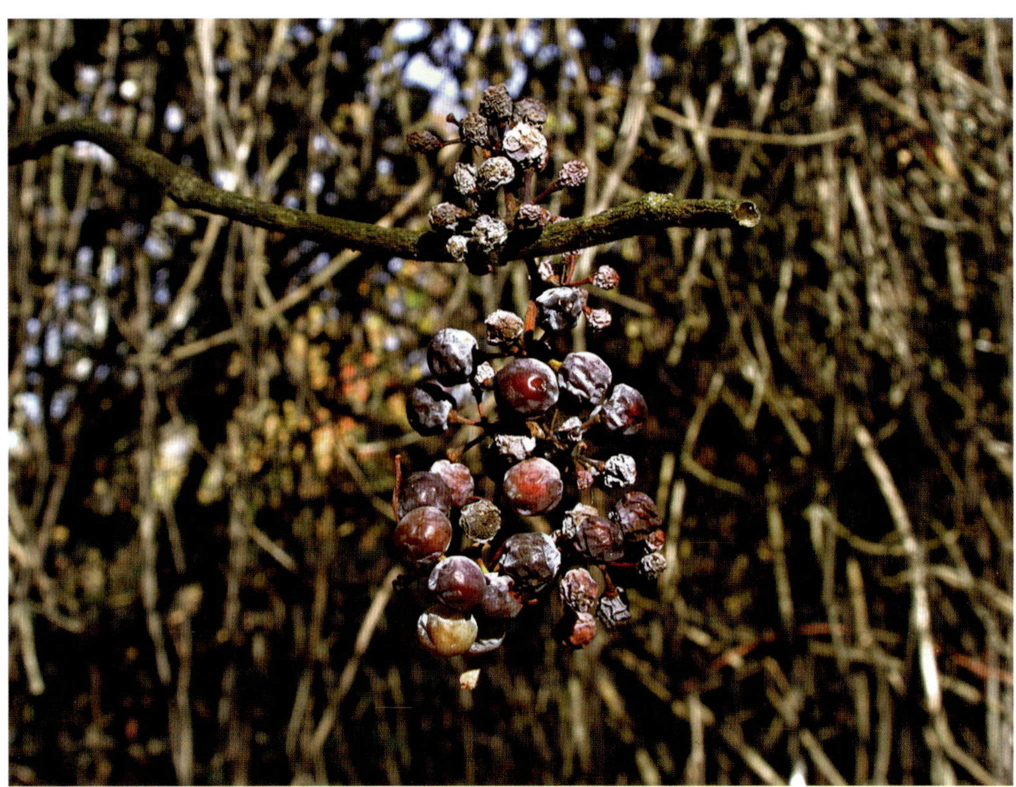

11.28.02

**Wild grapes on the path where you discovered poison oak**

11.29.02

**Cleaning out the gutters**

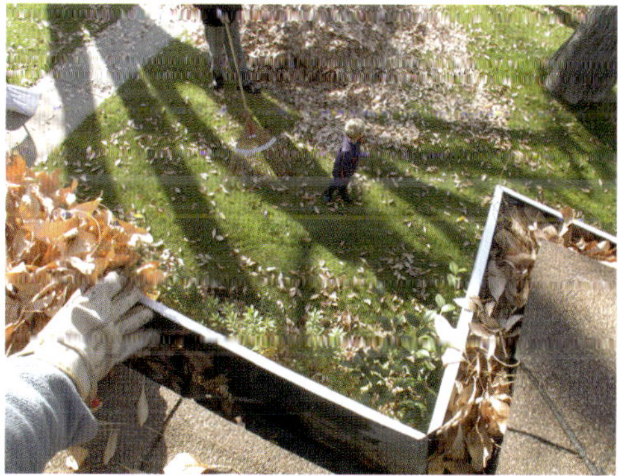

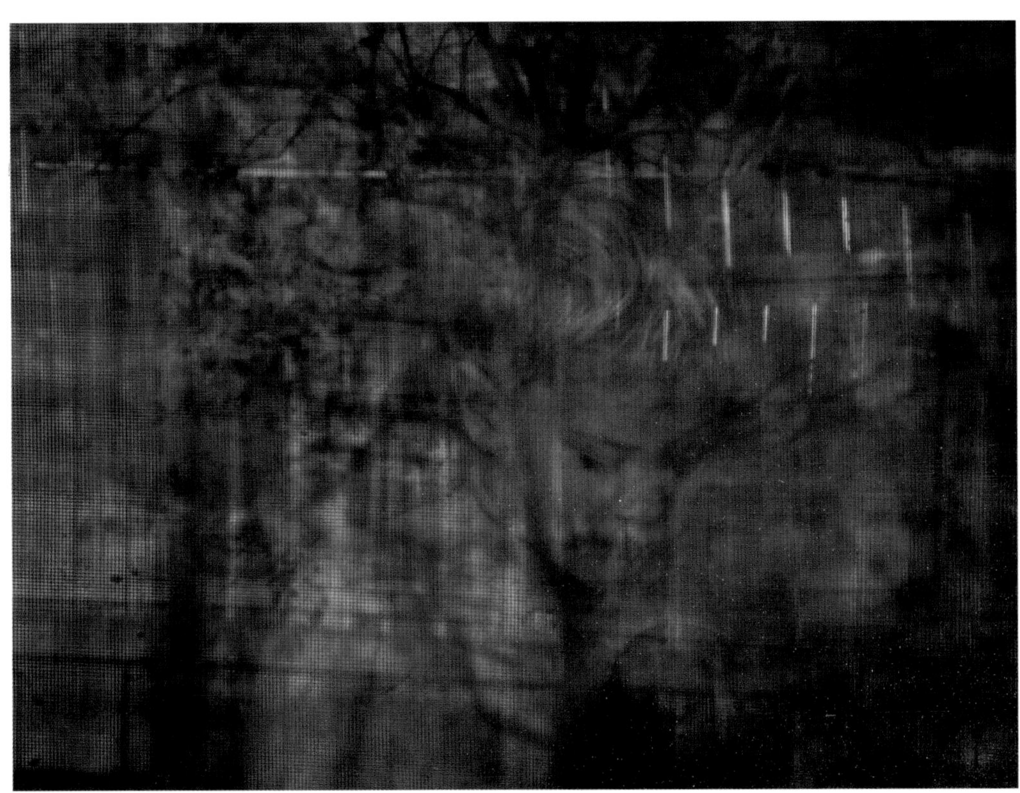

11.30.02

**While pruning the plum tree, I pause to watch you through the window**

12.01.02

**Sunday after sunset,**
**the end of Thanksgiving vacation,**
**a dirty house,**
**sleepless children,**
**empty trees,**
**blank sky**

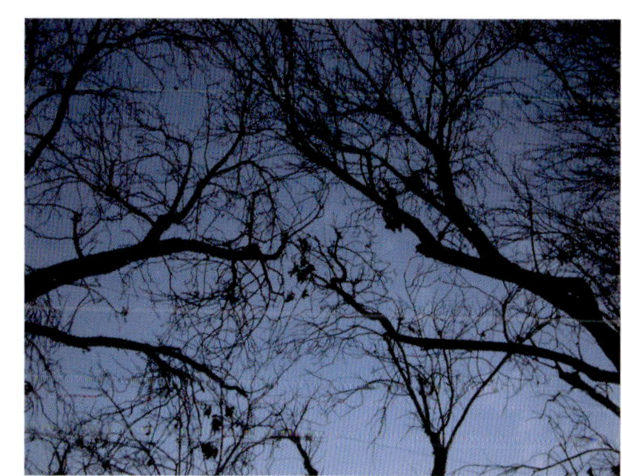

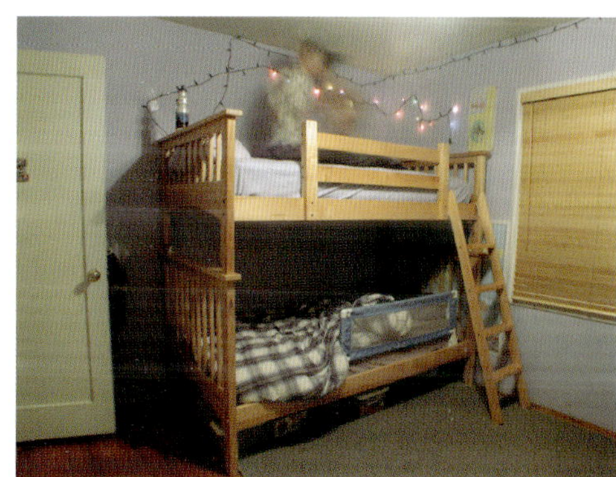

12.02.02

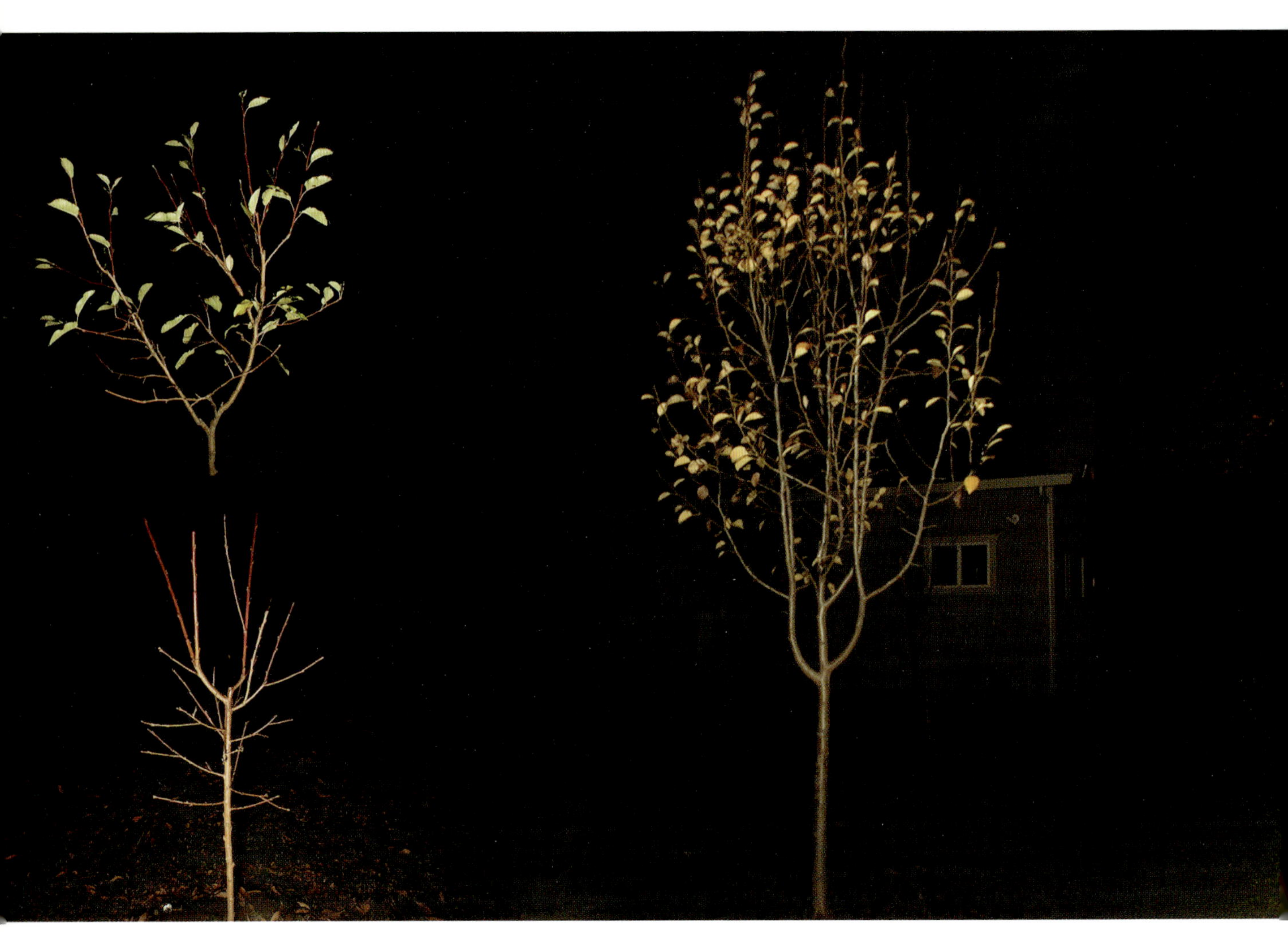

12.03.02–12.04.02

**Fruit trees in my yard**
**Whose names I say out loud**
**While wandering through the night:**

**Moorpark Apricot.**
**Chocolate Persimmon.**
**Warren Pear.**
**Montmorency Cherry.**
**Pink Lady Apple.**
**Liz's Late Nectarine.**
**Rio Oso Gem Peach**
**And my personal favorite,**
**The Weeping Santa Rosa Plum.**

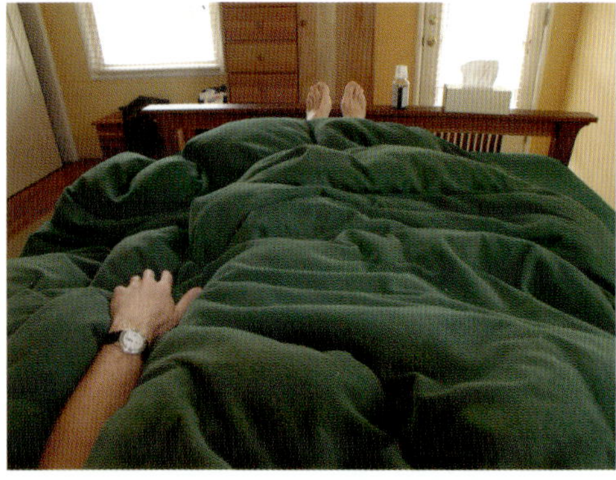

12.05.02

**At noon on a Thursday**

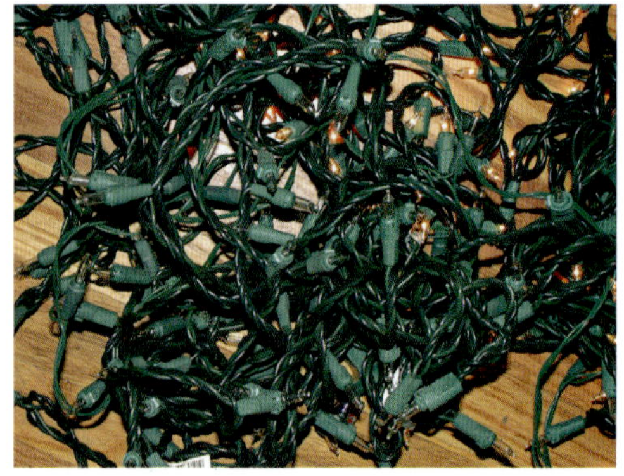

12.06.02

**Annual challenge**

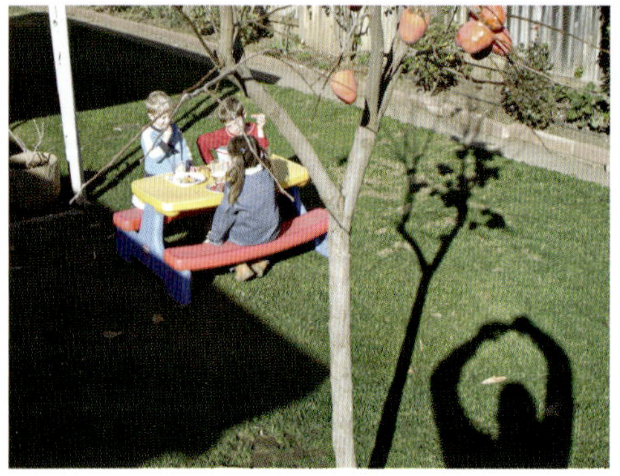

12.07.02

**In the backyard,
late autumn picnic**

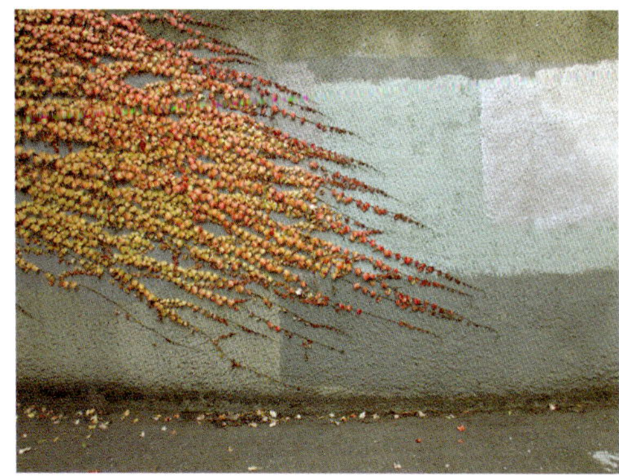

12.08.02

**Beneath the freeway**

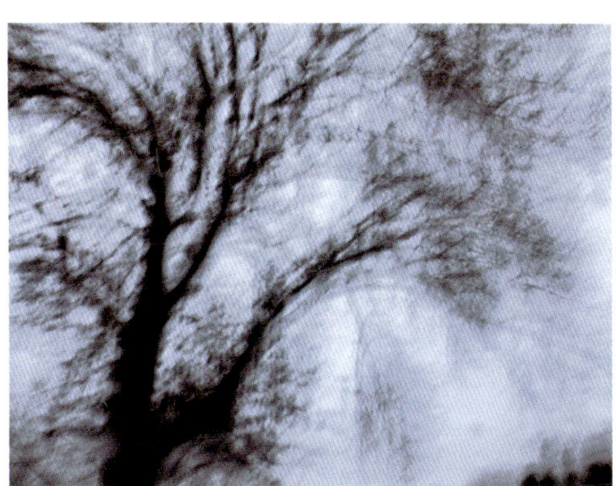

12.09.02

**The drive home**

after another difficult day at work

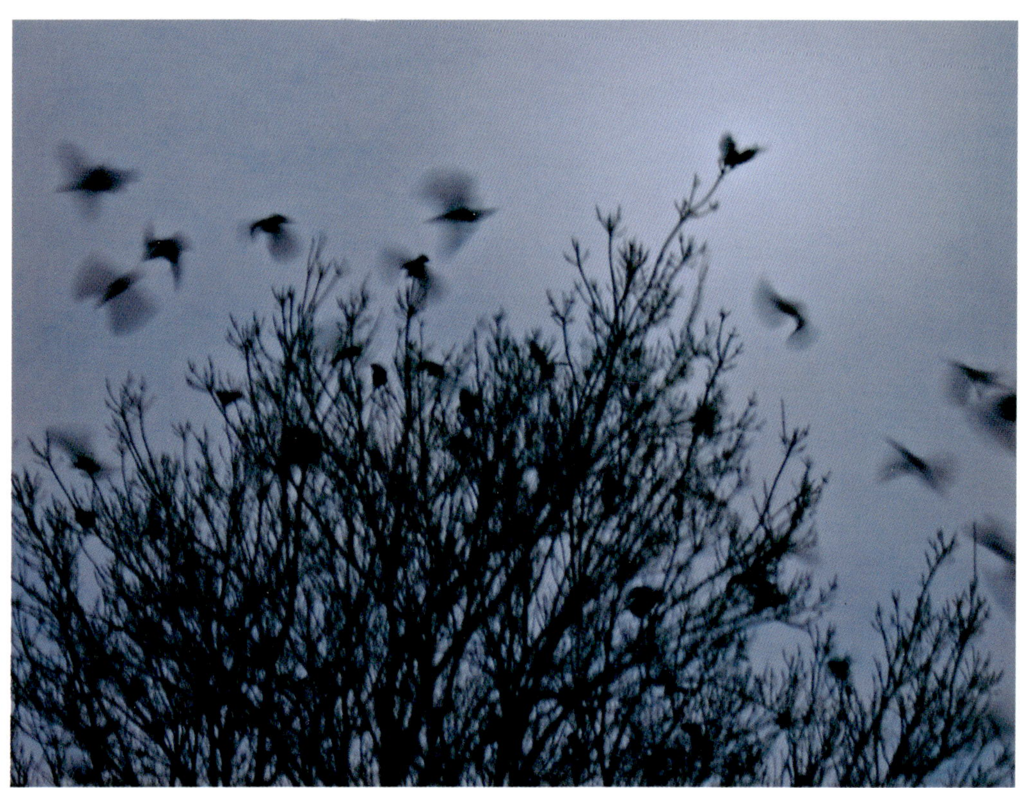

12.10.02

**Rainy weather, ravens at dawn**

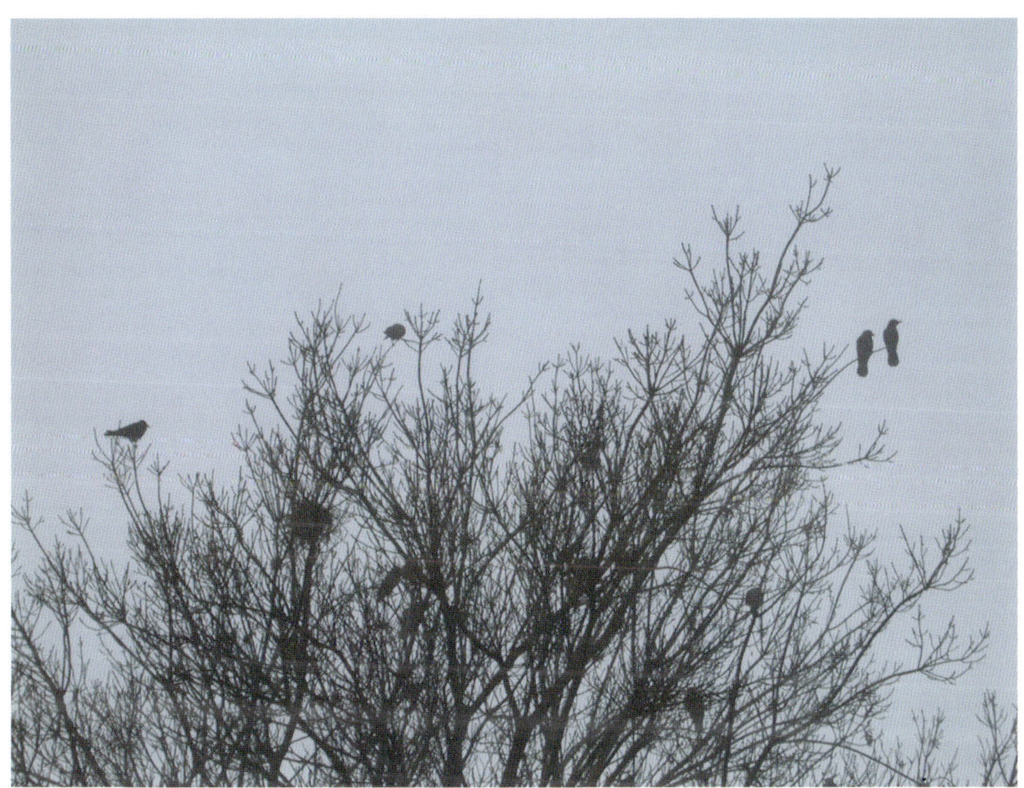

12.11.02

**Again with the ravens, now in a fog**

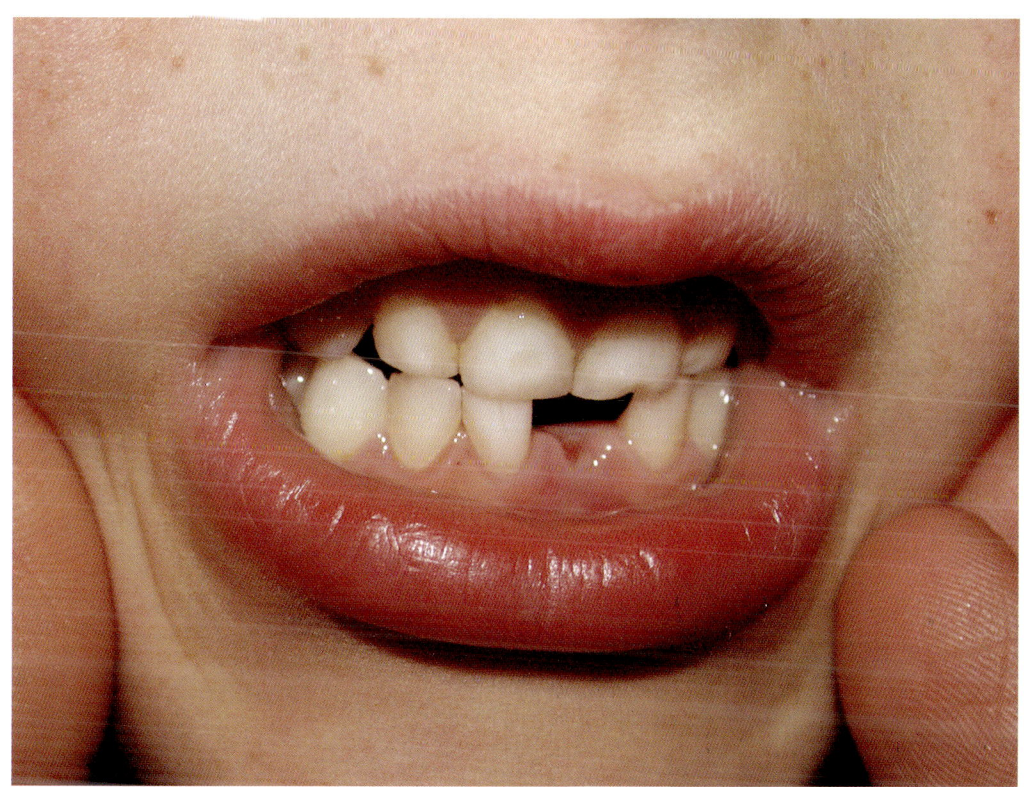

12.12.02
**Valued at $1.00**

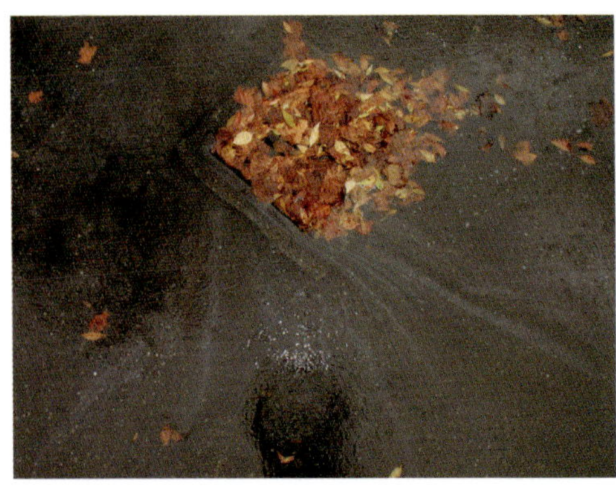

12.13.02
**Parking lot,**
**clogged storm drain,**
**the fourth straight day of rain**

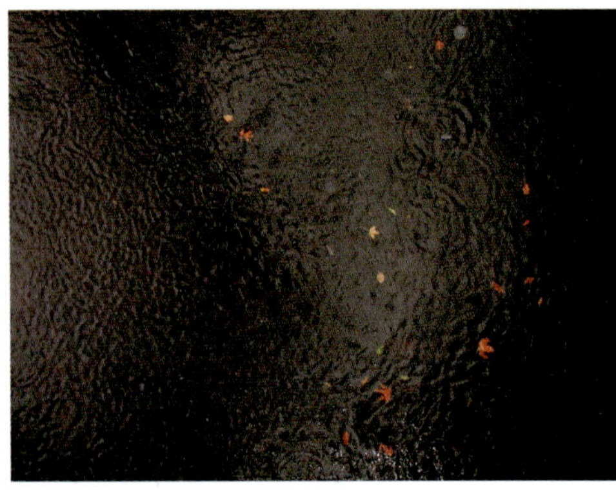

12.14.02
**Chico Creek in the rain**
**(day five)**

A major rainstorm (day six).

A minor depression.

What happened when I became more concerned with the destination

Than with the journey.

12.15.02

**The pictureless day**

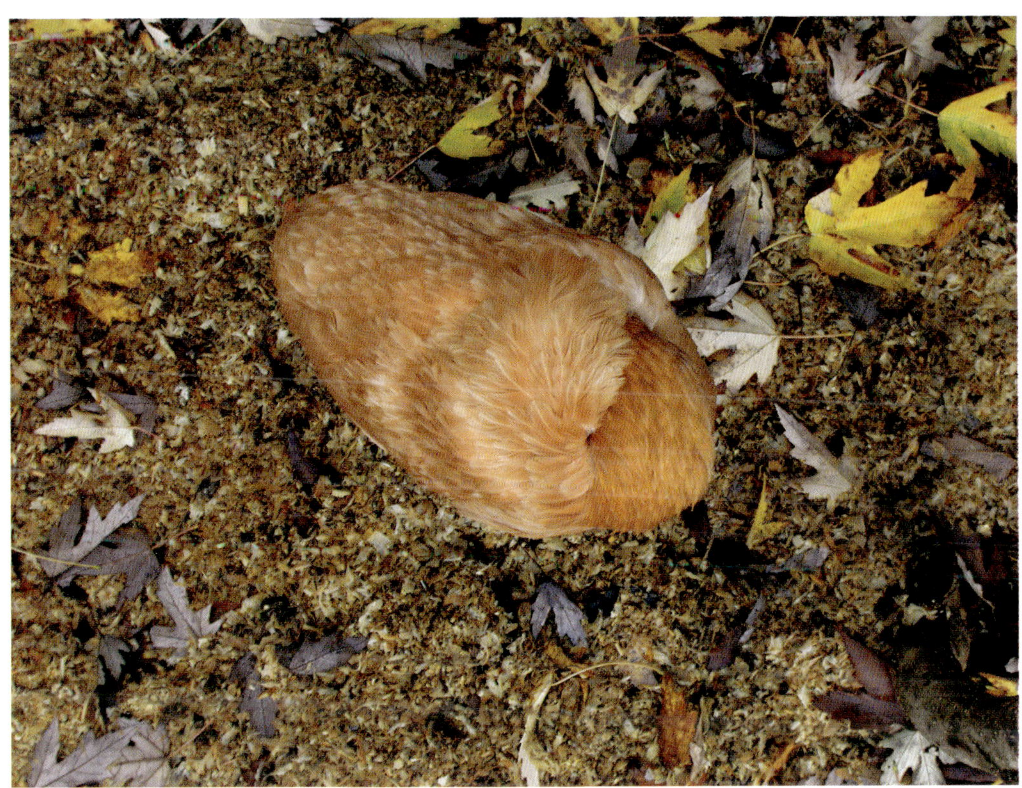

12.16.02

**"Yellow," resting quietly just hours before she passed away (cancer)**

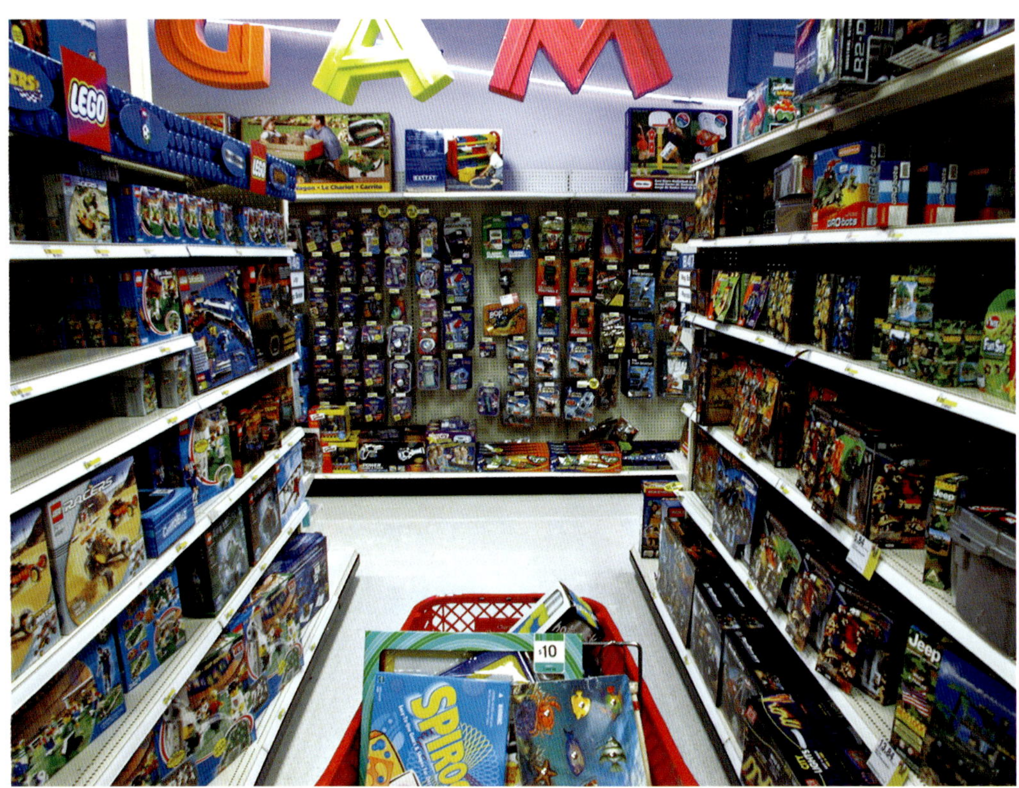


12.17.02

**Childless, on a rare date with my wife**

12.18.02

**The sky above the parking lot, Christmas shopping, day two**

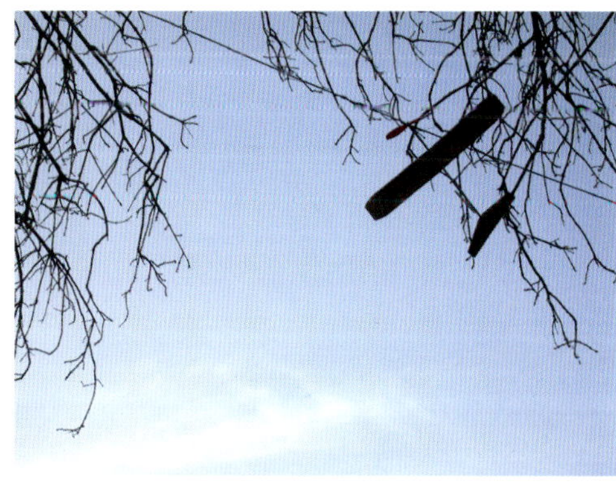

12.19.02

**Sky Streak's maiden flight**

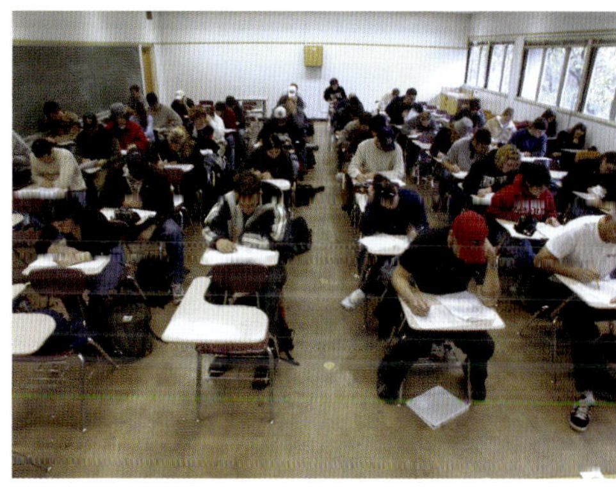

12.20.02

**Last class of the year**

# winter

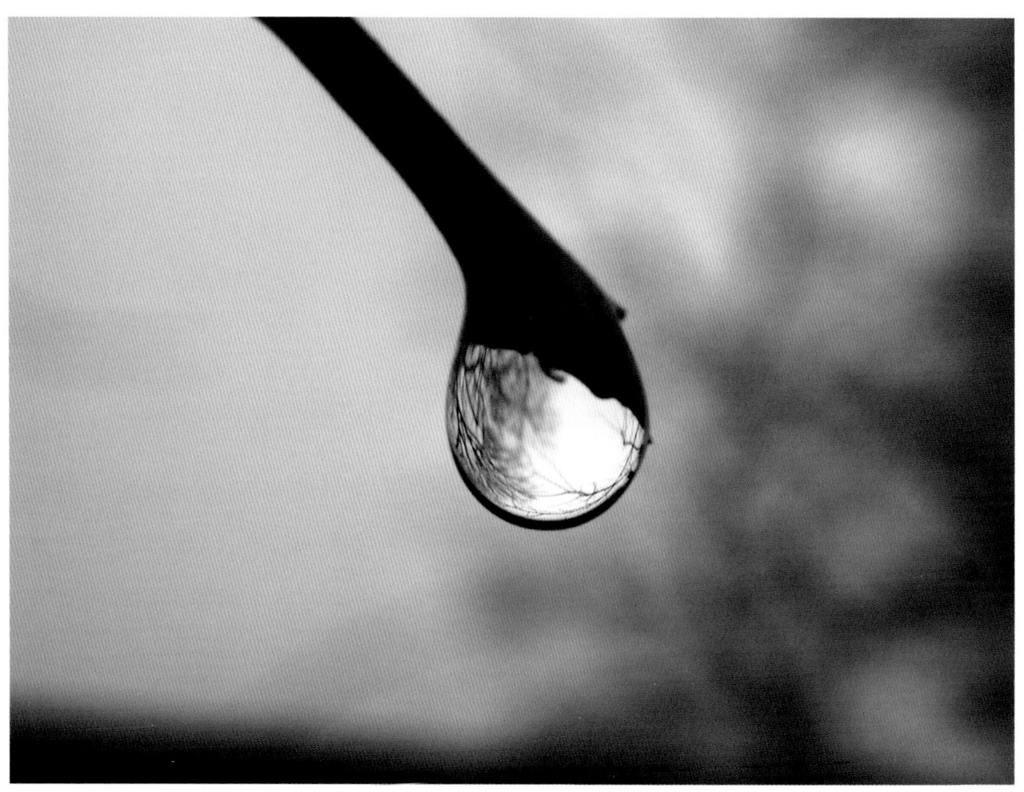

12.21.02

**Shortest day: at noon on the solstice, through the eyes of the Weeping Santa Rosa Plum**

12.22.02

**Minor turbulence**
**en route to Collinsville, Oklahoma**

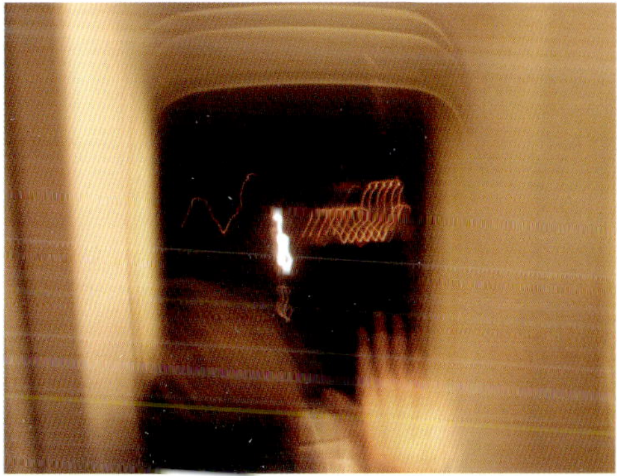

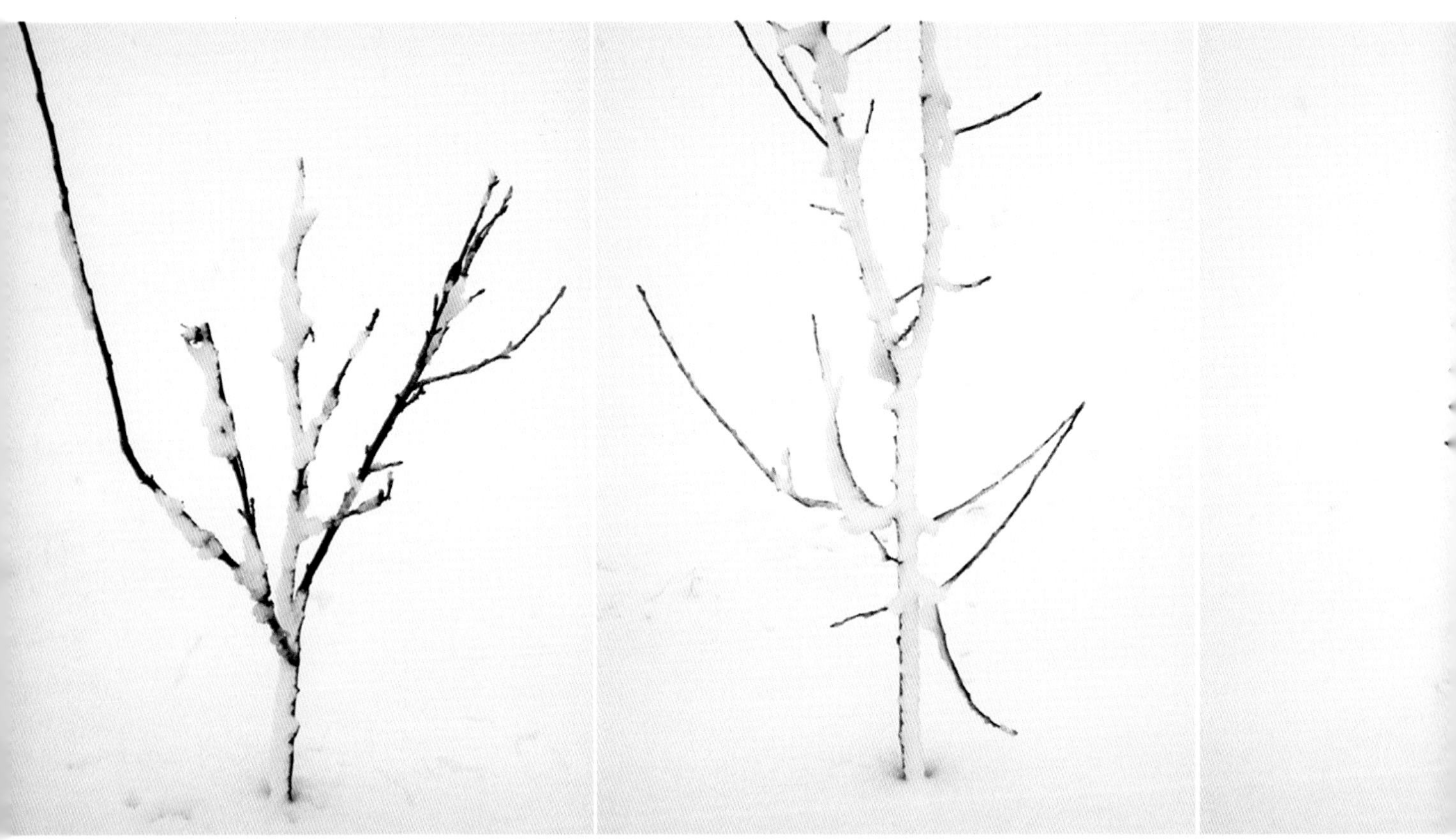

12.23.02

**1,875.5 miles—**
**The distance traveled**
**To photograph my father's trees**
**And watch them bend**
**From the weight of the day.**

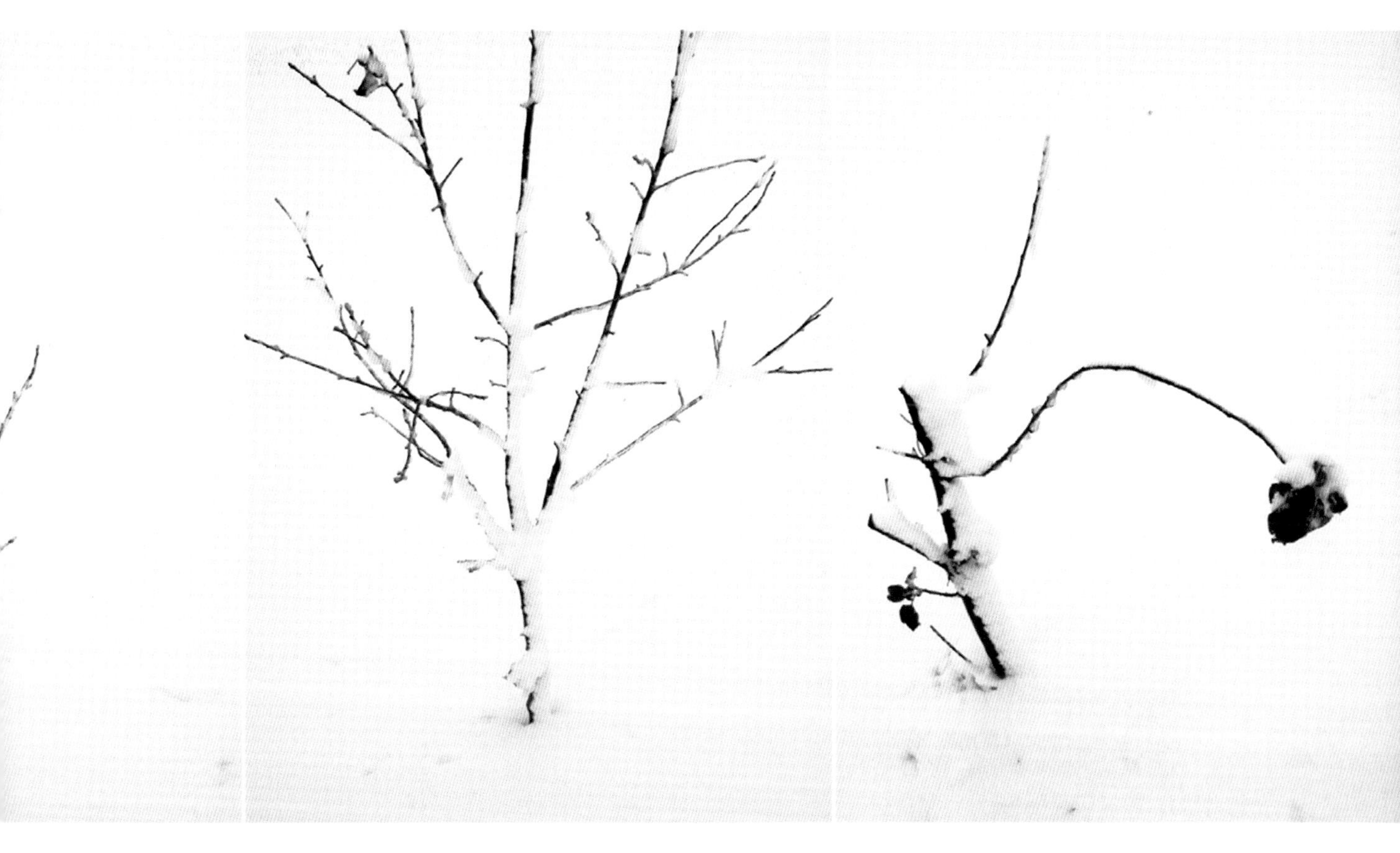

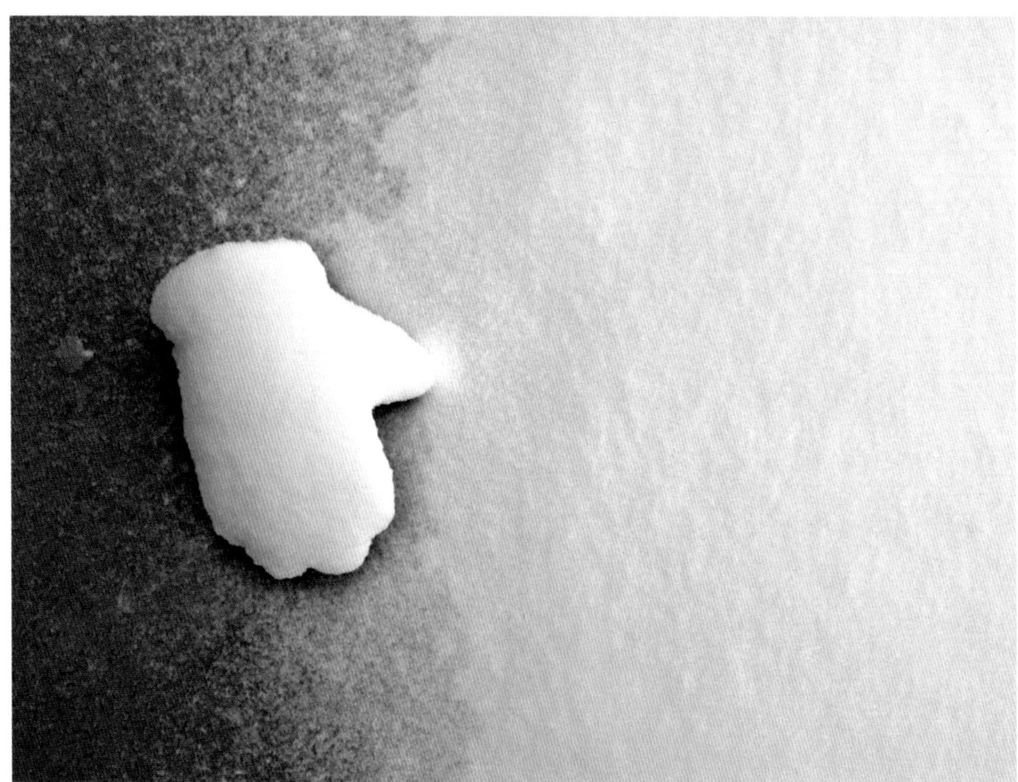

12.24.02

**Black mitten**

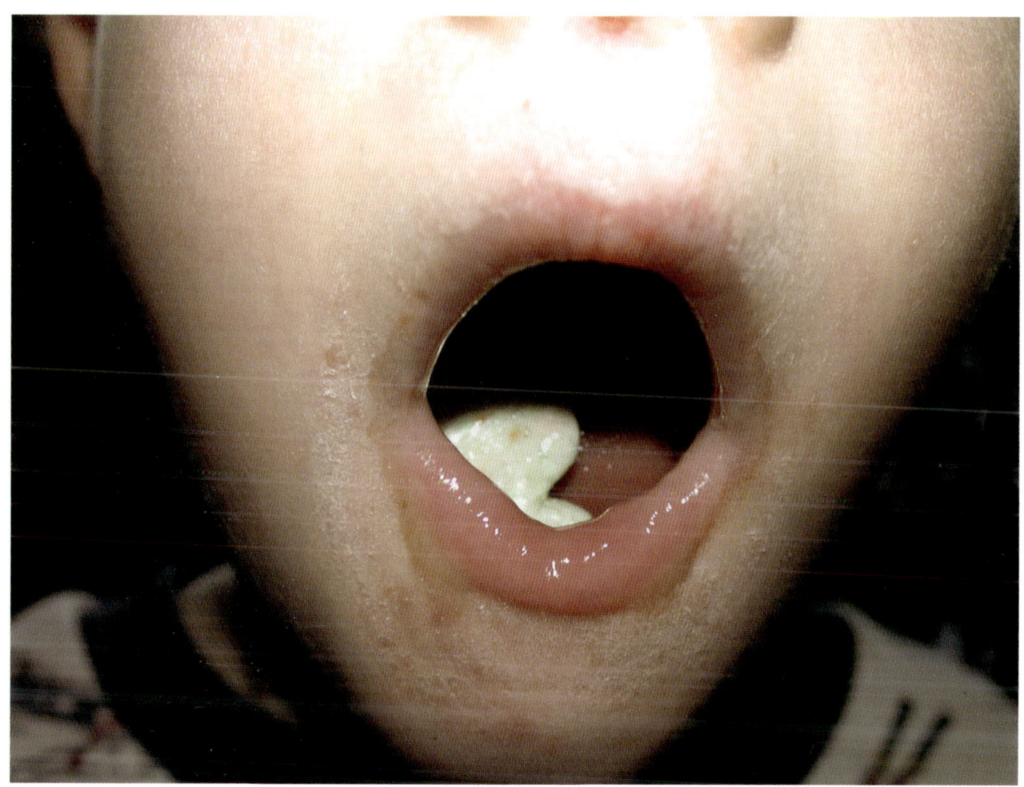

12.25.02

**Christmas morning, stockings emptied, an entire pack of Chiclets**

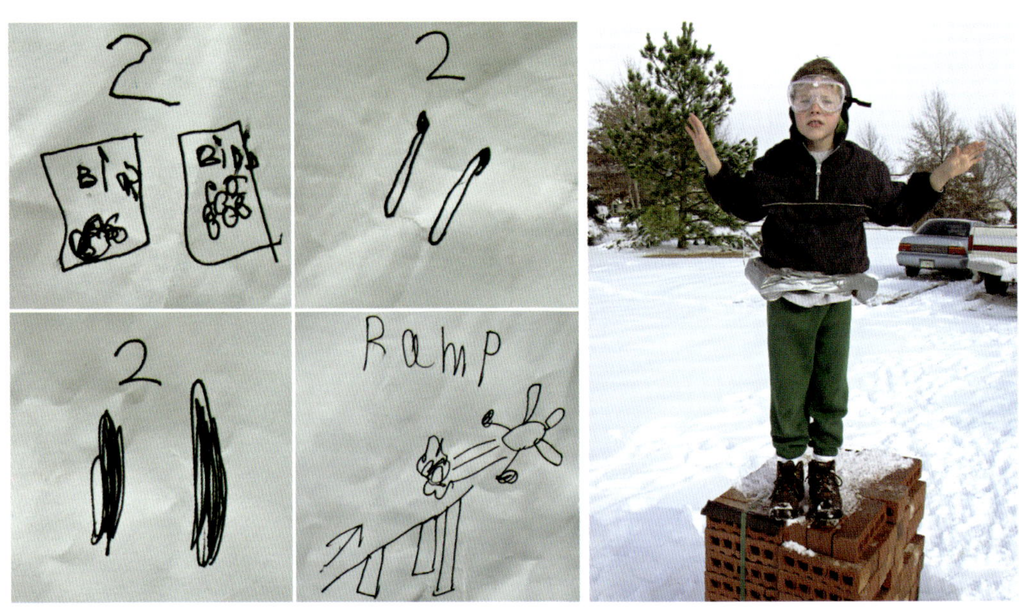


12.26.02

**Home-built jet-pack parts list: two empty bean cans, two matches, two pieces of duct tape, and one inclined ramp**

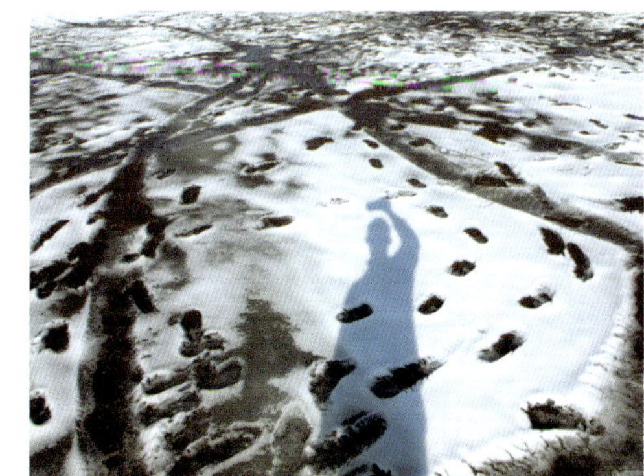

12.27.02
**Marks we made**
**on Christmas Day**

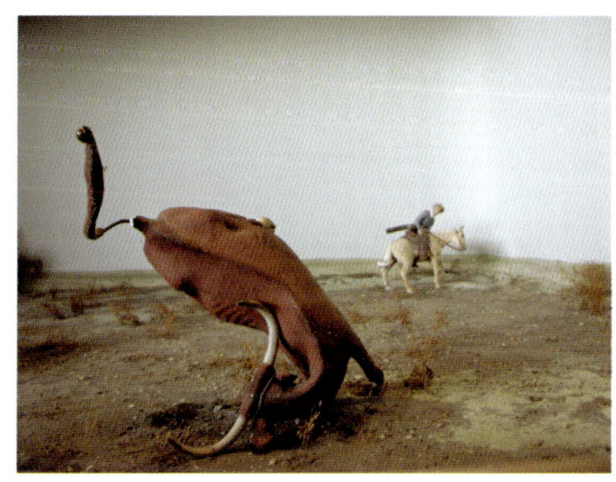

12.28.02
**Making history:**
**diorama from an Oklahoma sightseeing tour—**
**Will Rogers (1879–1935) roping a steer**

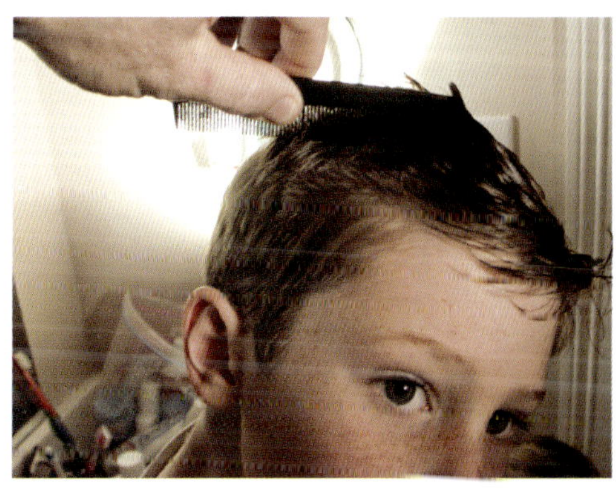

12.29.02
**Church**

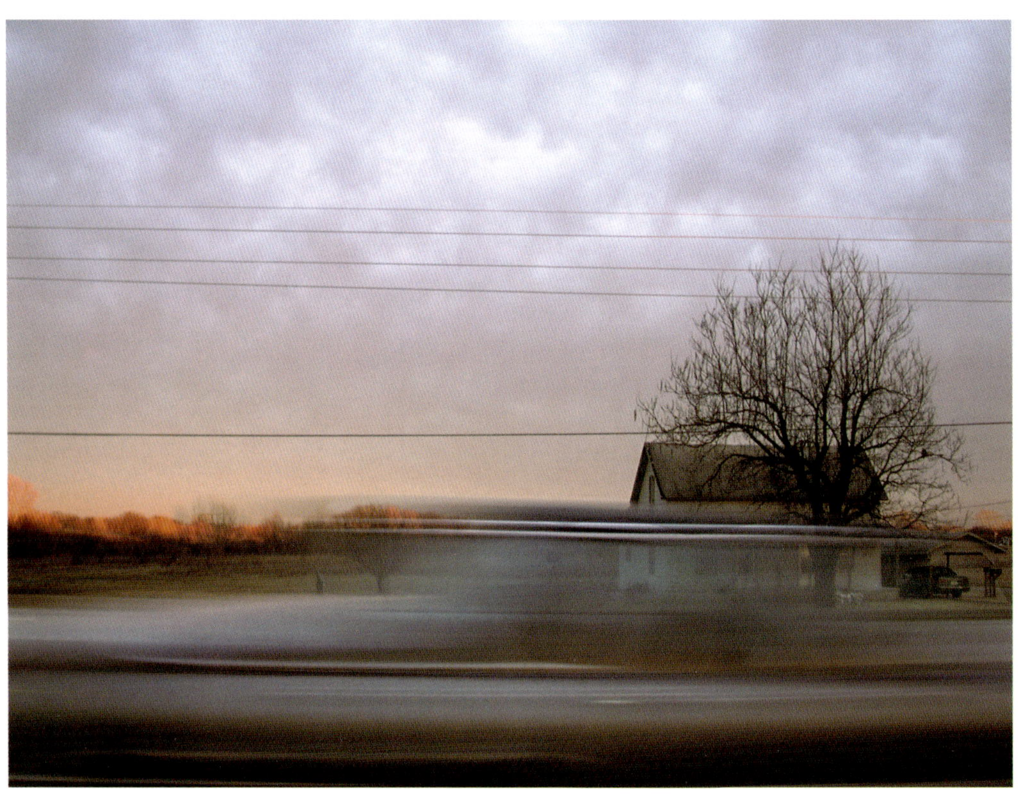

12.30.02

**Commuter traffic and farmhouse near my childhood home: standing in the parking lot of a franchised rib joint (when I was a kid, this was a field with pet buffalo), Tulsa, Oklahoma**

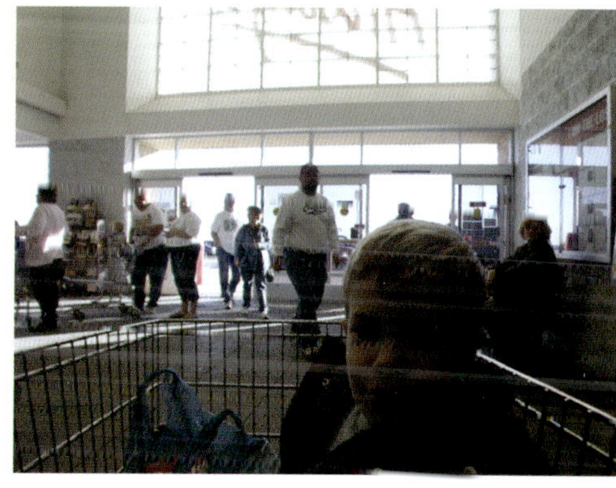

12.31.02

**Last-minute party supplies, Wal-Mart**

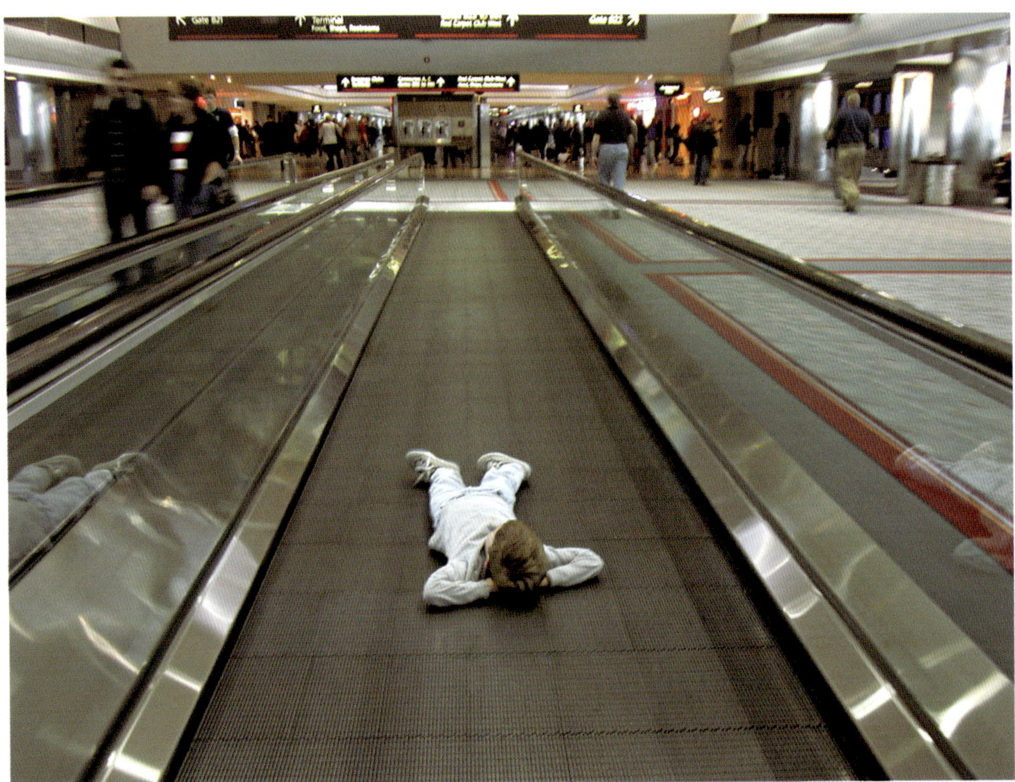


01.01.03

**New Year's Day, Denver International Airport**

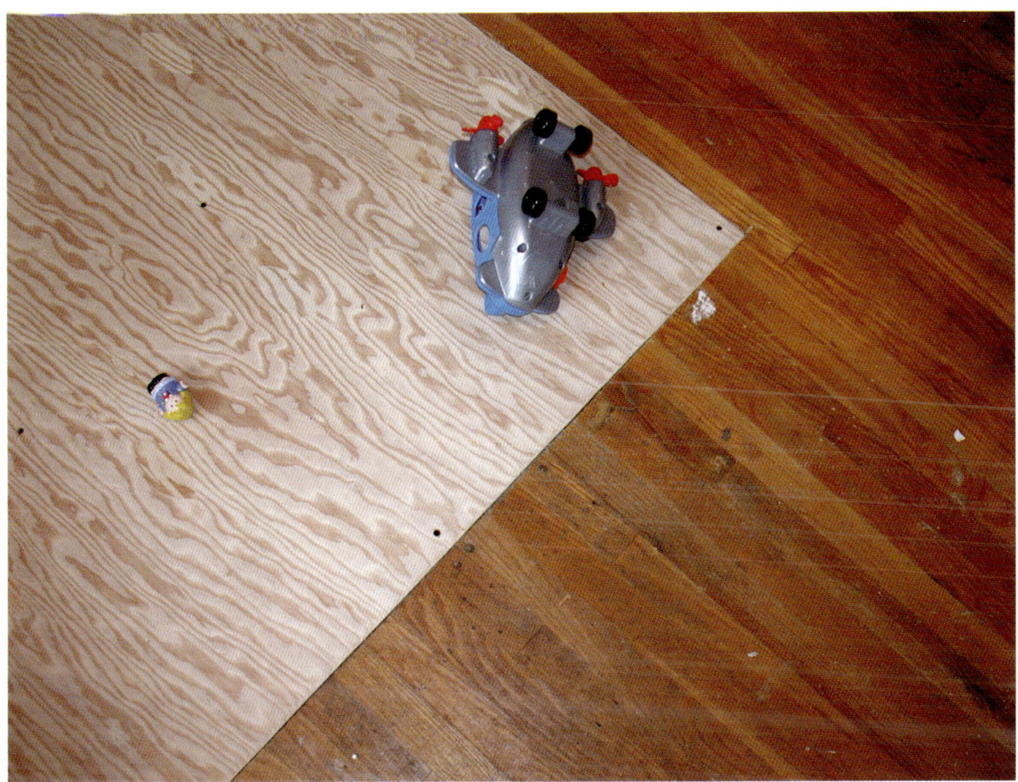

01.02.03

**Back home in Chico—where our roof leaked through seven days of heavy rain**

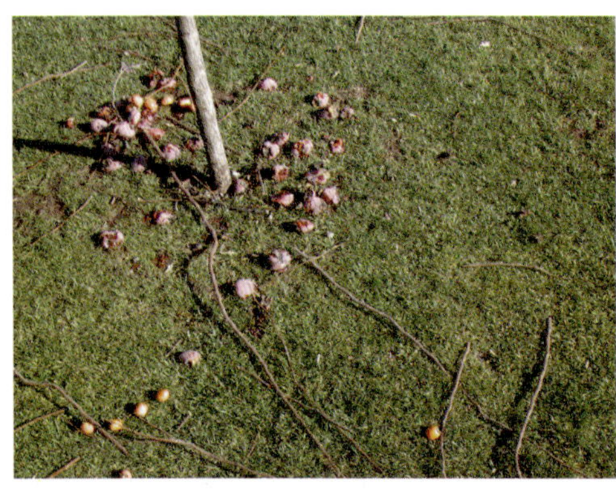

01.03.03

**Hen-pecked persimmons among recent cuttings**

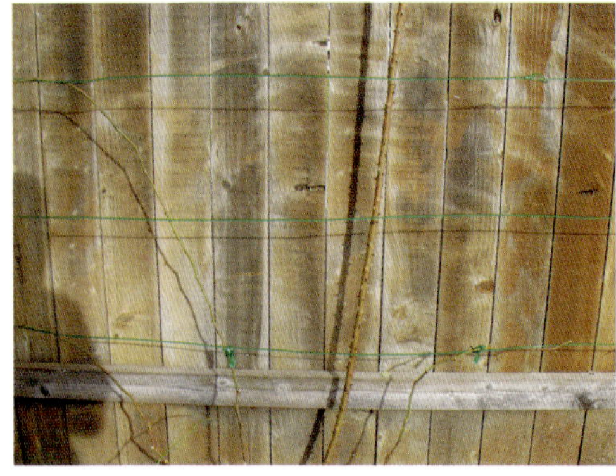

01.04.03

**January roses**

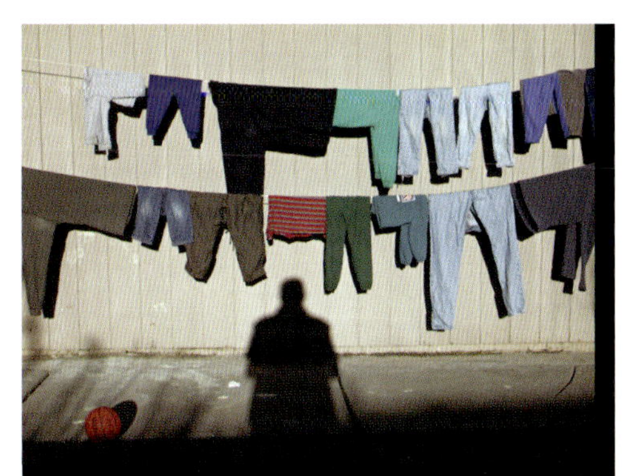
01.05.03

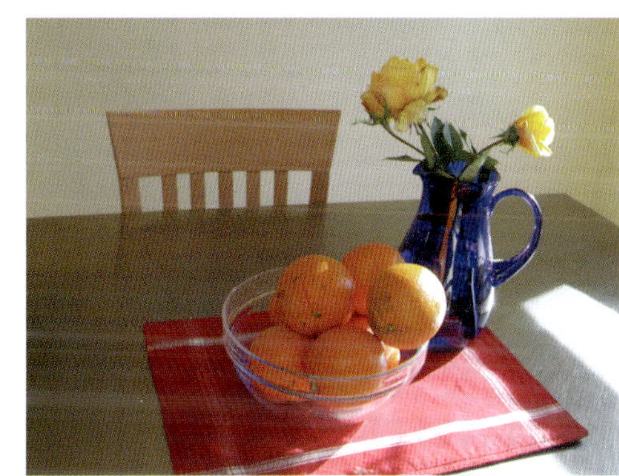
01.06.03

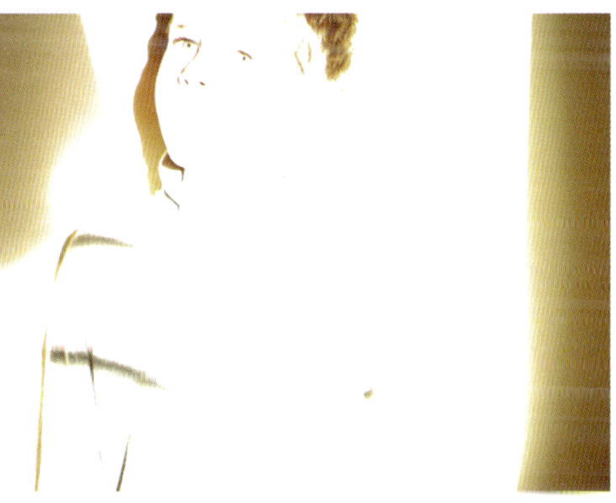
01.07.03

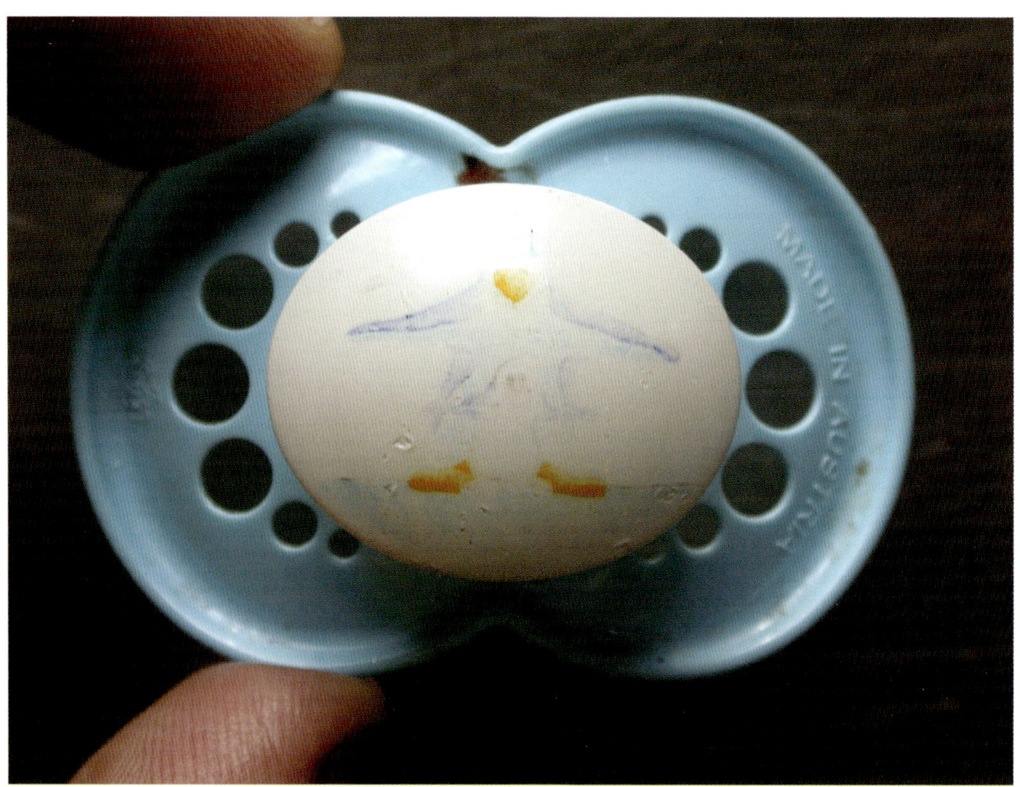

01.08.03

**My son's favorite binky**

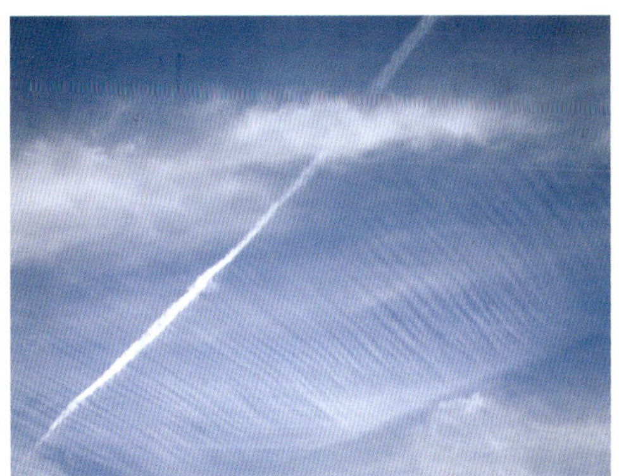

01.09.03

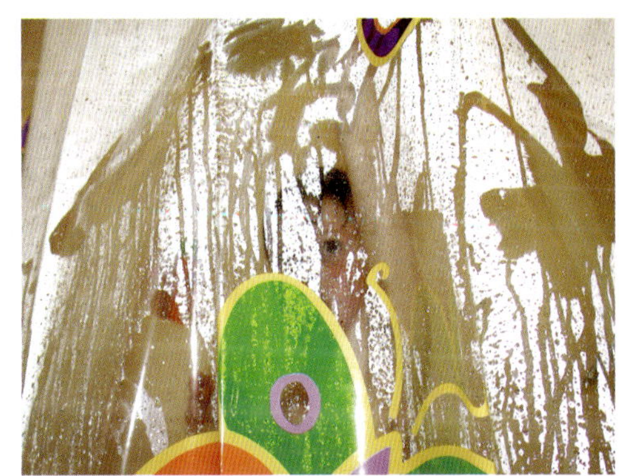

01.10.03

**New shower curtain!**

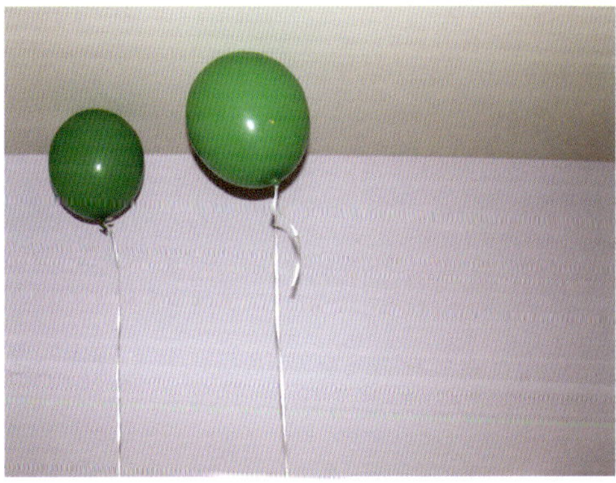

01.11.03

**The only toy guaranteed to end in tears**

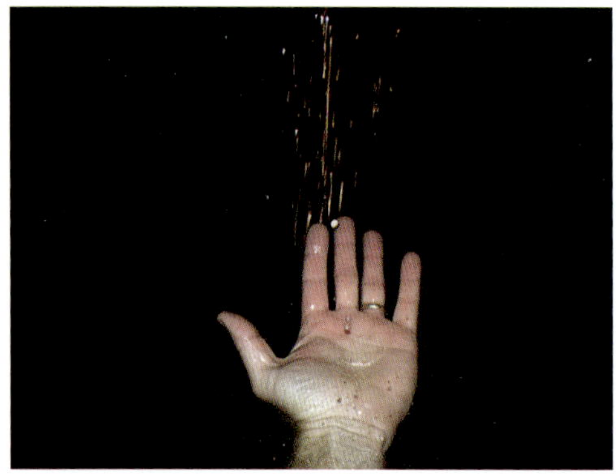

01.12.03

**More winter rain**
**(probably leaking into the attic)**

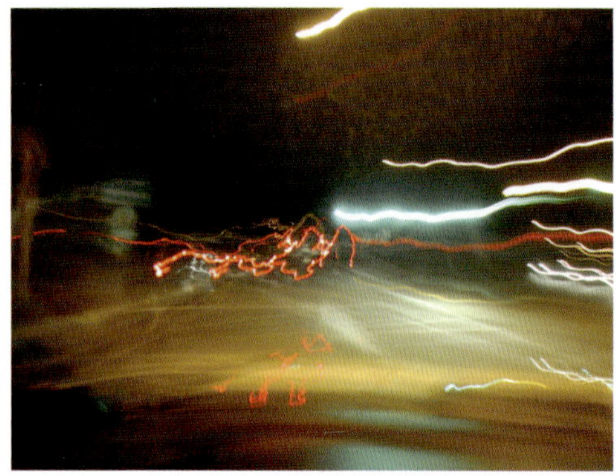

01.13.03

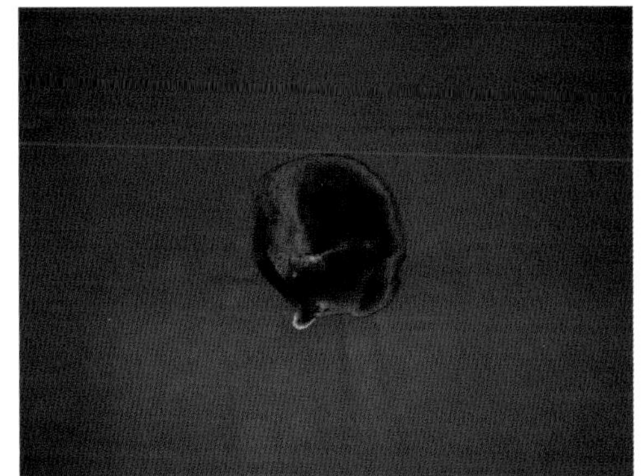

01.14.03
**11:00 PM,**
**cat in the center of our bed**

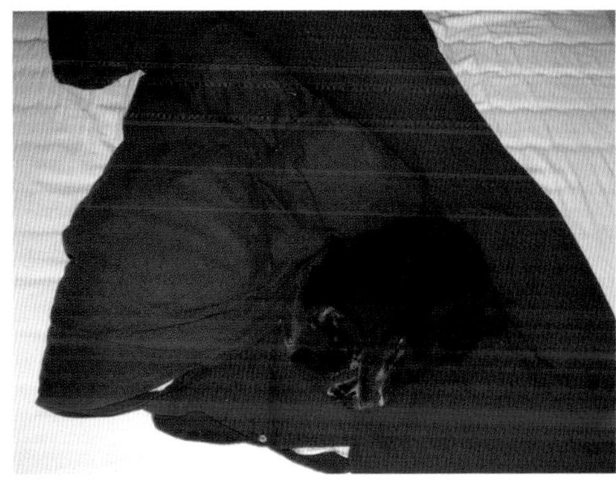

01.15.03
**8:23 AM,**
**cat at the foot of our bed**

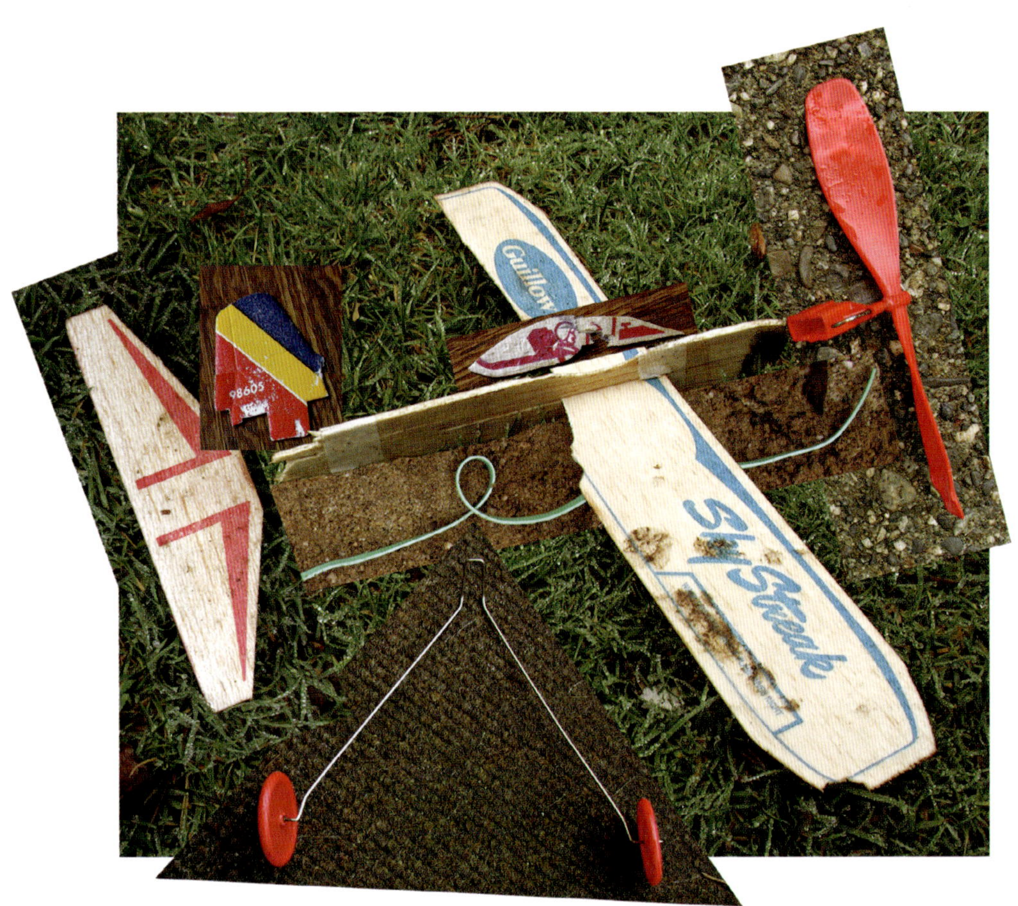


01.16.03

**Reconstructing the legendary Sky Streak from parts around the house**

01.17.03

**A rare moment of sun**

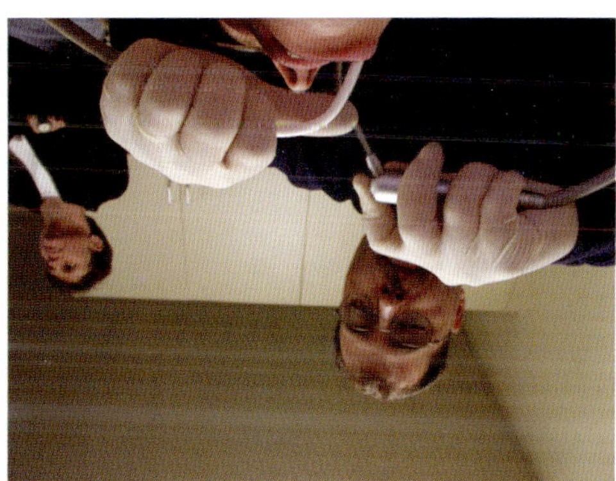

01.18.03

**My dentist**

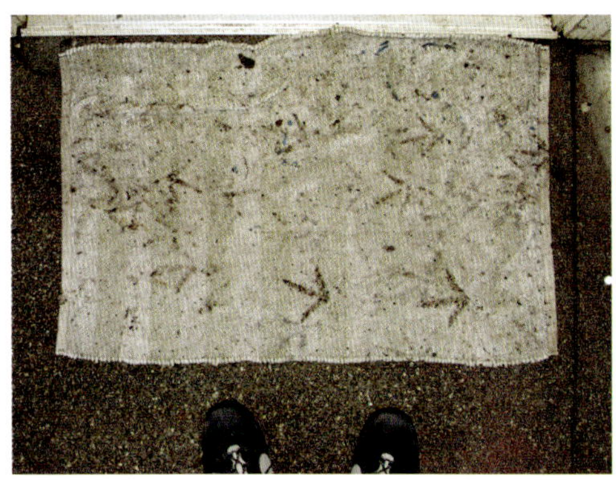

01.19.03
**Damn chickens**

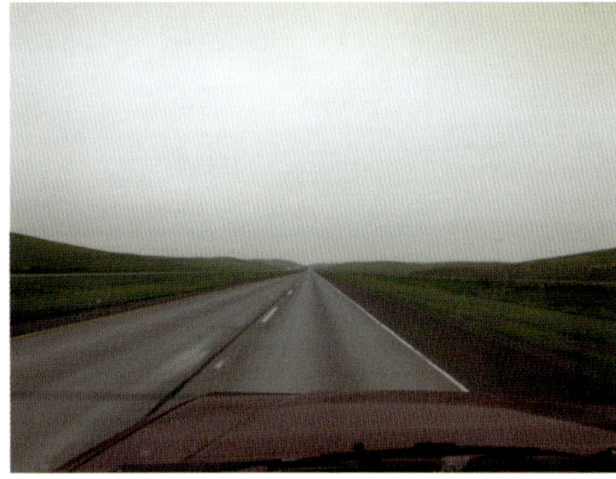

01.20.03
**The valley fog at noon, on California Highway 99**

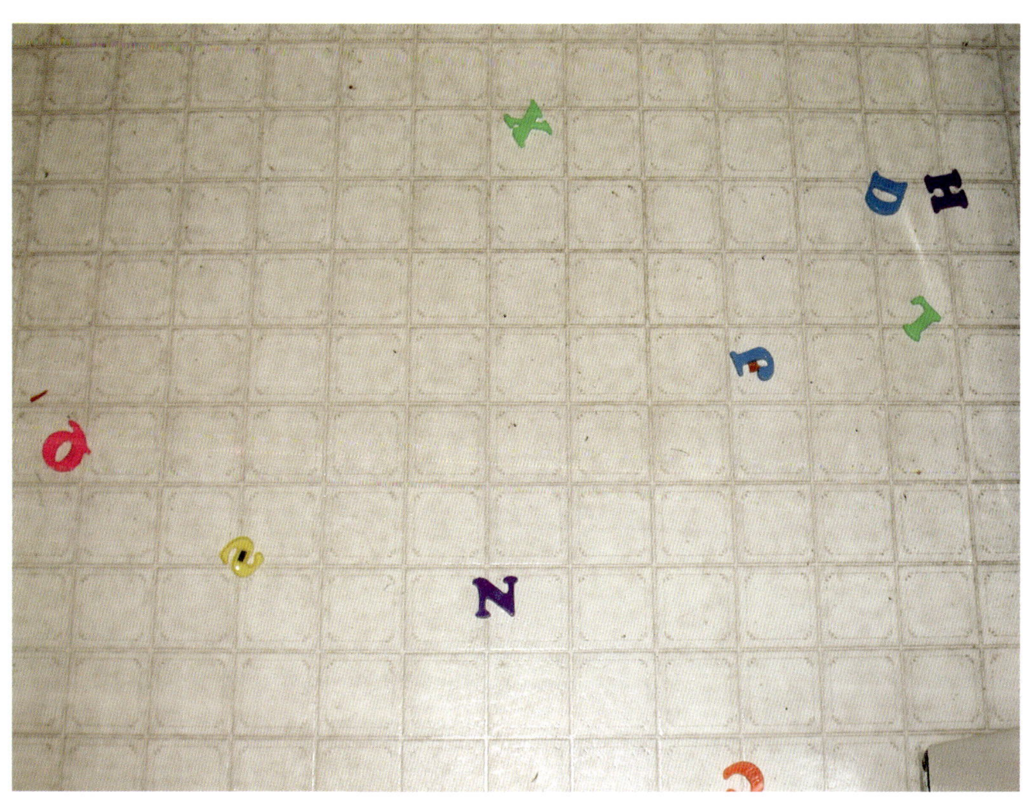

01.21.03

**O, S, N, C, X, J, L, D, and H**

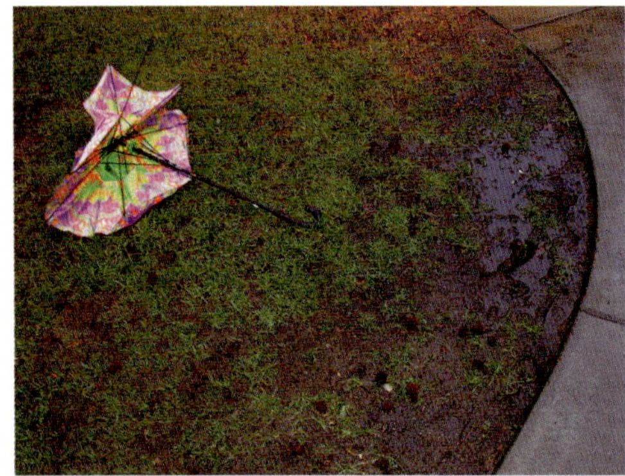

01.22.03

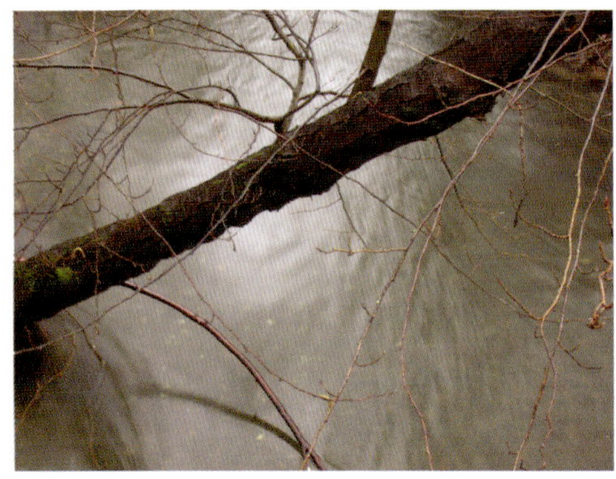

01.23.03

**Fallen tree,**
**Chico Creek in the rain**

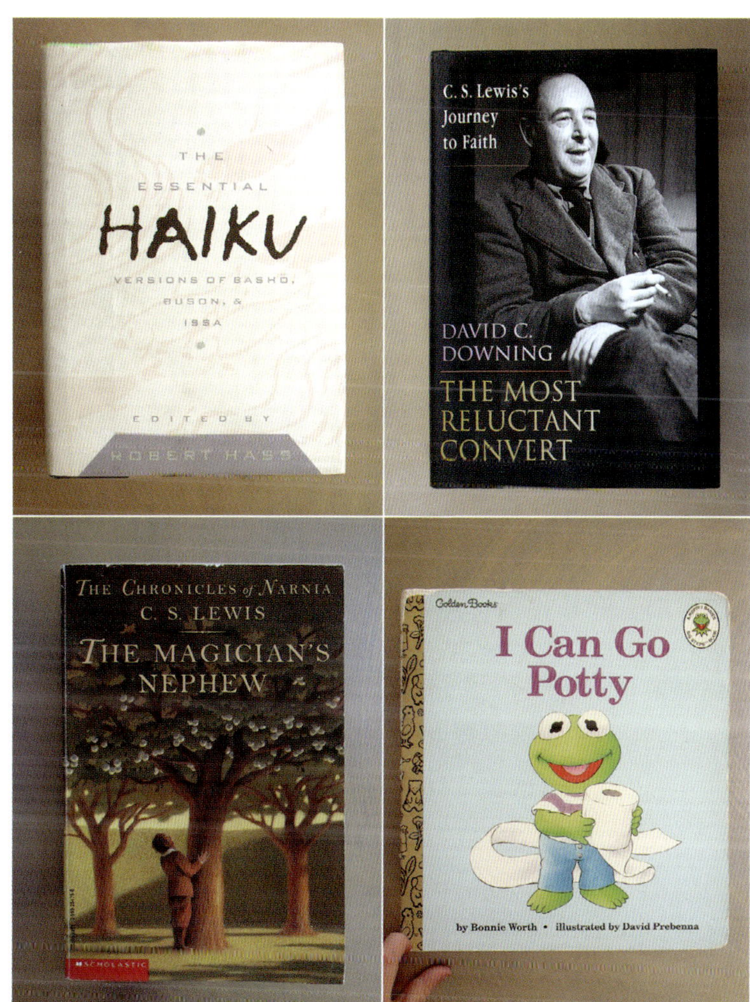


01.24.03

**What the family is reading**

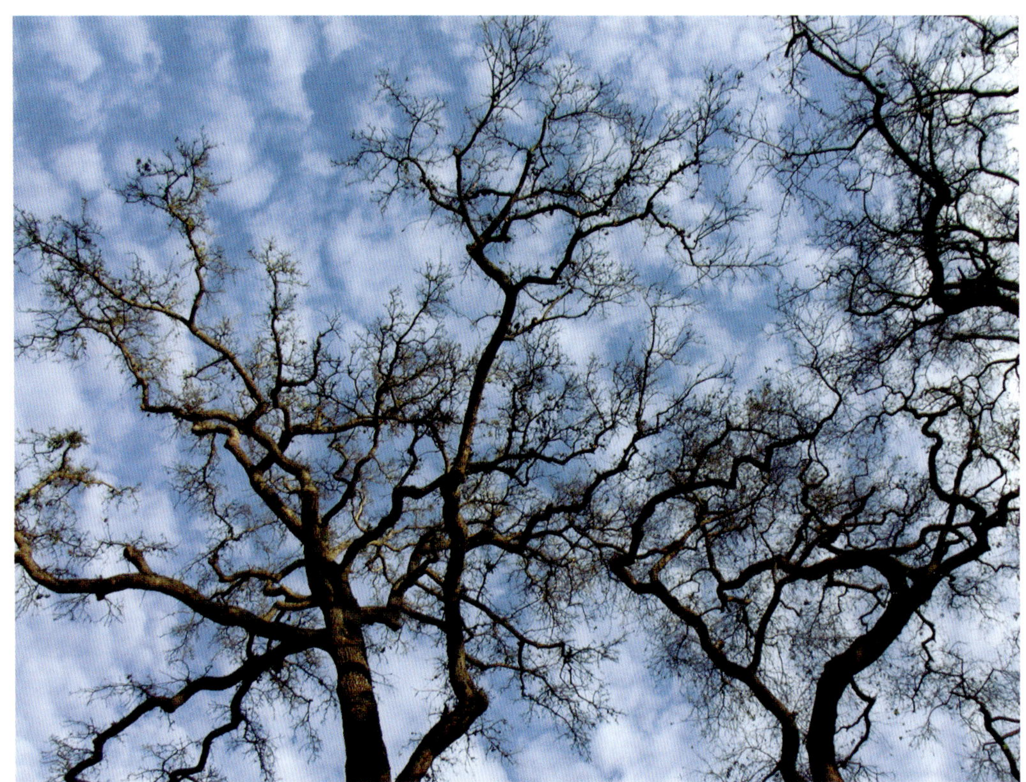

01.25.03

**While on a walk with a friend who leaves tomorrow to go to a probable war**

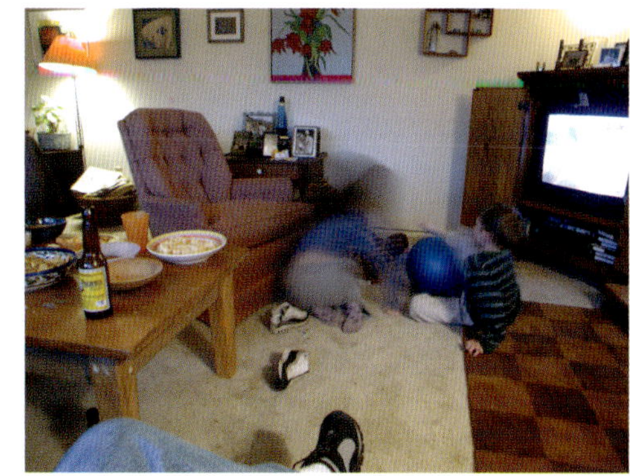

01.26.03

**Super Bowl Sunday**

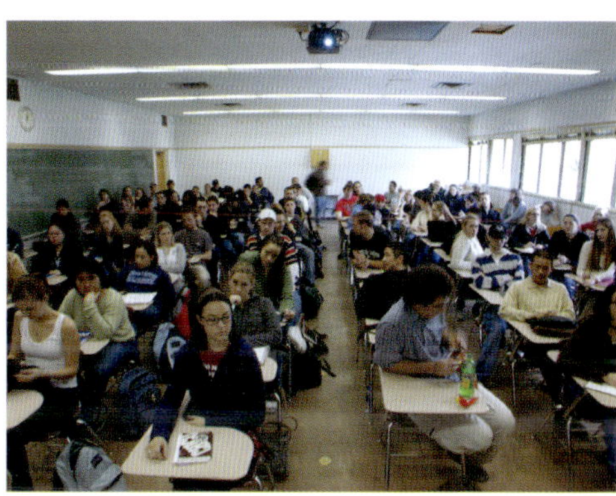

01.27.03

**Back to work**

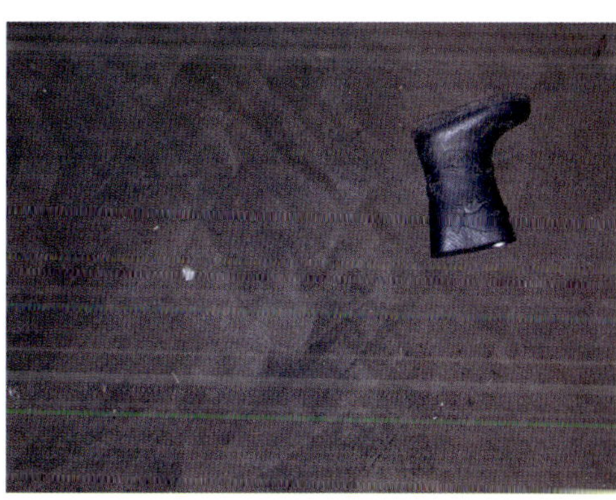

01.28.03

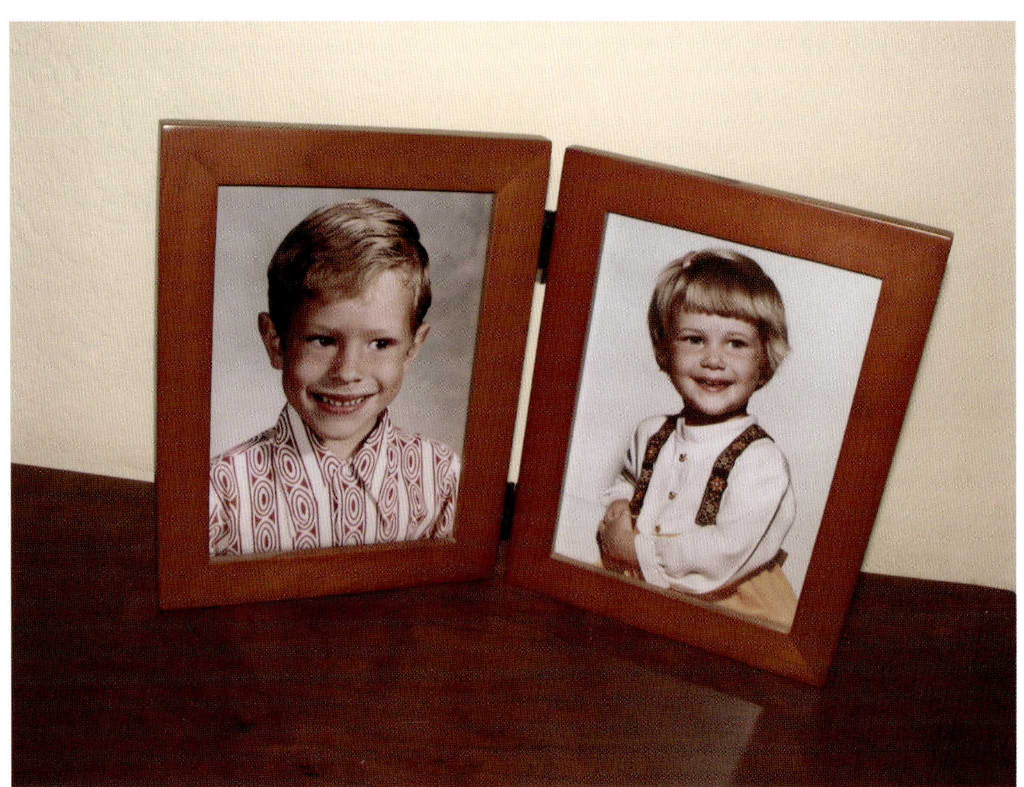

01.29.03

**When we were kids**

01.30.03

**Another foggy morning**

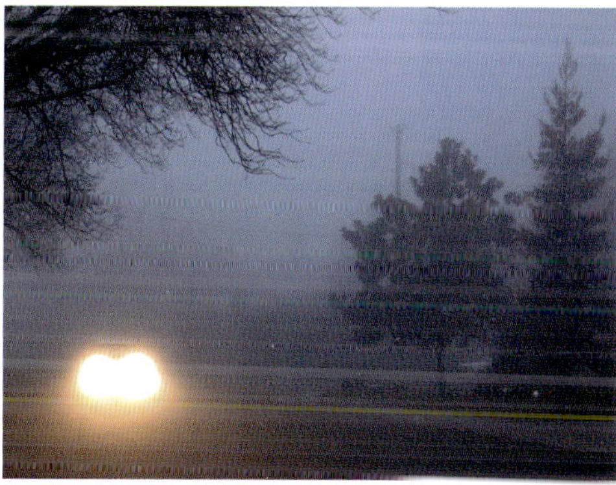

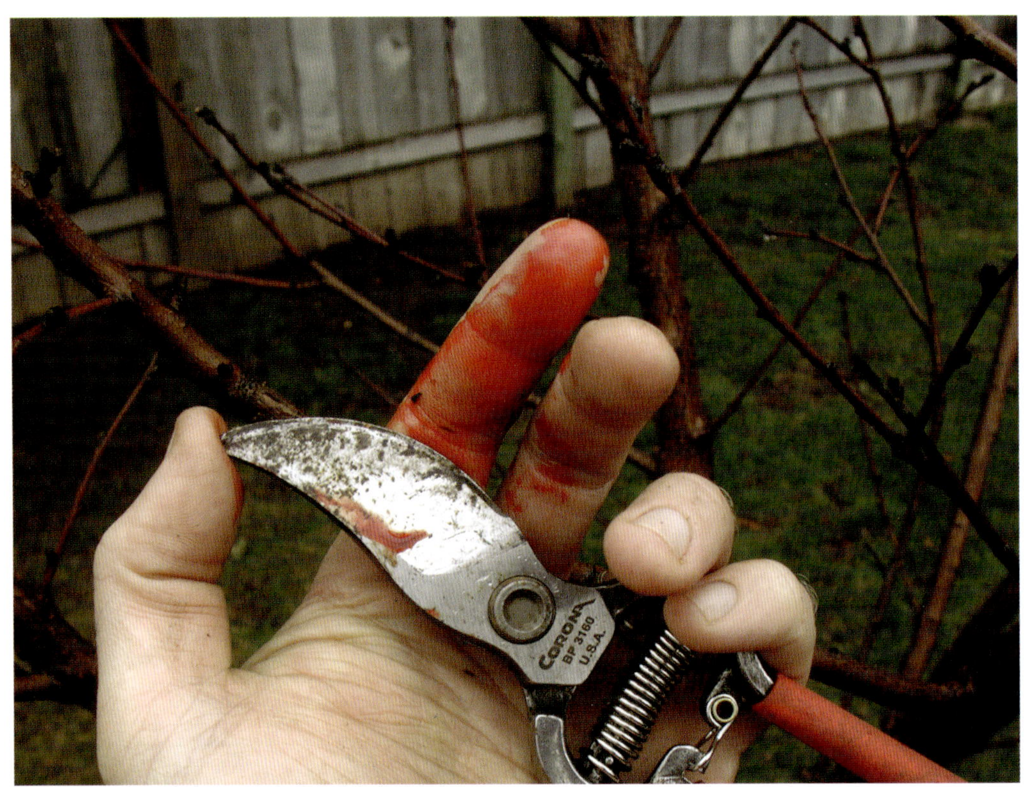


01.31.03

**Pruning the peach tree**

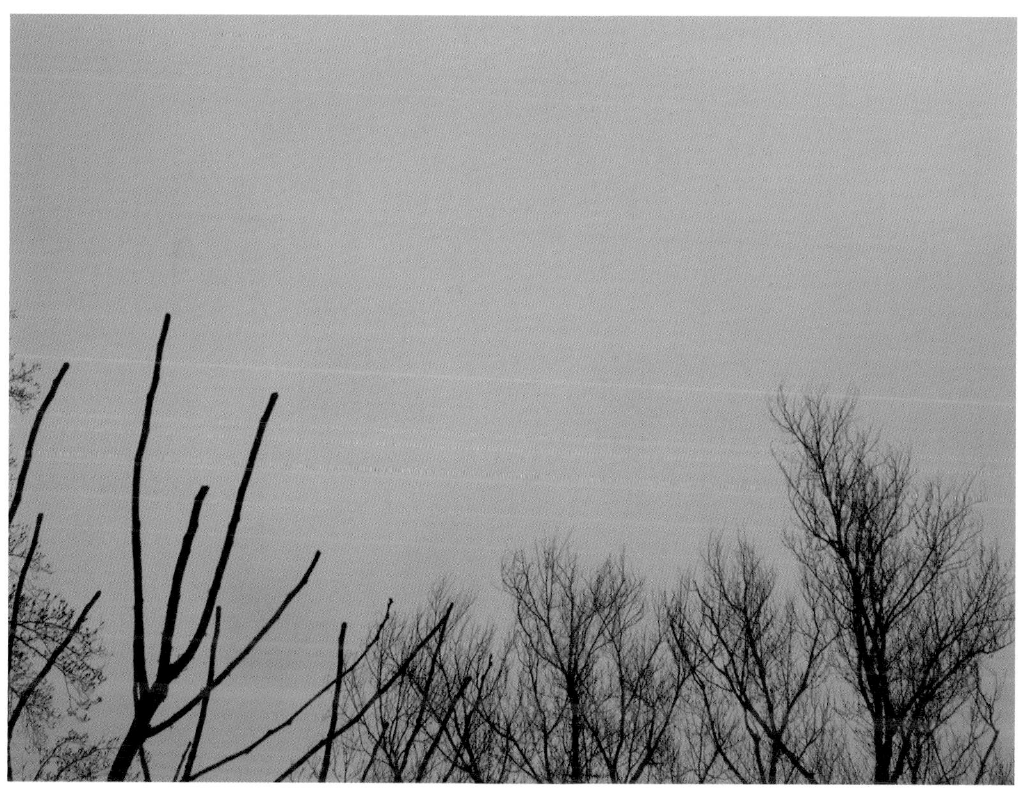

02.01.03

**Early morning, looking toward a Texas sky and the lost space shuttle**

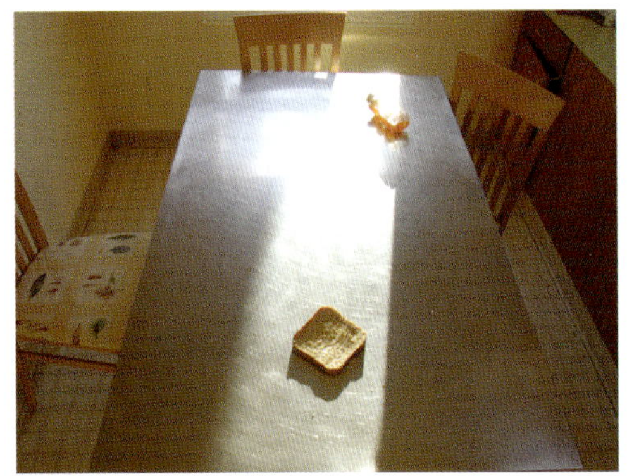

02.02.03

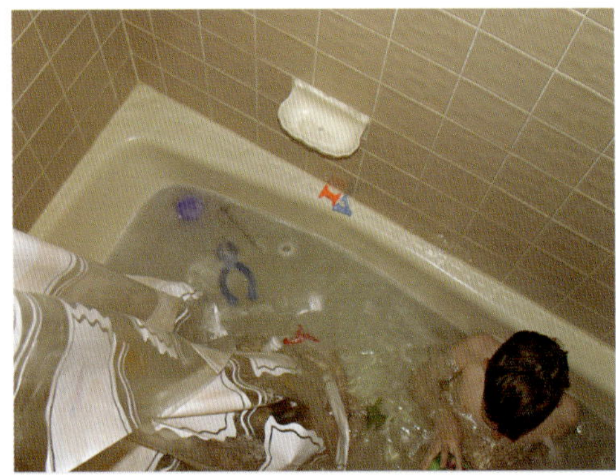

02.03.03

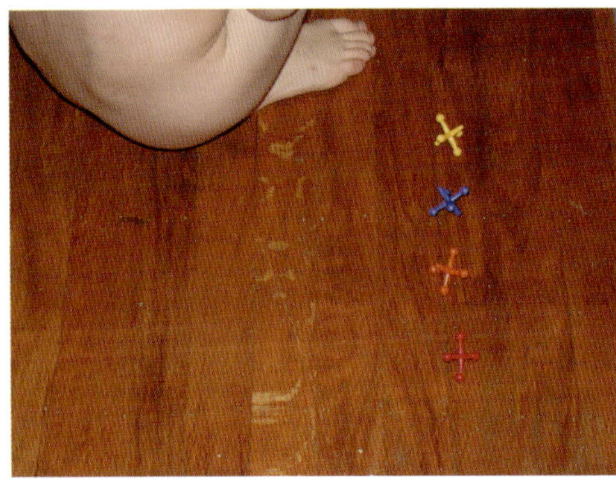

02.04.03

02.05.03

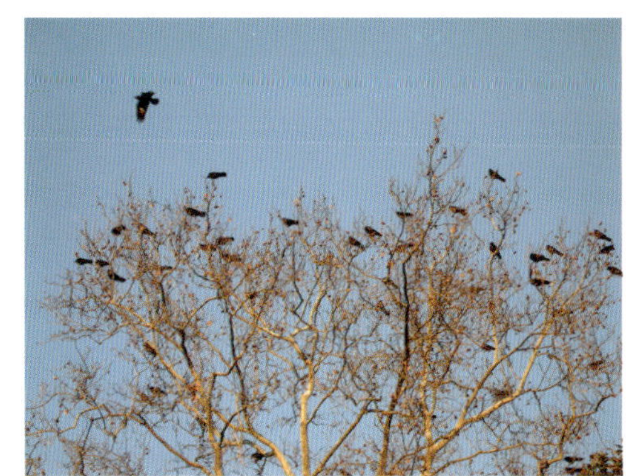

02.06.03

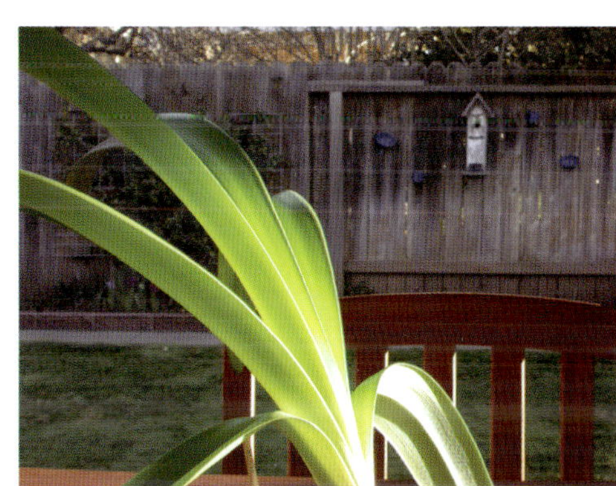

02.07.03

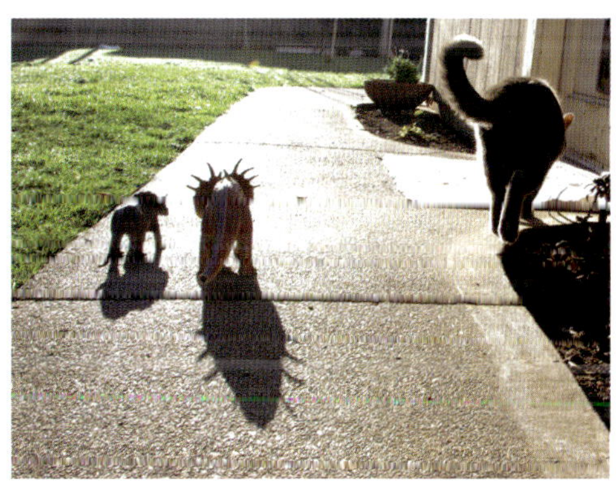

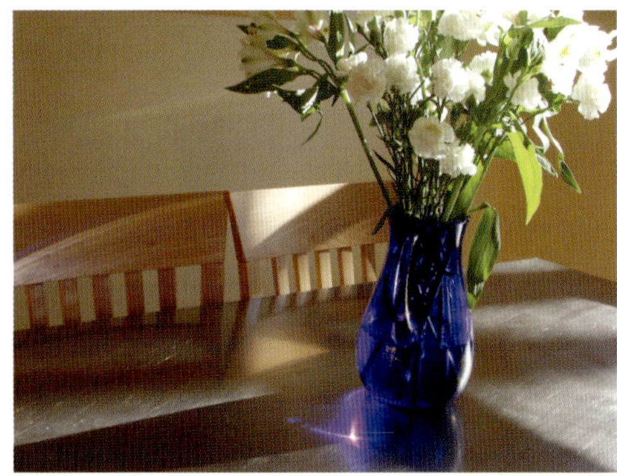

02.08.03

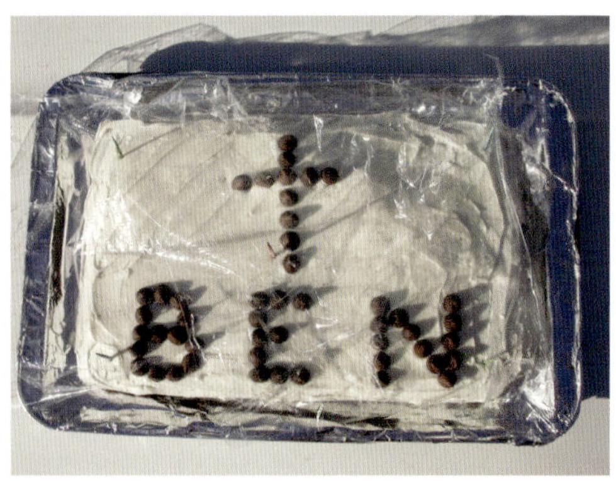


02.09.03

**Baked by a friend for Ben’s baptism**

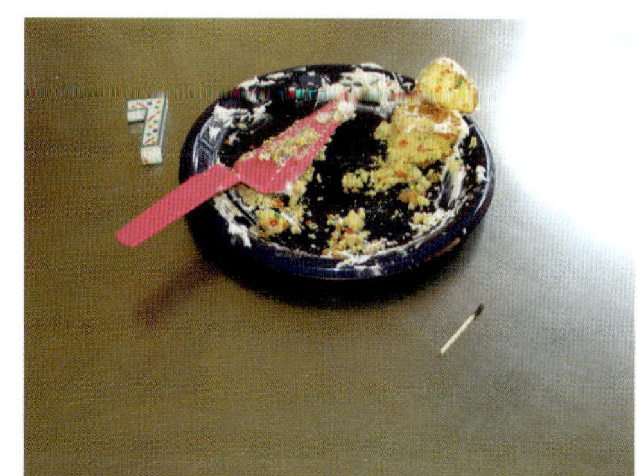

02.10.03

02.11.03

**Moonrise**

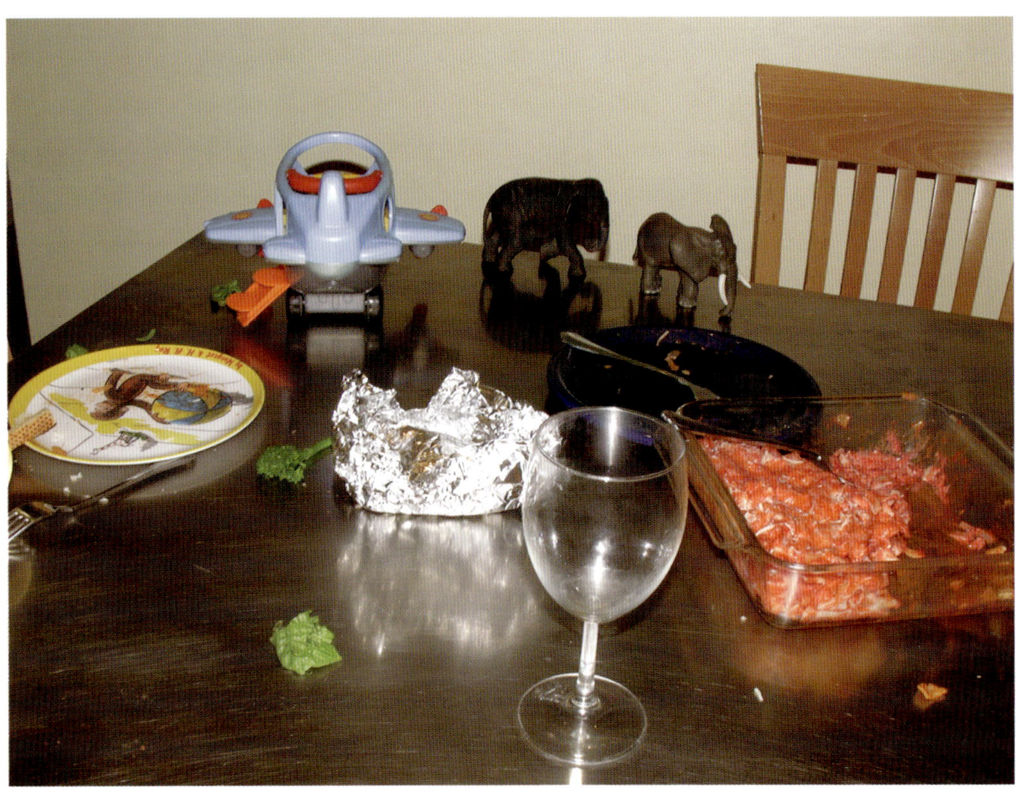

02.12.03

**Another typical dinner**

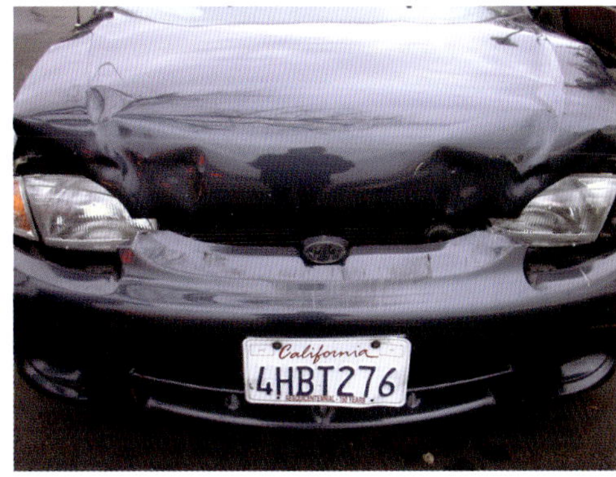


02.13.03

**The car that rear-ended me**

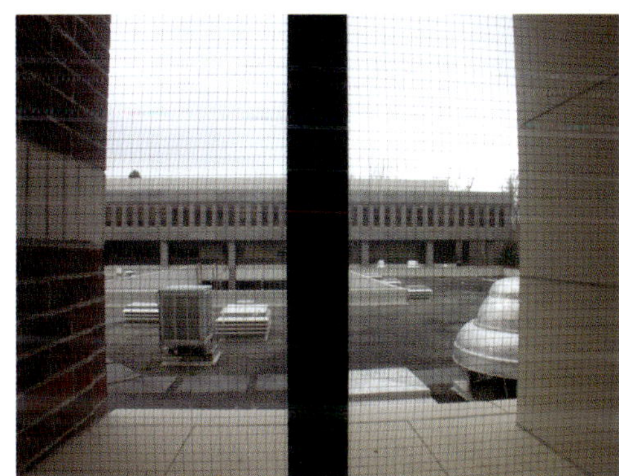

02.14.03

**Rainy day from "Institution Point"
(my locked office window)**

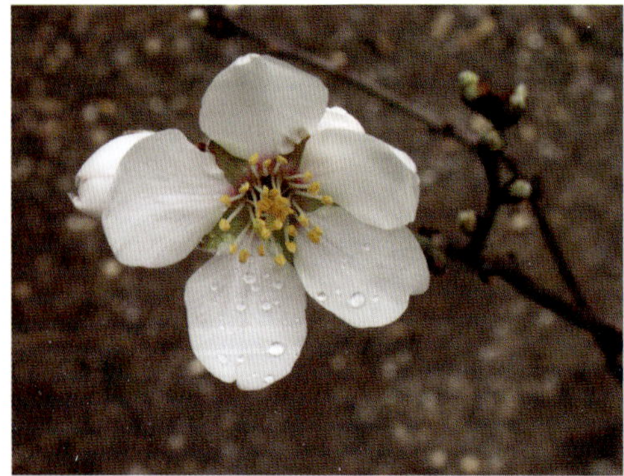

02.15.03

**First almond blossom**

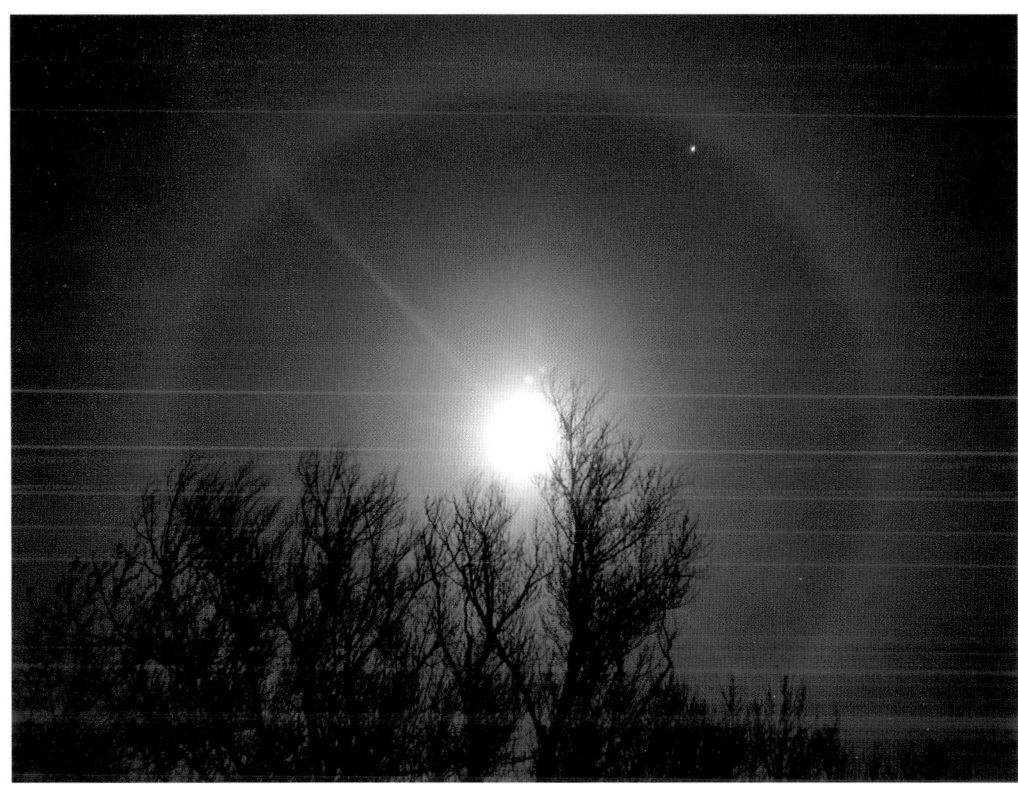

02.16.03

**Jupiter within the full moon's halo**

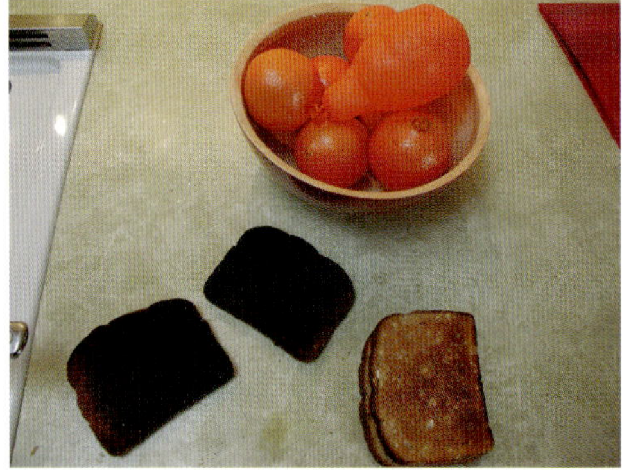

02.17.03

**Breakfast,**
**late to work,**
**and the only picture I made all day**

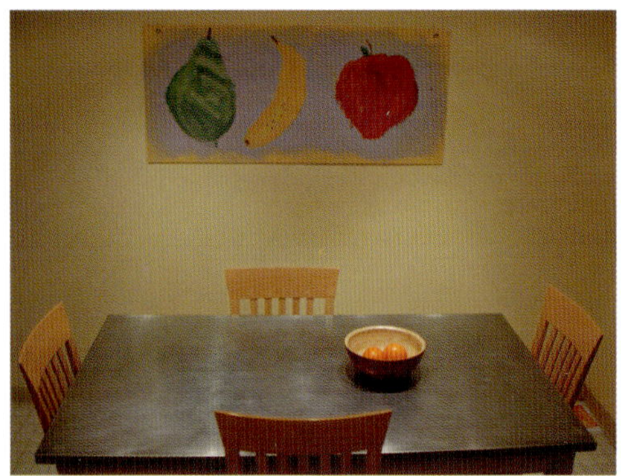

02.18.03

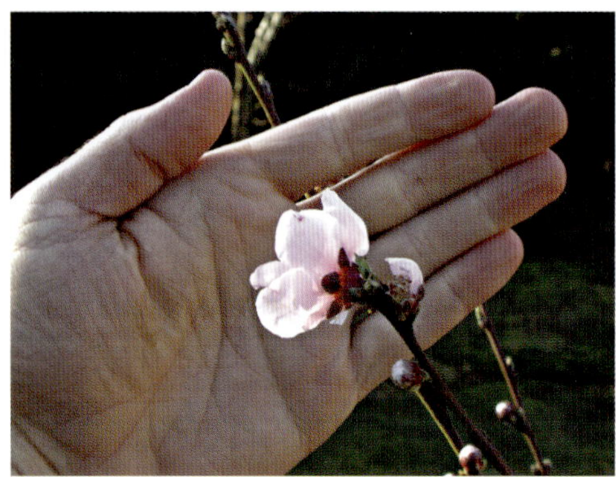

02.19.03

**First nectarine blossom**

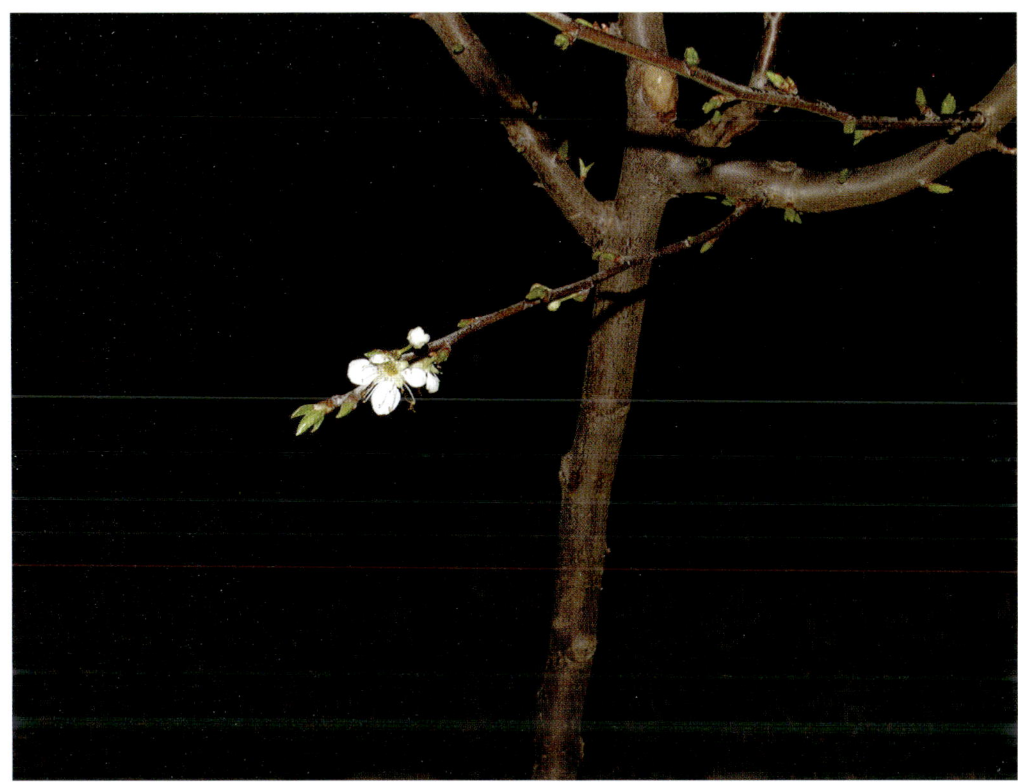

02.20.03

**Only six Mariposa plum blossoms, each one damaged in a gentle rain**

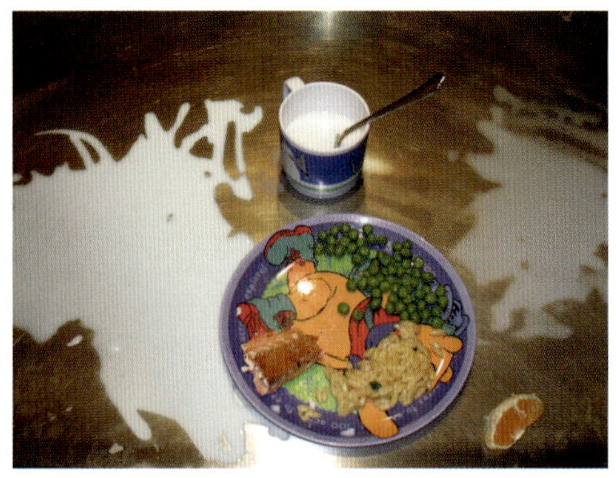

02.21.03

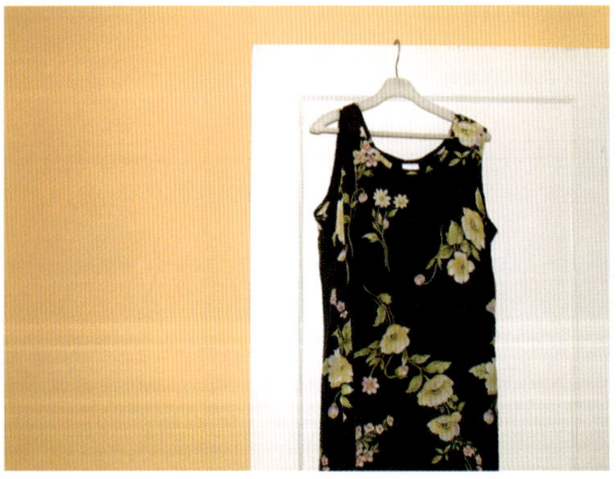

02.22.03
**Saturday night**

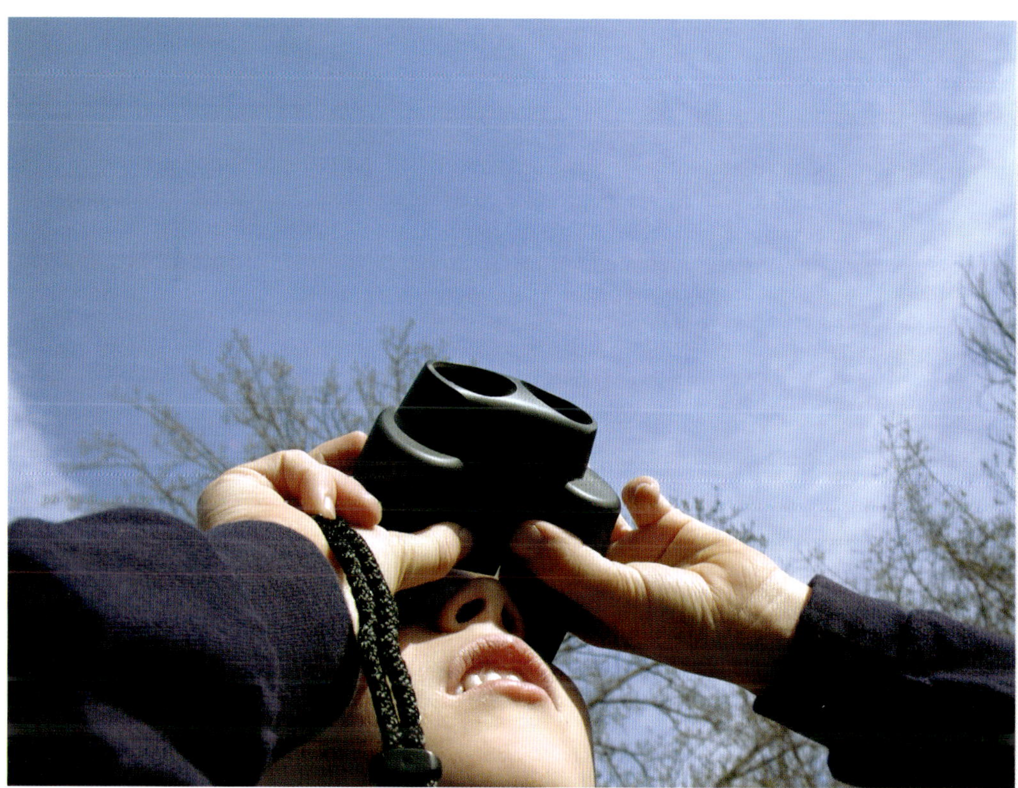

02.23.03

**Sunday morning in the backyard, beneath a snow goose flyway**

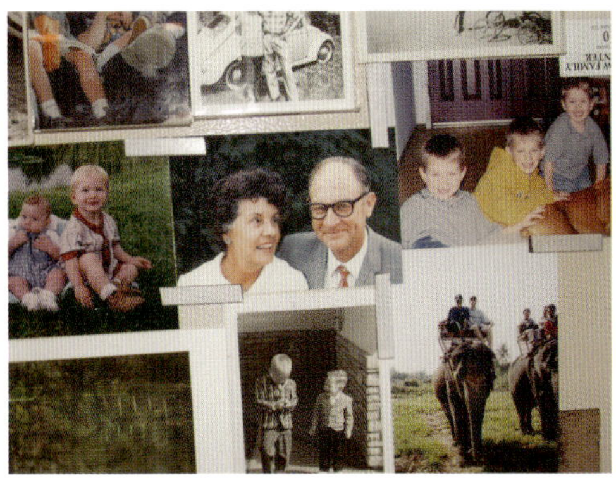

02.24.03

**More refrigerator photos**

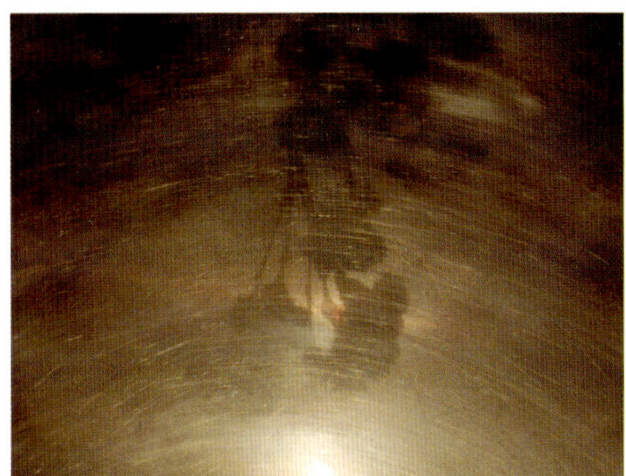

02.25.03

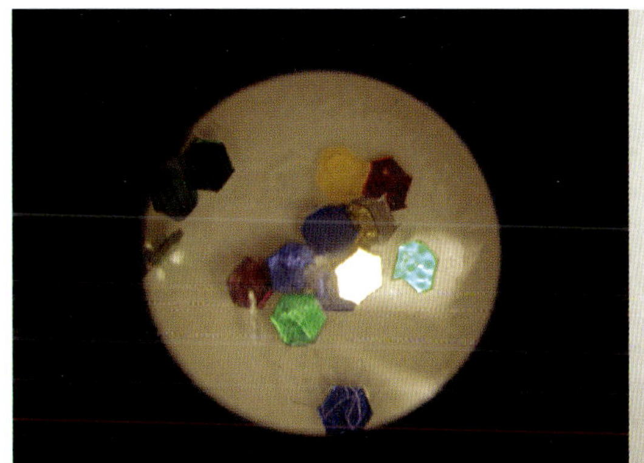

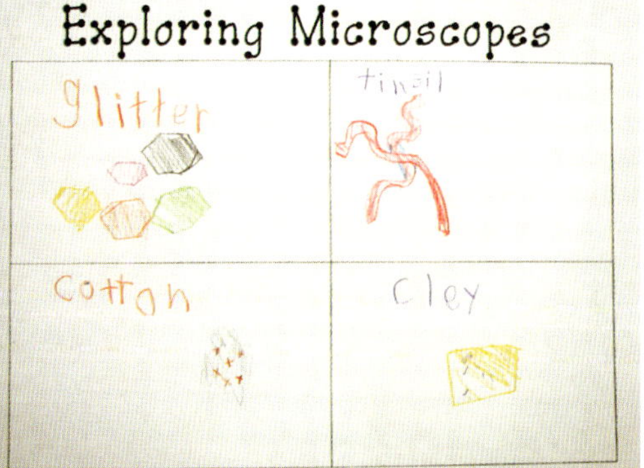


02.26.03

**Observations from family science night at elementary school**

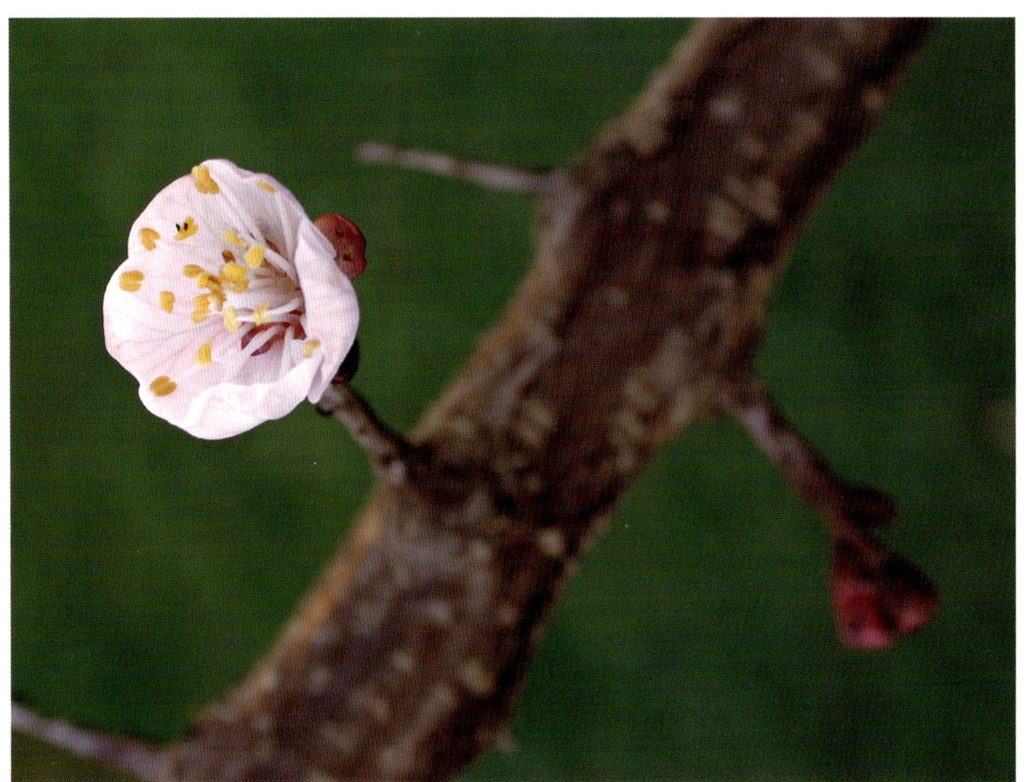

02.27.03

**First apricot blossom**

02.28.03

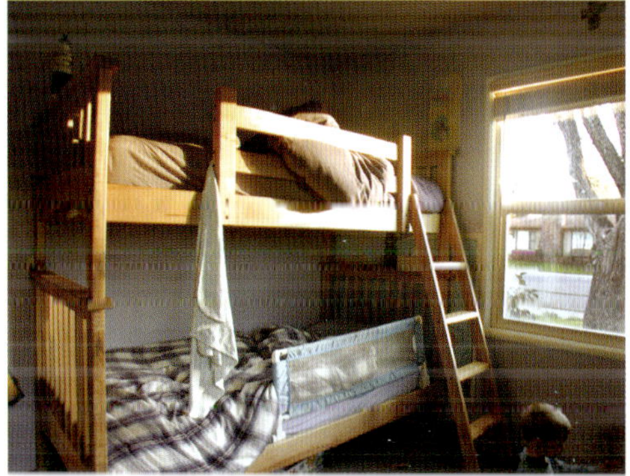

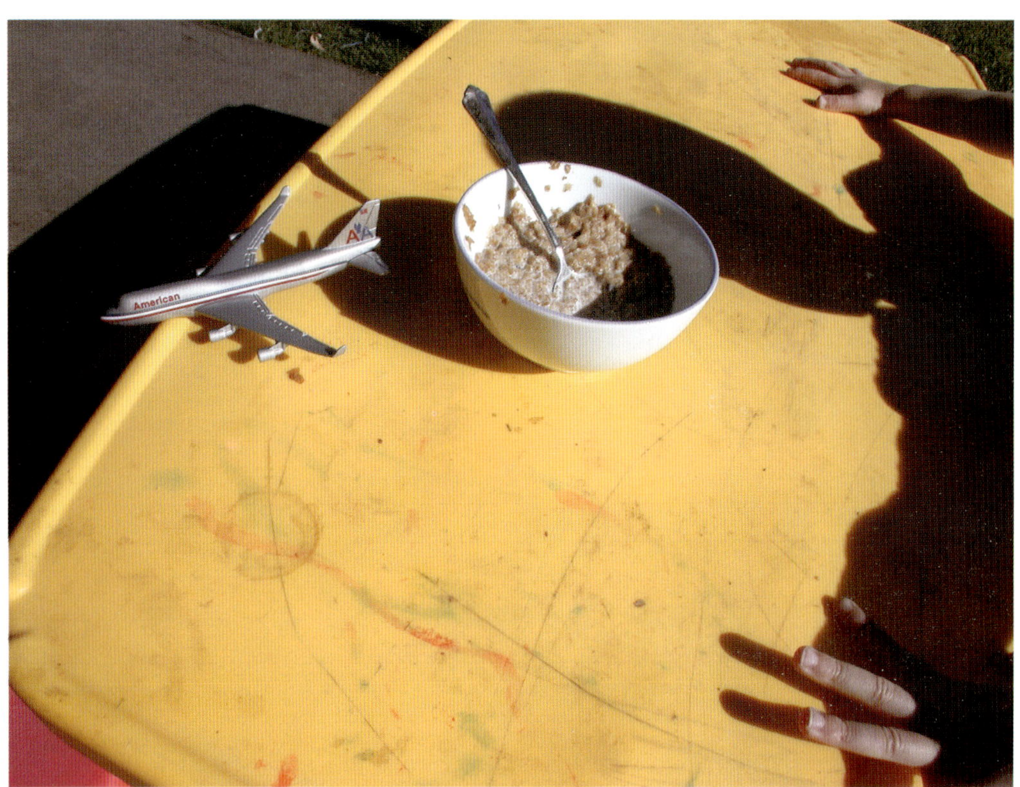


03.01.03

**Another downed plane just after breakfast**

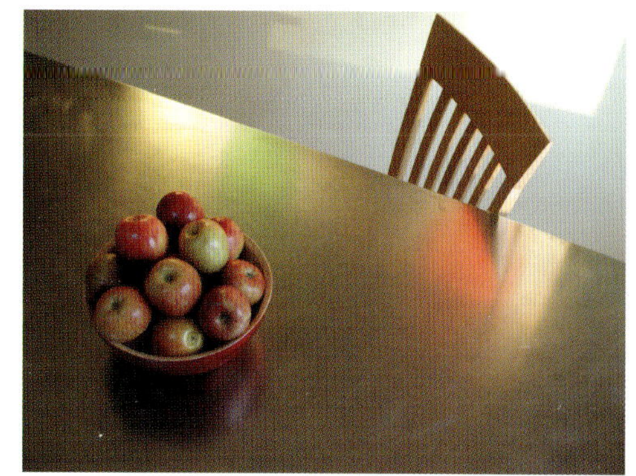

03.02.03

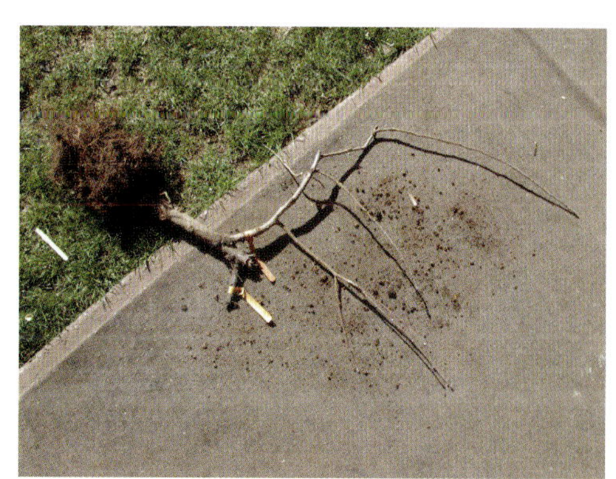

03.03.03

**An apple tree that didn't survive the winter**

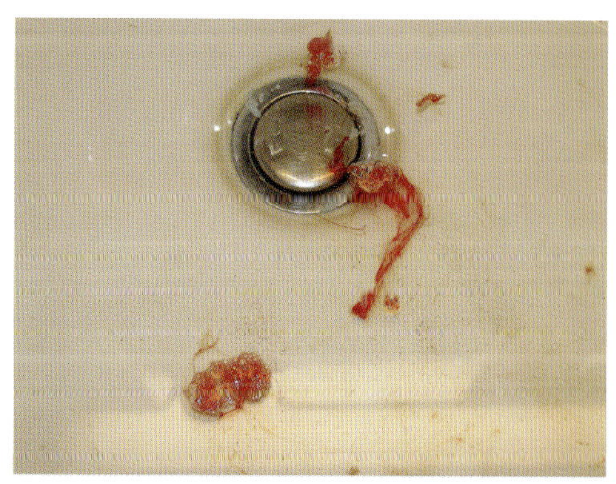

03.04.03

**Prelude to our second visit from the tooth fairy**

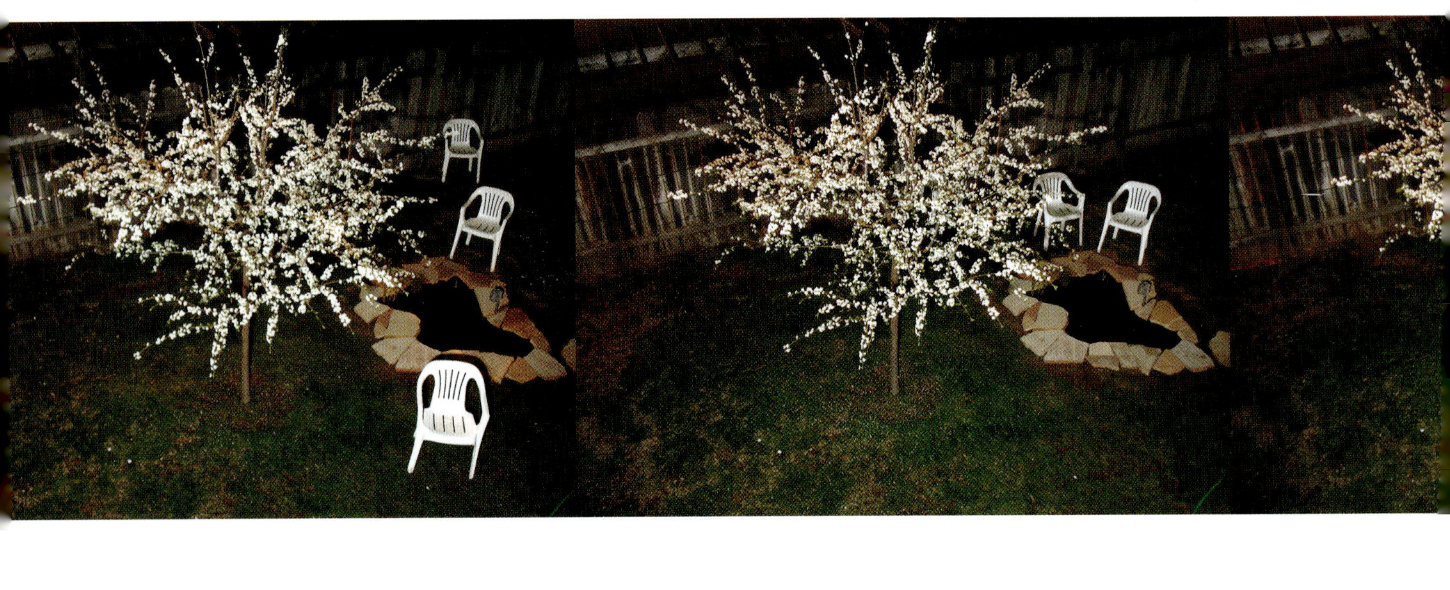

03.05.03–03.11.03

**Seven nights of falling plum blossoms, ending in a chilling rain**

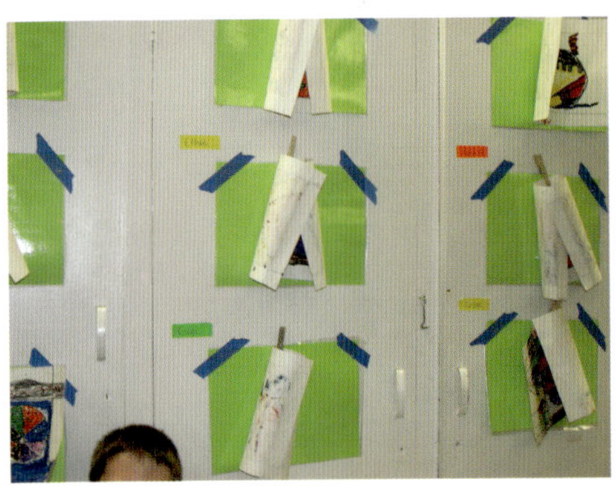

03.12.03

**Back-to-school night**

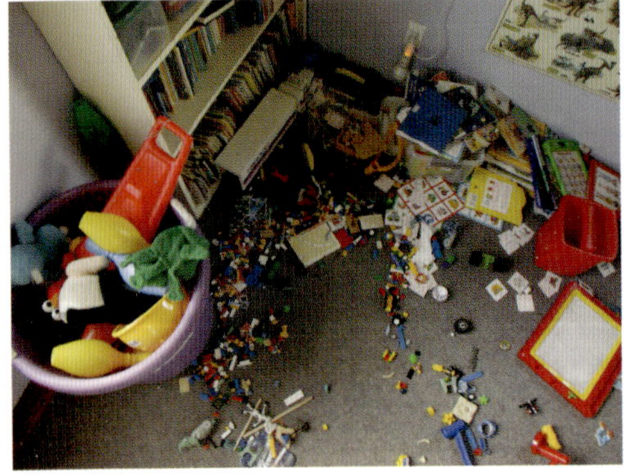

03.13.03

**LEGO land**

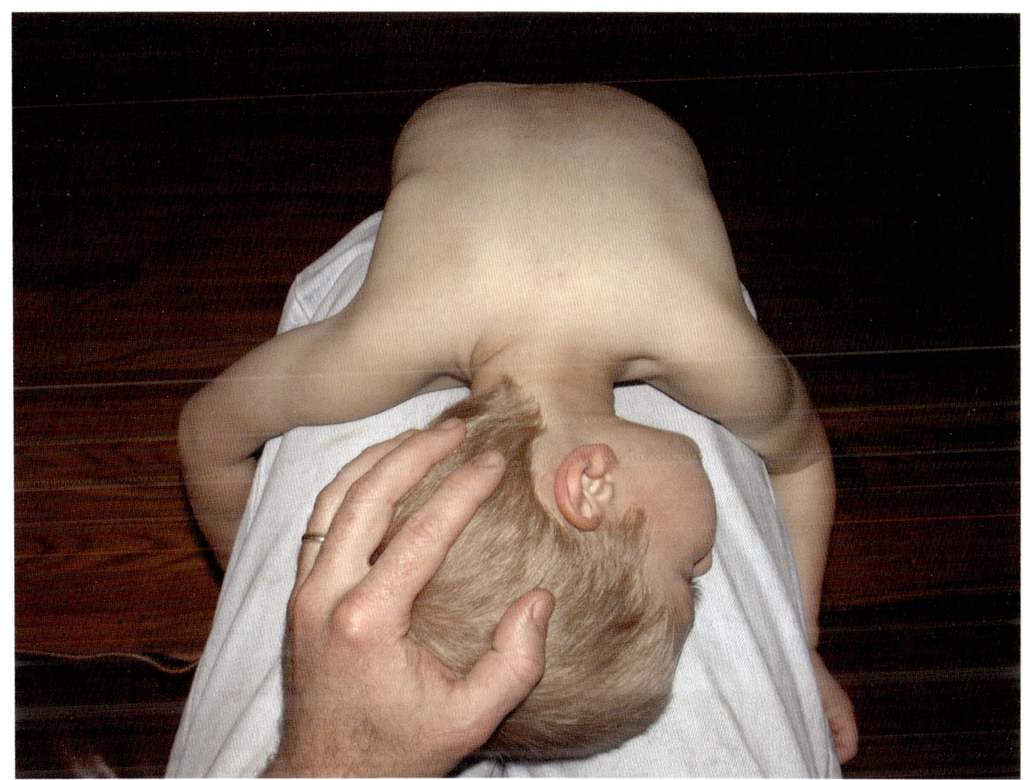

03.14.03

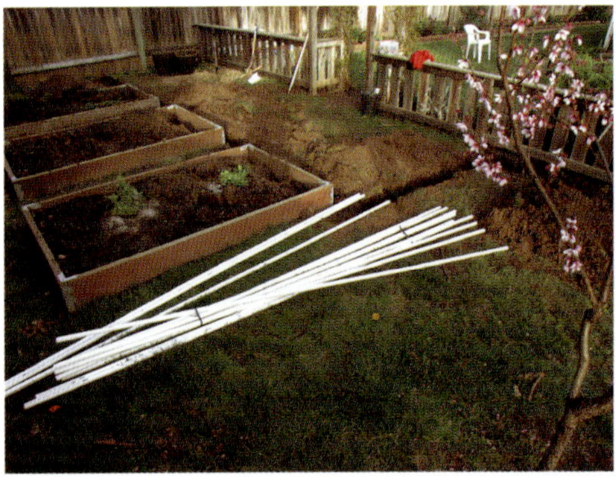

03.15.03

**Gardening infrastructure**

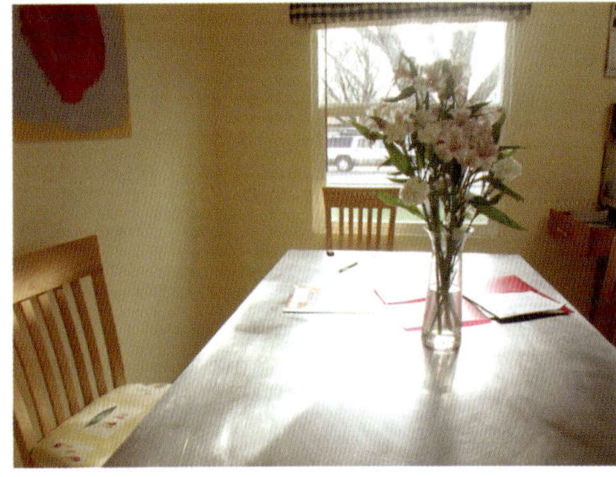

03.16.03

**Sunday afternoon,
homework on the kitchen table**

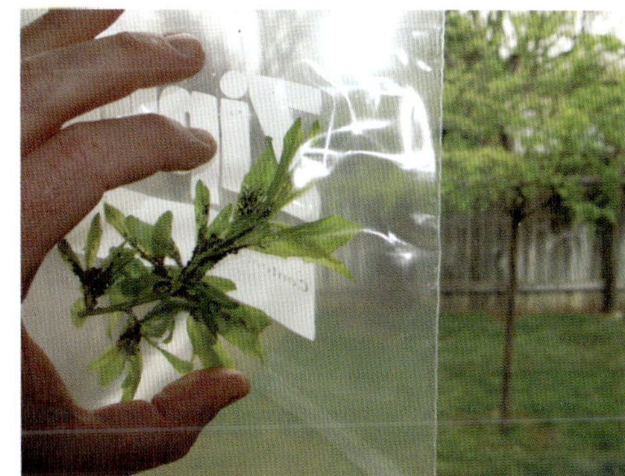

03.17.03

**Aphids attacking my plum tree!**

03.18.03

**Moonrise and lens flare**

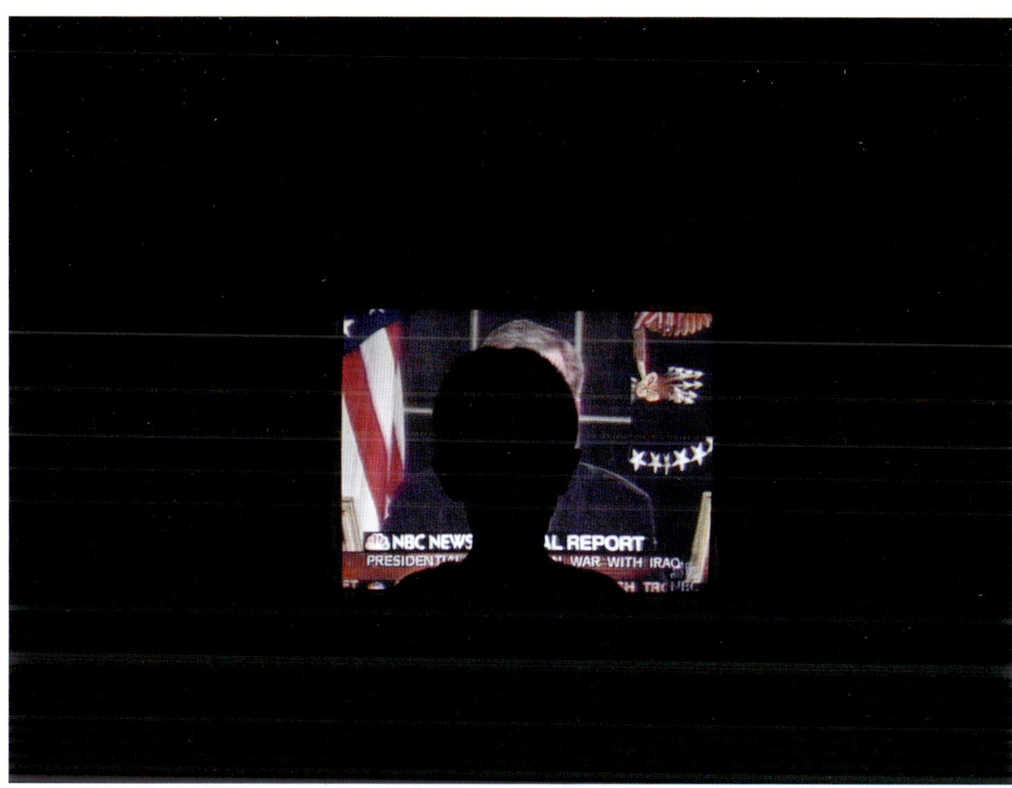


03.10.03

**War at 7:15 PM Pacific (10:15 PM Eastern)**

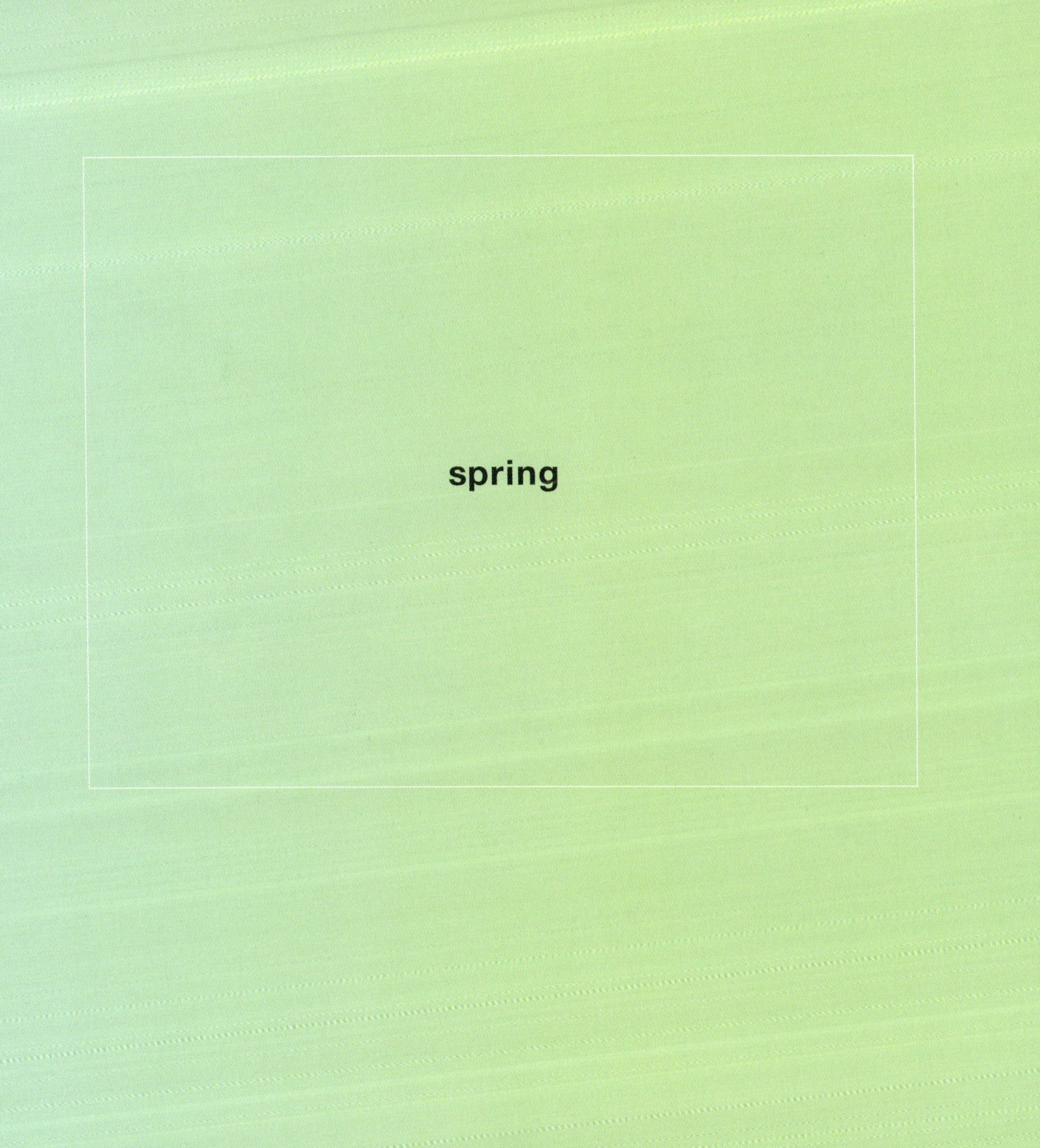

# spring

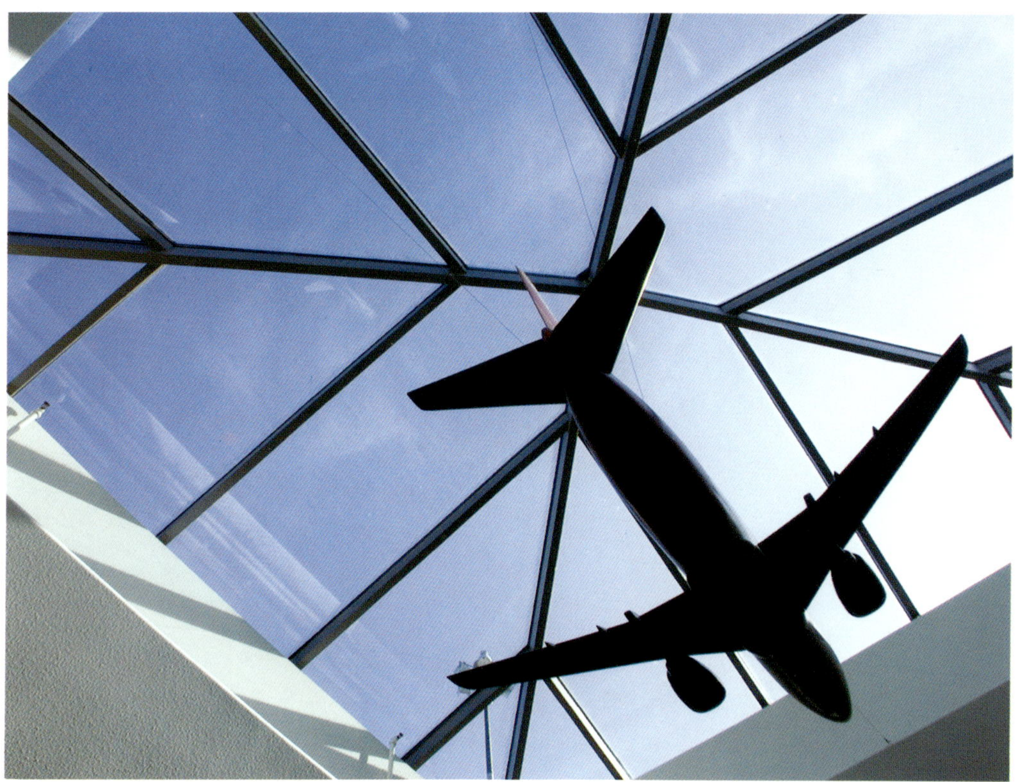

03.20.03

**Airport display and unsettling reminder at the start of a journey**

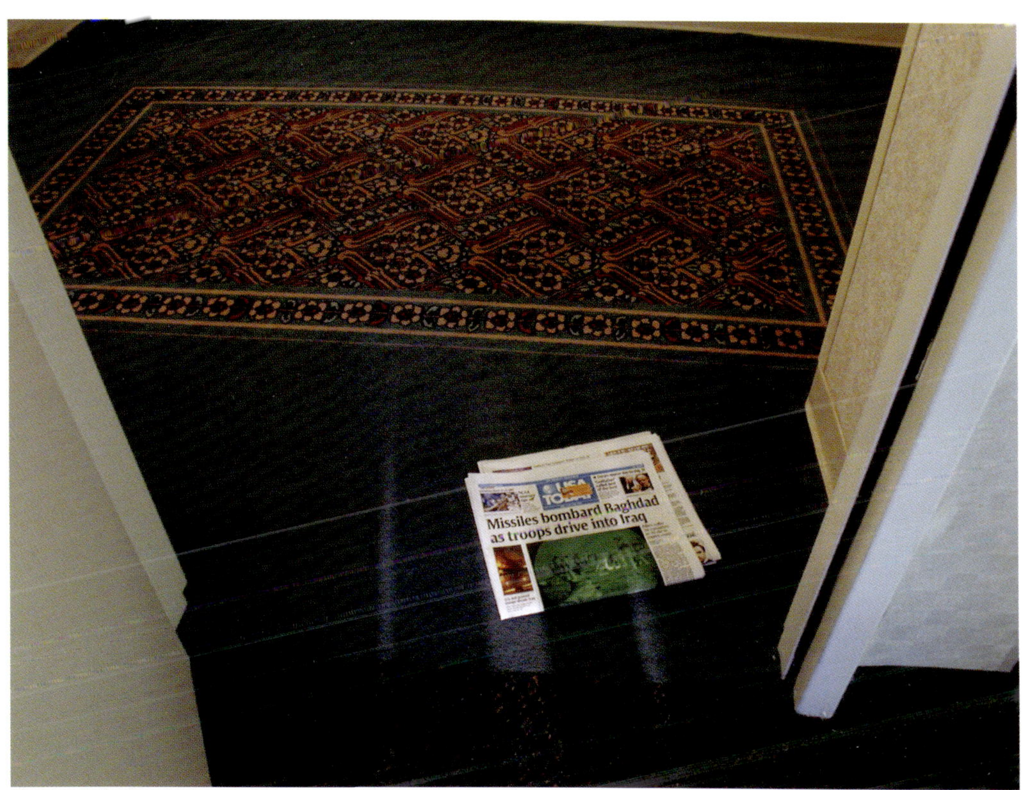


03.21.03

**My complimentary copy, the USA today**

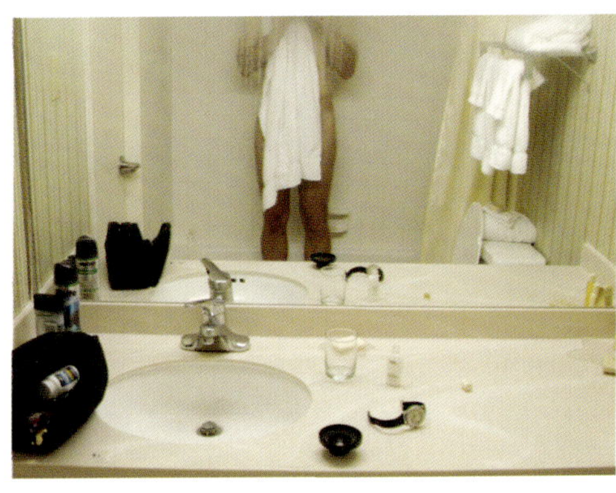

03.22.03

**Embedded in a strange hotel: after a sleepless night of TV war on CNNMSNBCCBSABCFOX**

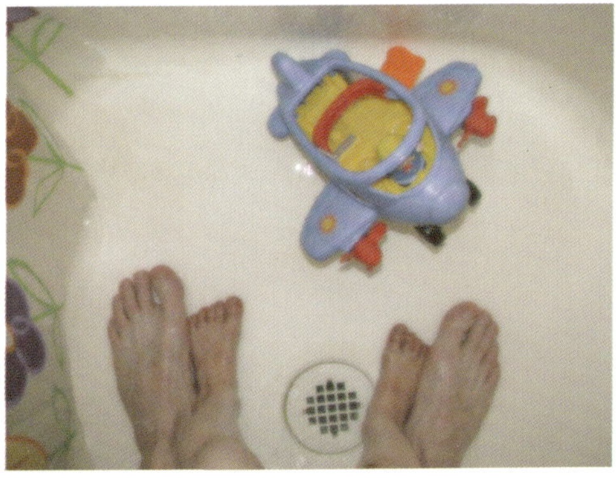

03.23.03

**Back home in Chico**

03.24.03

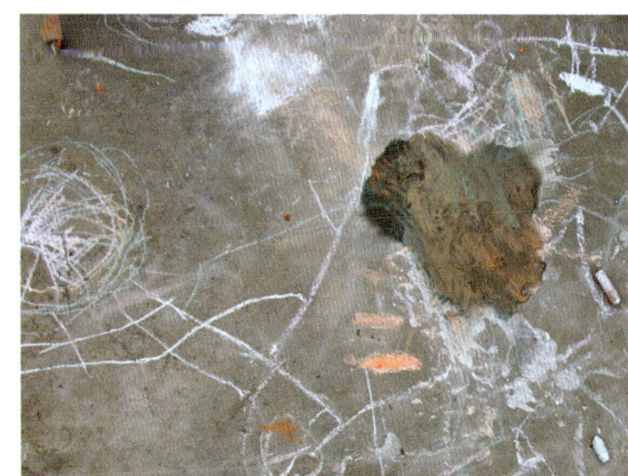

03.25.03

**Dinner for a sick seven-year-old**

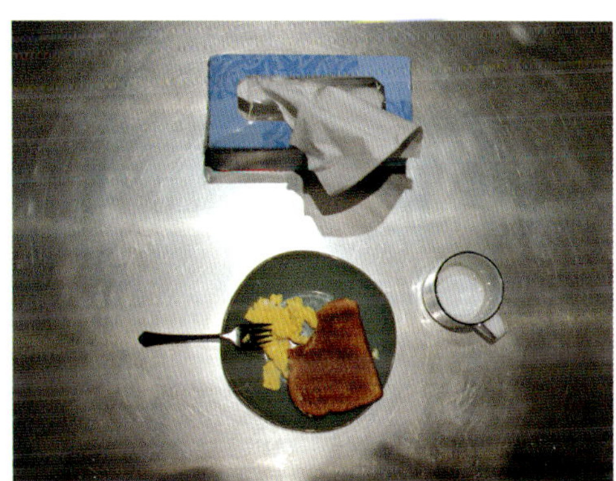

03.26.03

**Waking from a black dream at midnight:**
**disconsolate visions of laser-guided missiles, bomb craters, and flying debris**

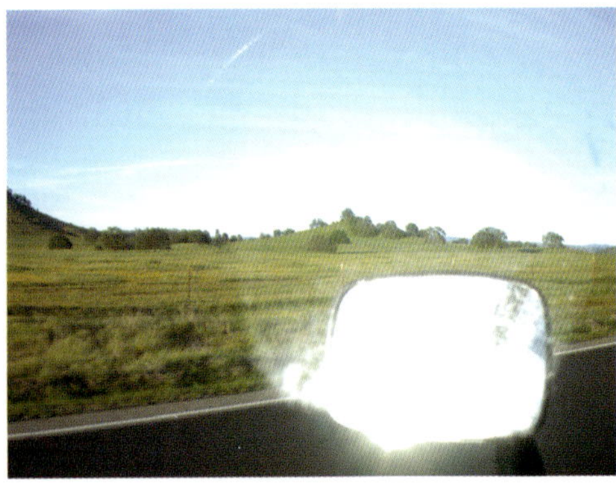

03.27.03

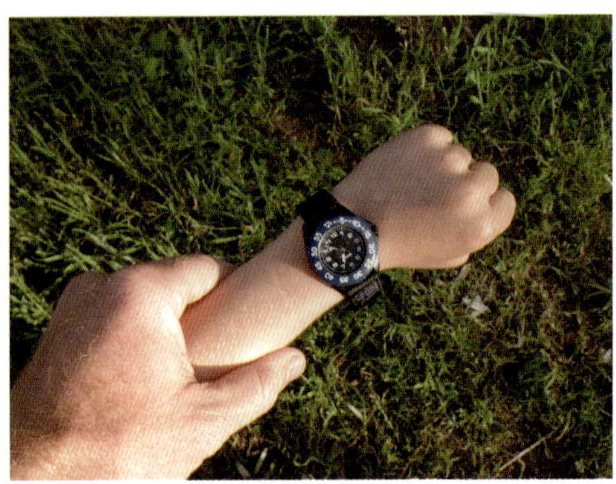

03.28.03
**First watch**

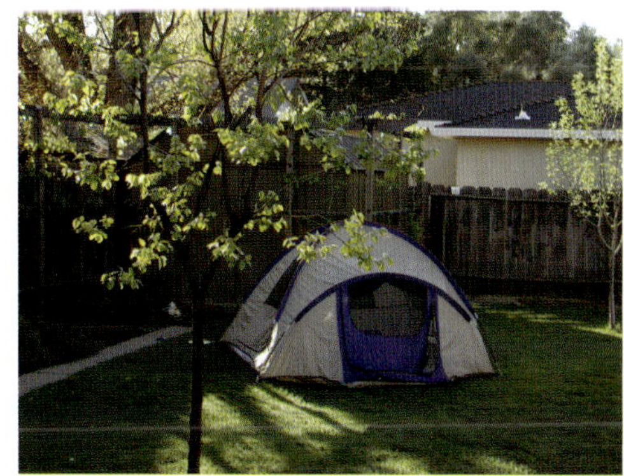

03.29.03
**In the backyard:**
**first spring camp**

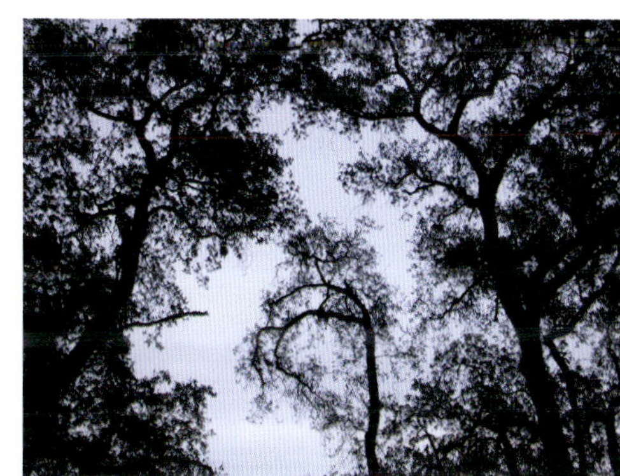

03.30.03
**Second camp, now in the woods:**
**the sky above our tent,**
**momentarily free from bugs**

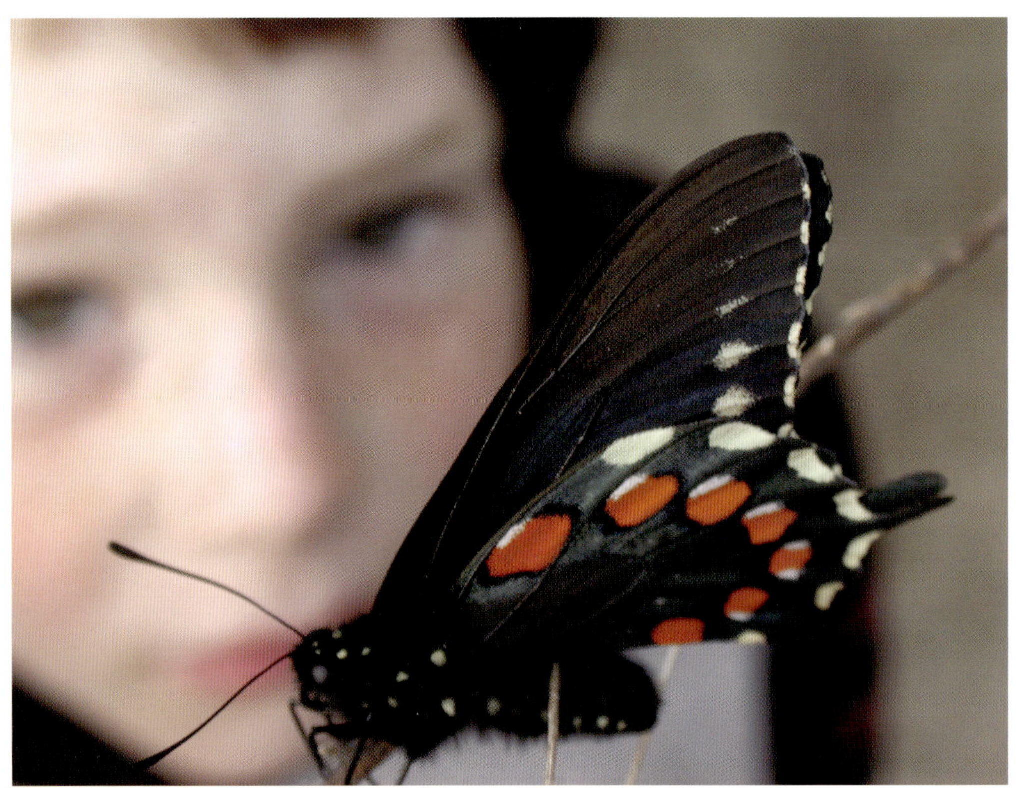

03.31.03

**Camp life**

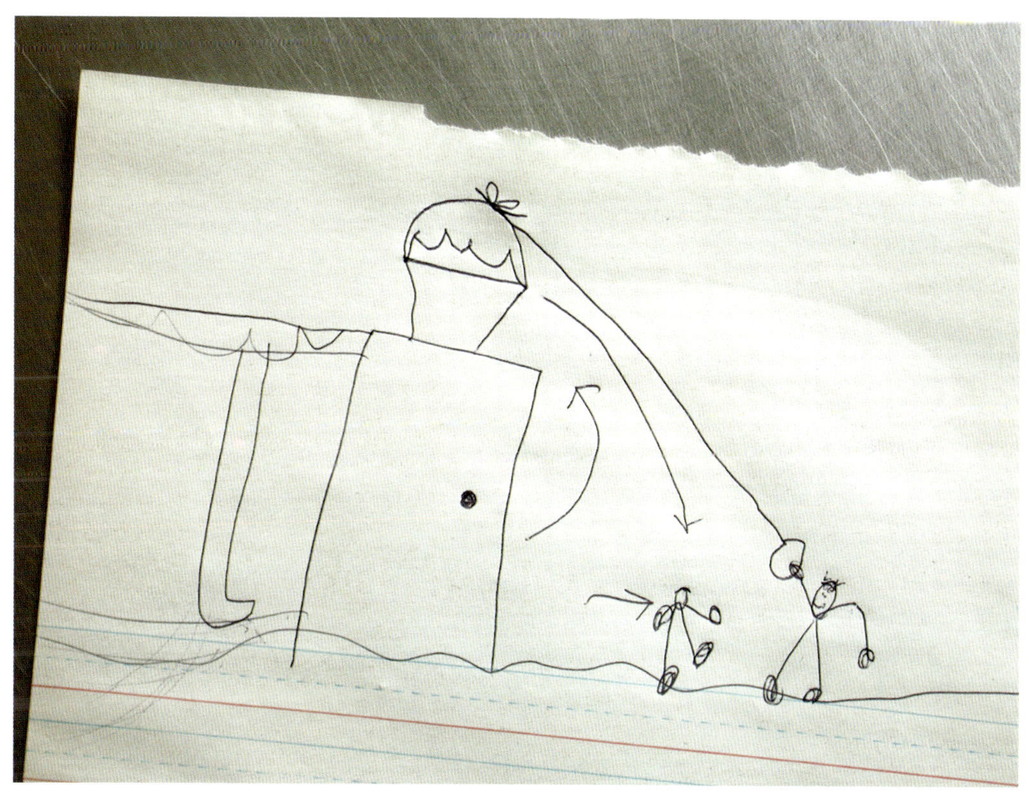

04.01.03

**April Fool's Day plan**

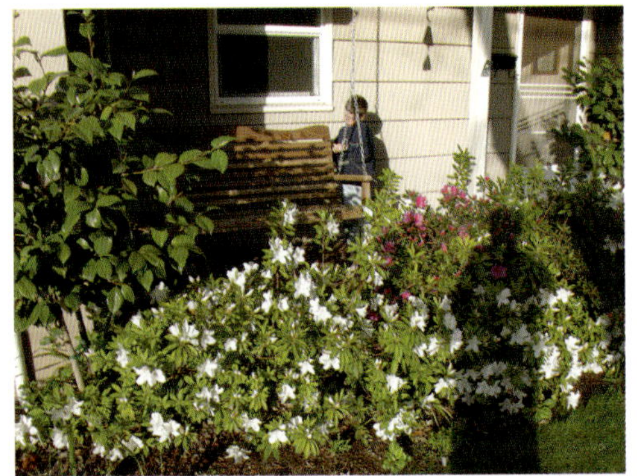

04.02.03

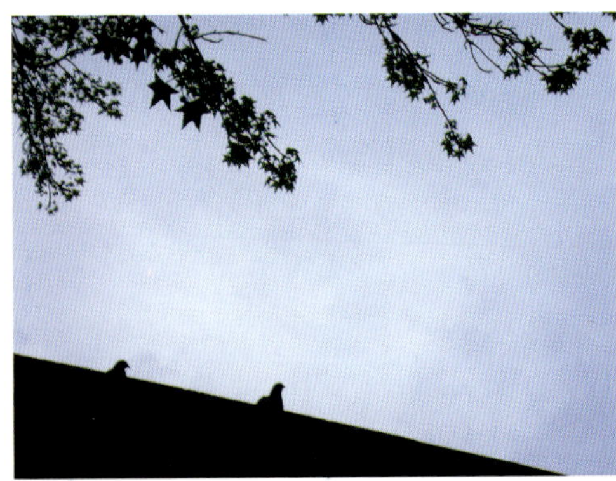

04.03.03

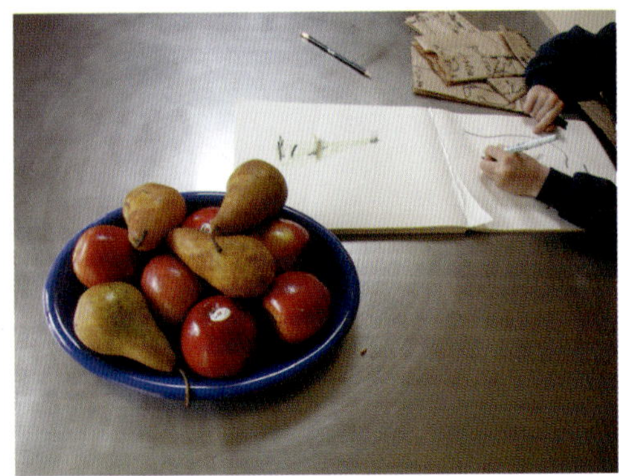

04.04.03

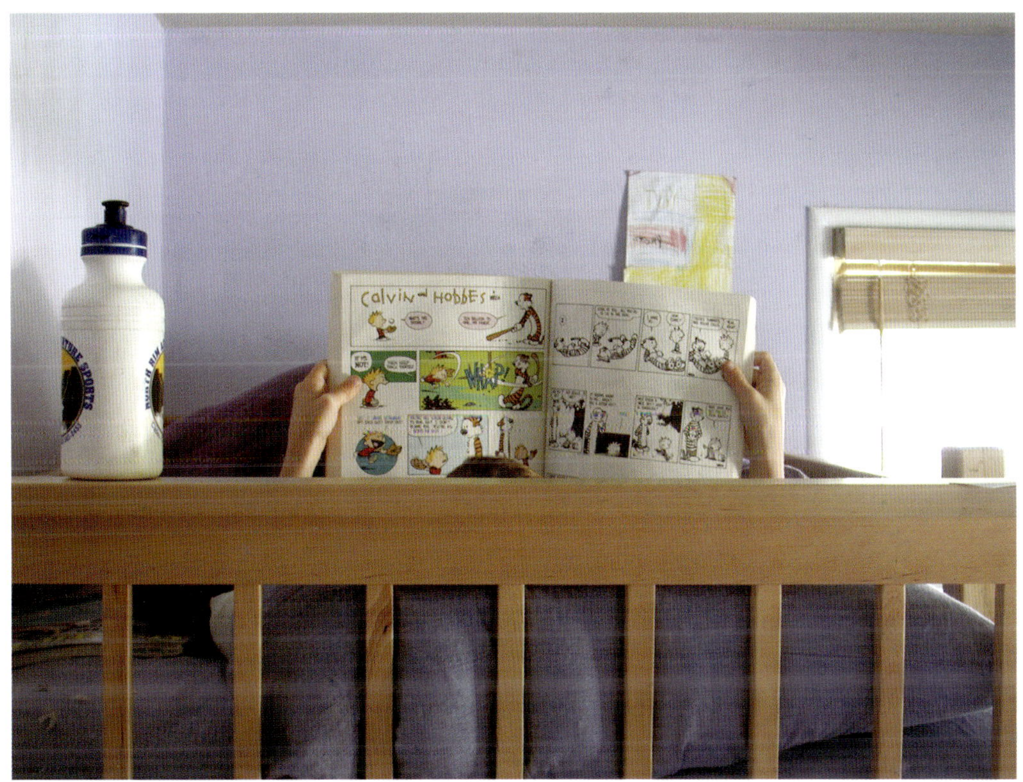


04.05.03

**Saturday, 9:00 AM**

04.06.03

**Domestic Excavations**

**(a partial list of stuff that clutters the top of our dresser)**

01 **Large river stone (provenance unknown)**

02 **Schematic for our garden irrigation project (still in progress)**

03 **A piece of your jewelry box (broken years ago)**

04 **Pocket knife from my brother (c. 1990)**

05 **Father's Day card—"PARA MI PAPÁ" (2002)**

06 **Ethan's handmade piggy bank (c. June 2001)**

07 **A newer bank that you made (for the boys' allowance)**

08 **My first home-run baseball (inscribed as such on June 2, 1979)**

09 **Autographed baseball from a high school classmate (now in the majors)**

10 **Hand-painted envelopes that held cash for flowers (my Christmas gift to you, 2001)**

11 **Baby clothes (purchased months ago as gifts for others)**

12 **Ben's baptism certificate (lost for weeks, then recovered)**

13 **Your homecoming tiara (the one from high school, not college)**

14 **Your grandmother's pearls**

15 **My grandfather's obituary**

16 **Our portrait, before we were married and had furniture to clutter**

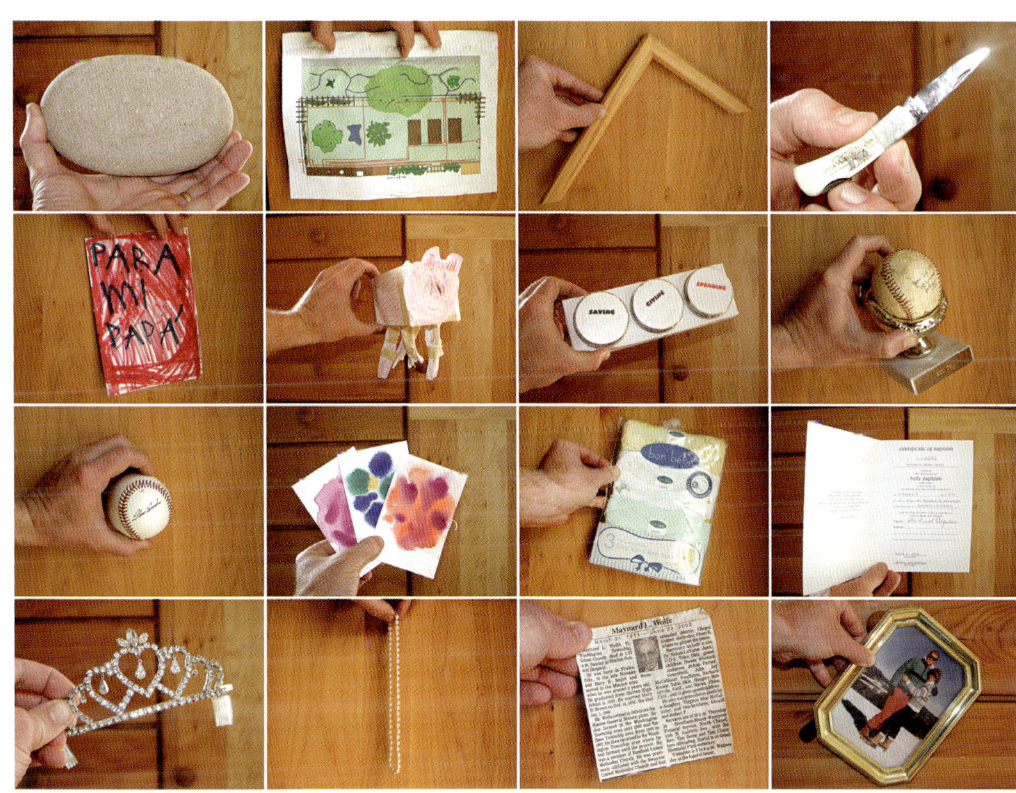
PARA
MI
PAPÁ
SAVING
GIVING
SPENDING
Maynard L. Wolfe

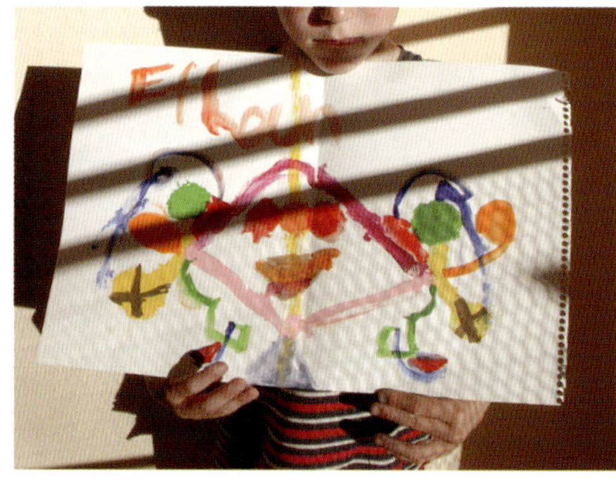

04.07.03

**A modern portrait the creator hopes will someday be displayed in a museum**

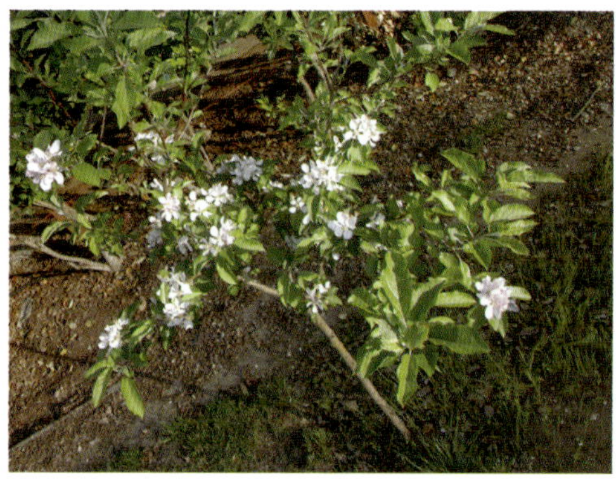

04.08.03

**The tree that produced last year's apple**

04.09.03

**Site of the wet and foggy December ravens**

Things I want to photograph, but don't know how:

The war.

A wobbly economy.

Budget cuts.

Our direct-deposit tax return.

Interminable and unproductive meetings.

Every beautiful sky I missed while standing at the front of a classroom,

Or staring at a computer screen.

My youngest son's voice.

04.10.03

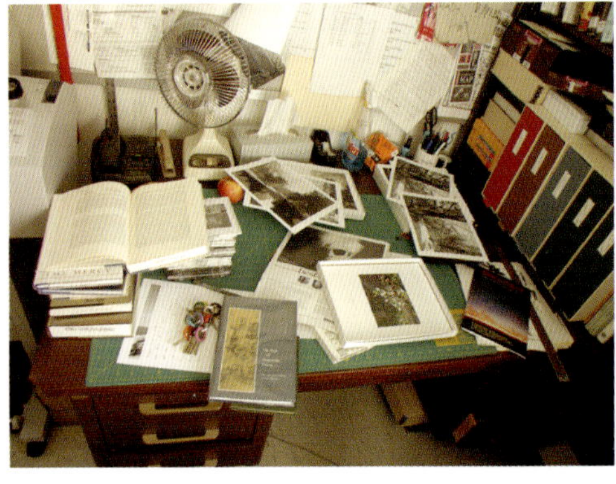

04.11.03

**The landscape of my office**

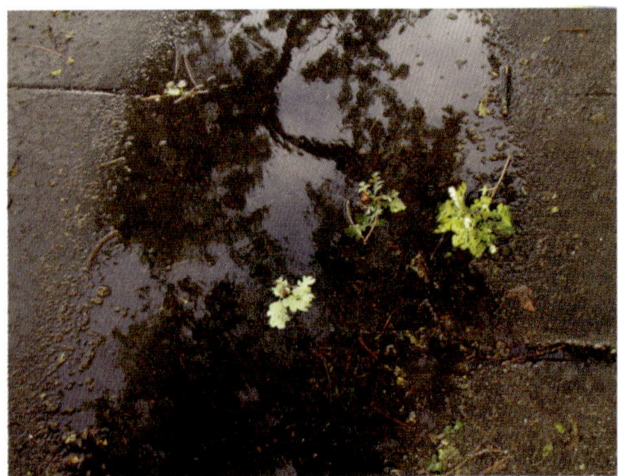

04.12.03

**More rain**

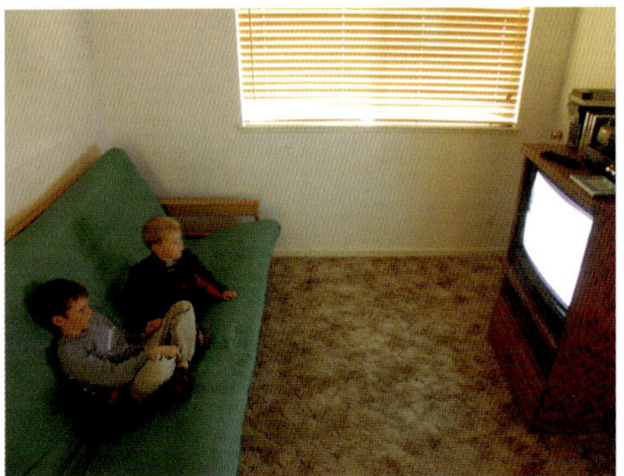

04.13.03

**Eight seconds of *Charlotte's Web* on a rainy Sunday afternoon**

04.14.03
**Paper butterfly**

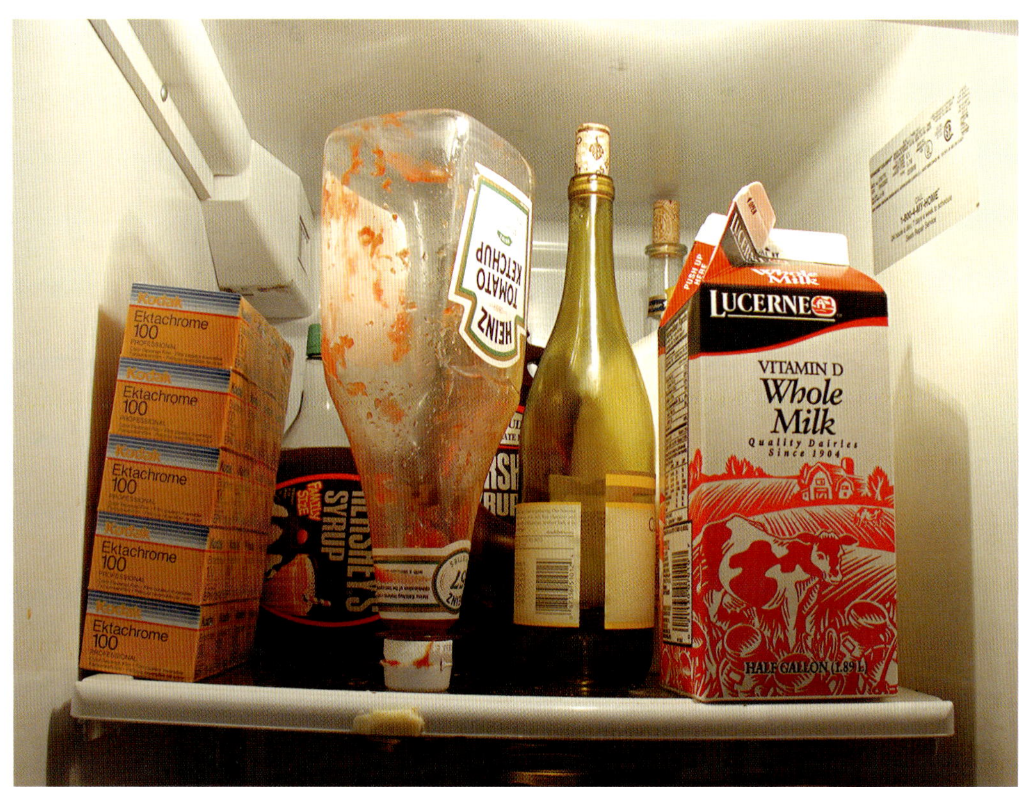


04.15.03

**The top shelf**

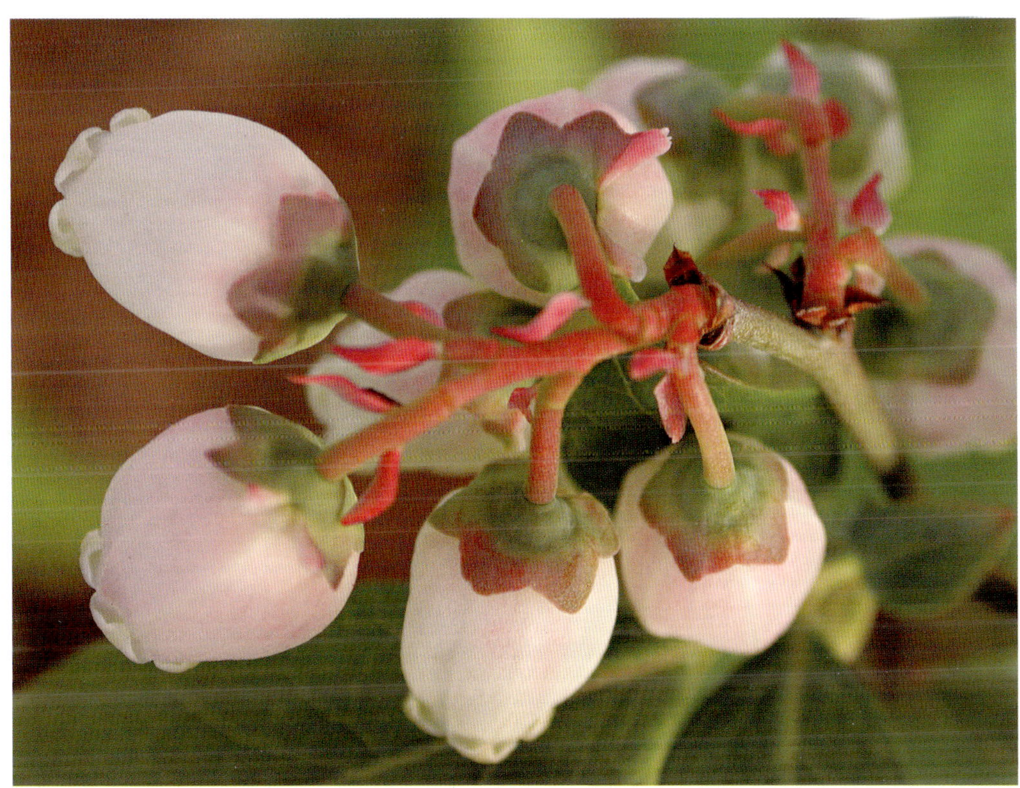

04.16.03

**Blueberry blossoms**

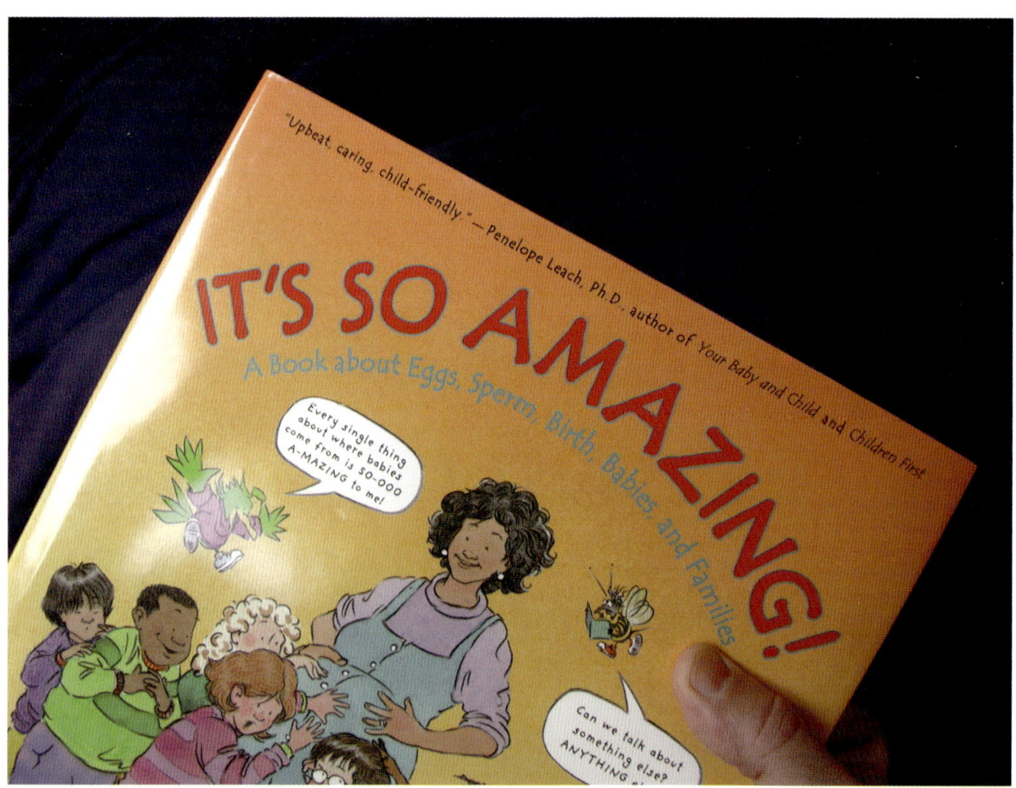


04.17.03

**Assigned reading for an upcoming discussion**

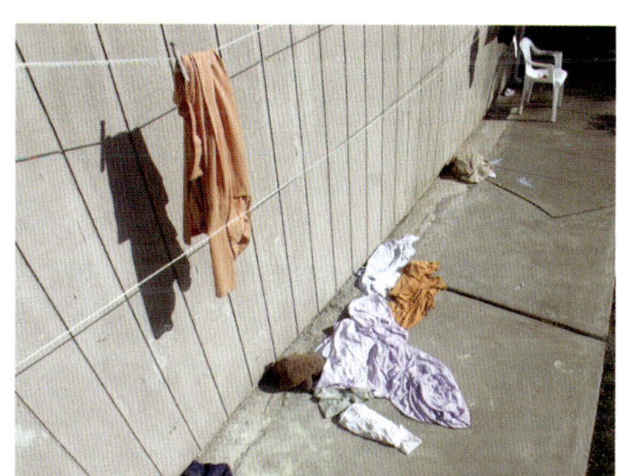

04.18.03

**When you were away for the week**

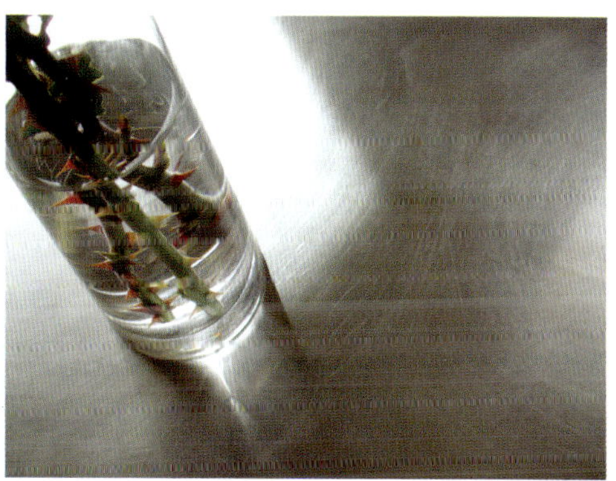

04.19.03

**First cuttings of the year**

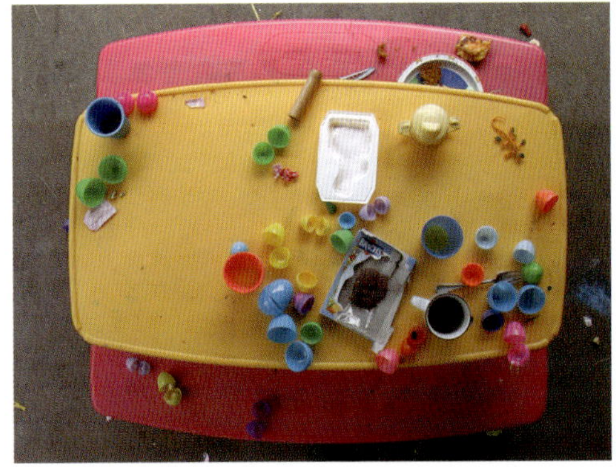

04.20.03

**Sunday morning**

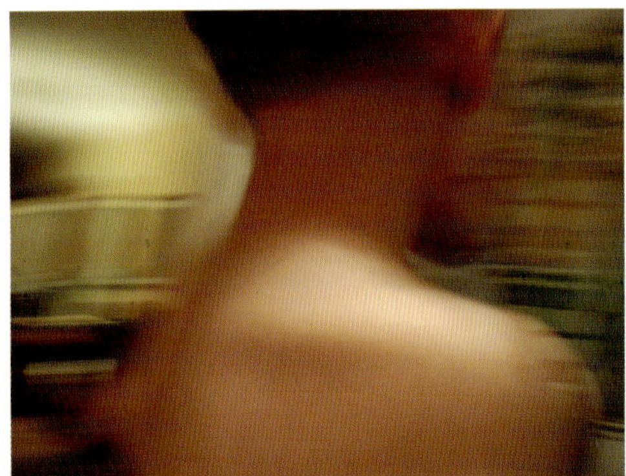

04.21.03

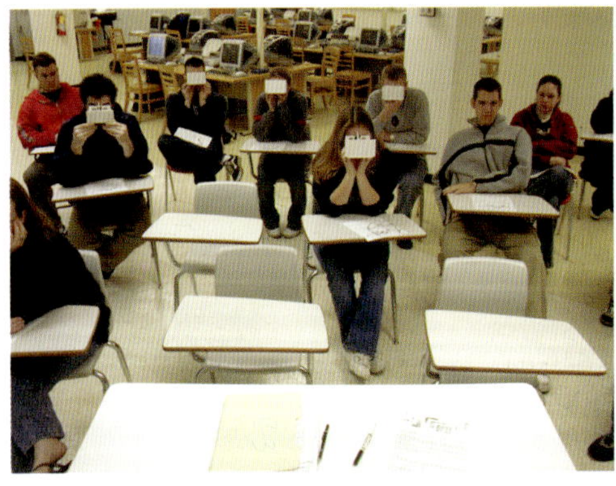

04.22.03

**Watching my students**

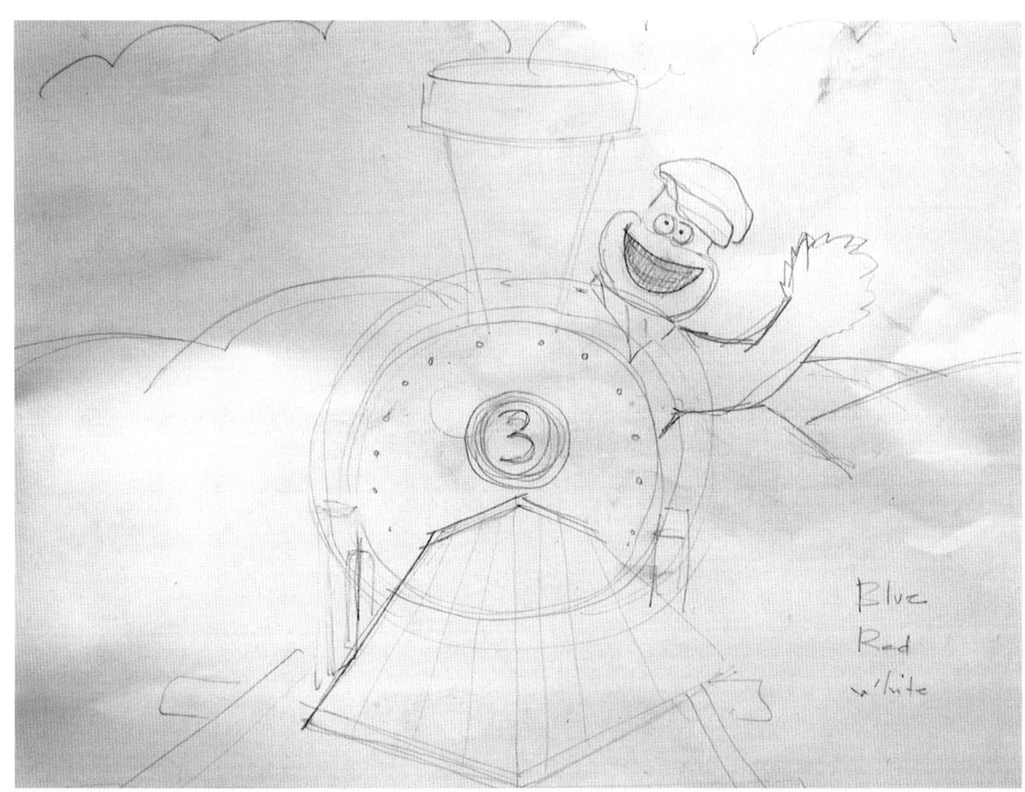


04.23.03

**Preliminary sketch**

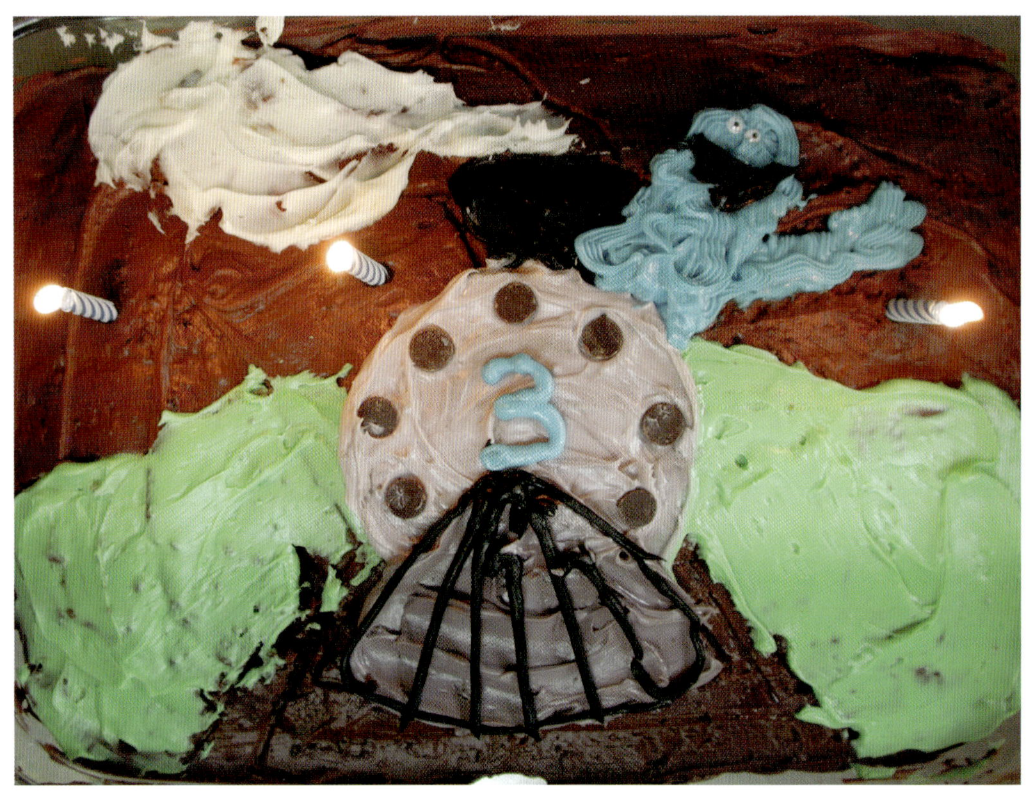

04.24.03

**“Cookie Monster on a train” in mixed media**

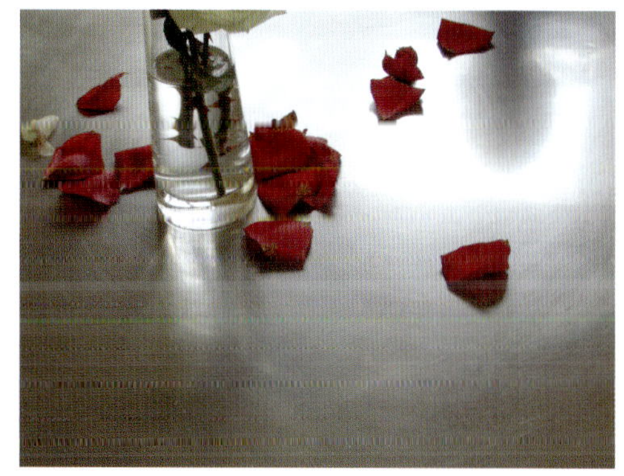

04.25.03

**First cuttings, day seven**

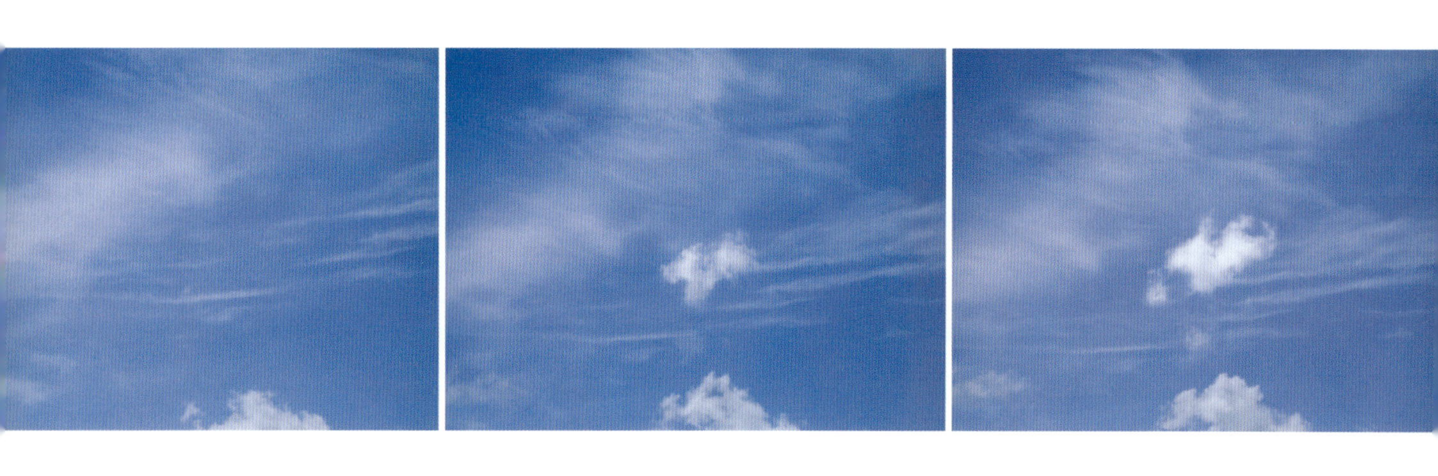

04.26.03

**The life of a cloud (1:58–2:03 PM)**

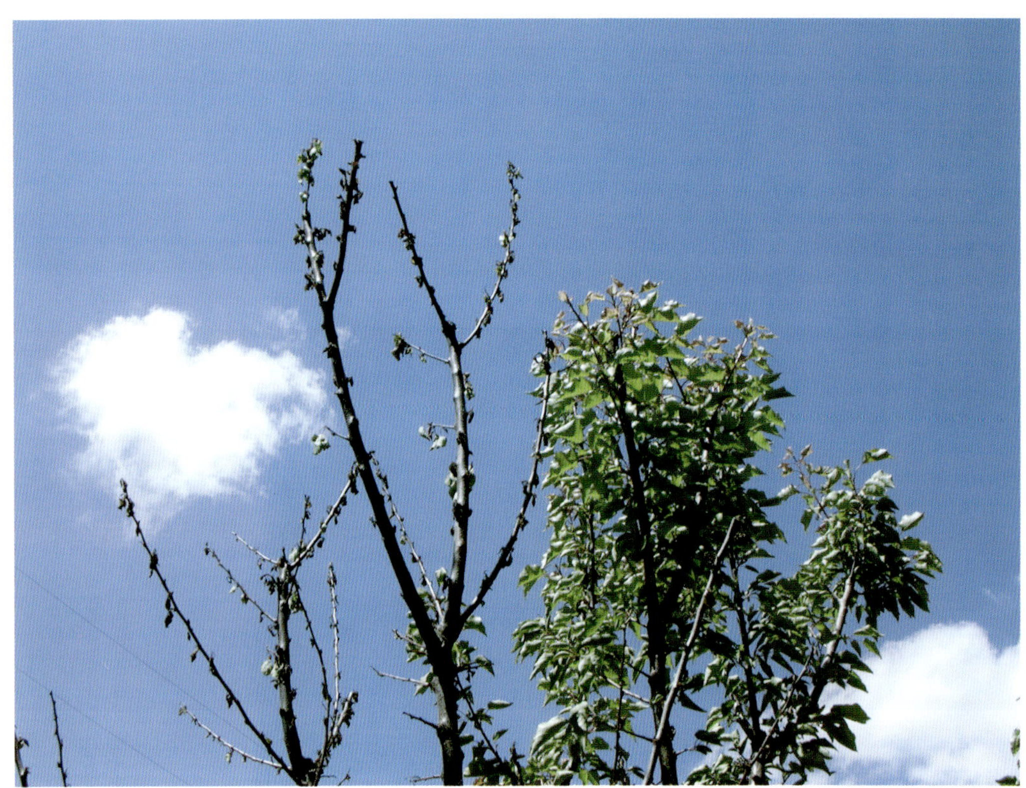

04.27.03

**Our slowly dying apricot tree**

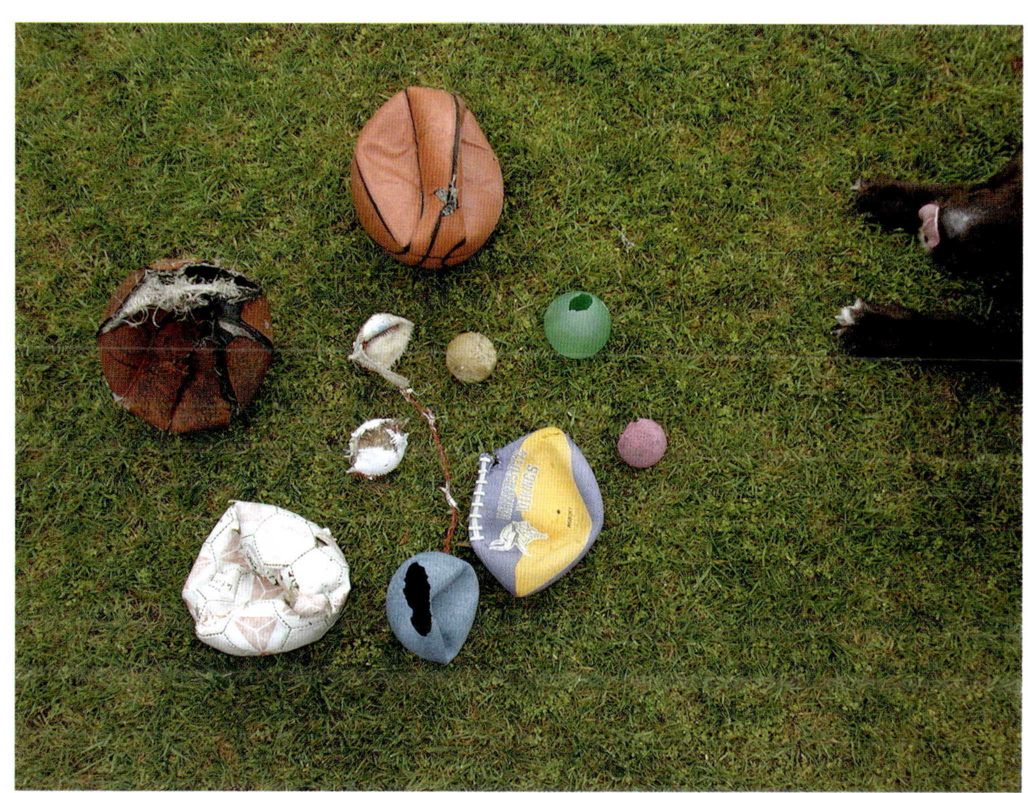

04.30.03

**All in one day**

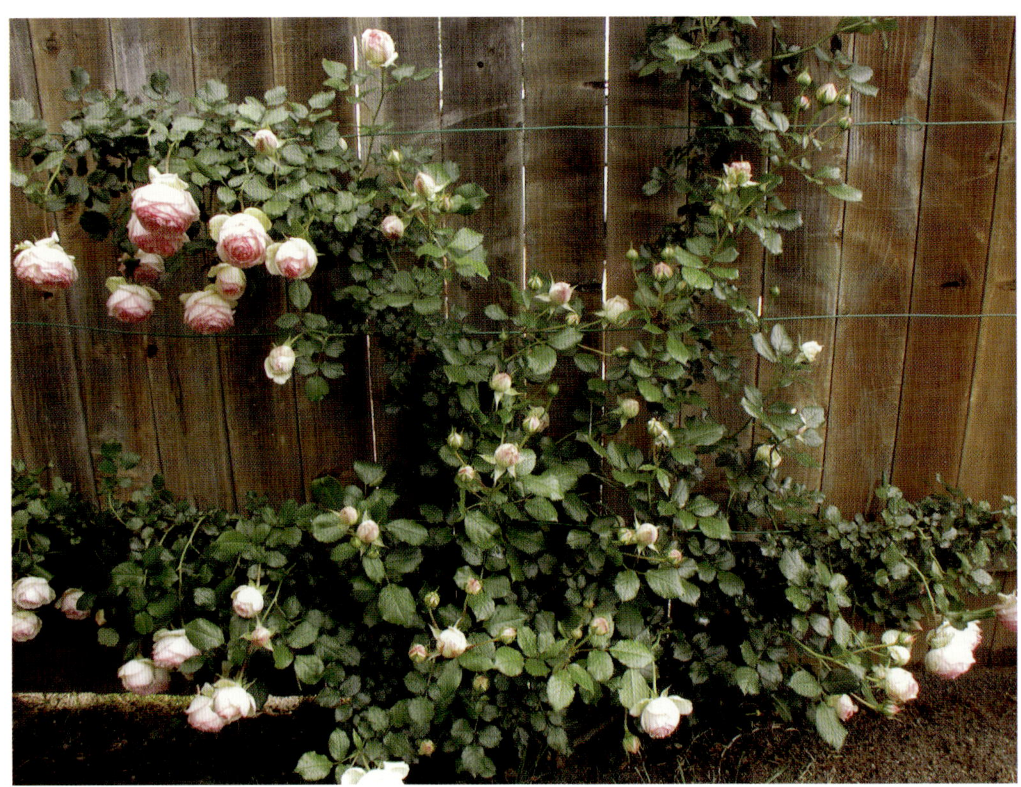

05.01.03

**May roses**

05.02.03

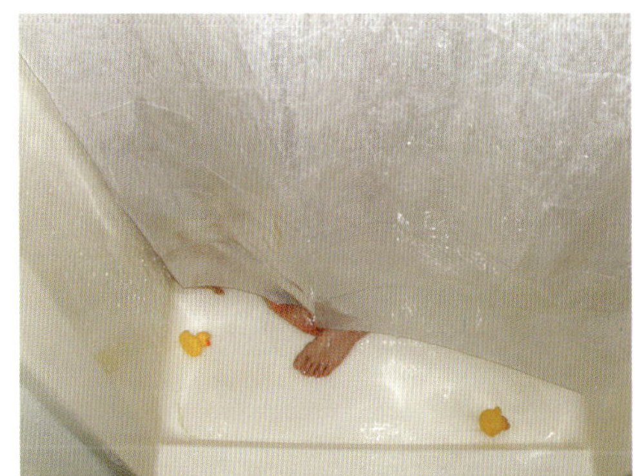

05.03.03

**Under new ownership**

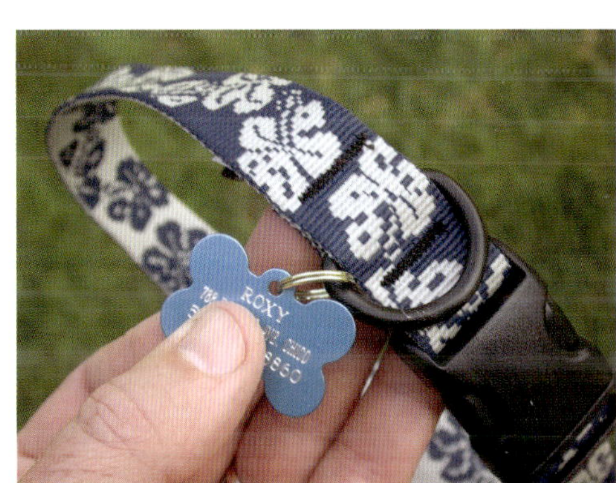


05.04.03

**Fallen plums**

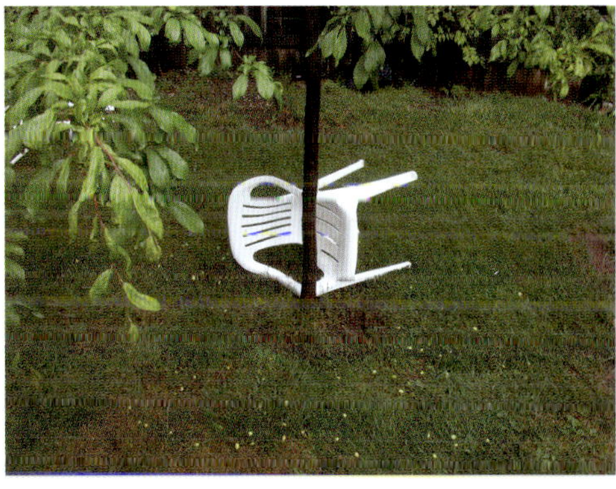

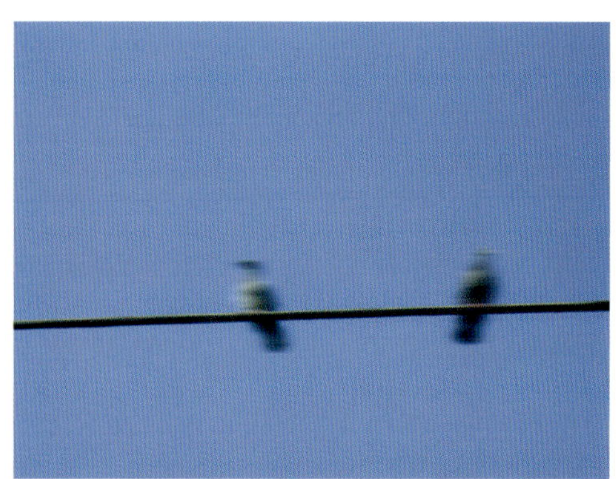

05.05.03

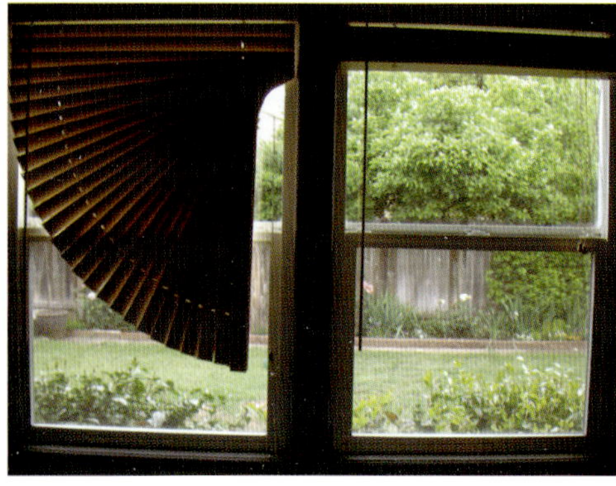

05.06.03

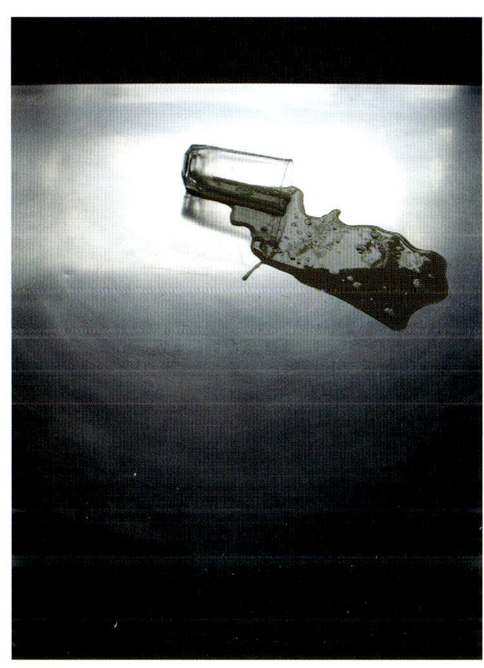

05.07.03

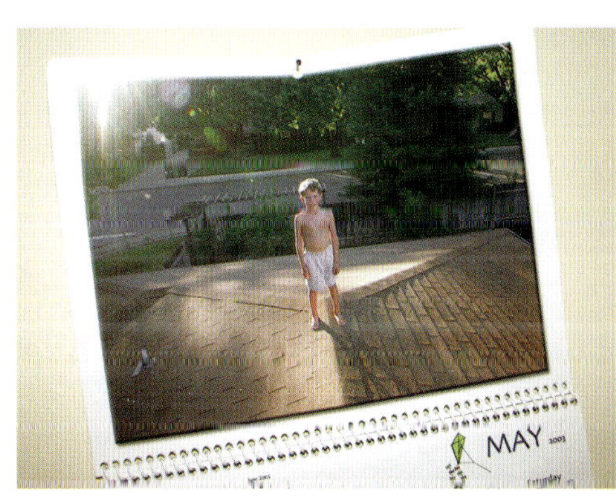


05.08.03

**Sometime last year**

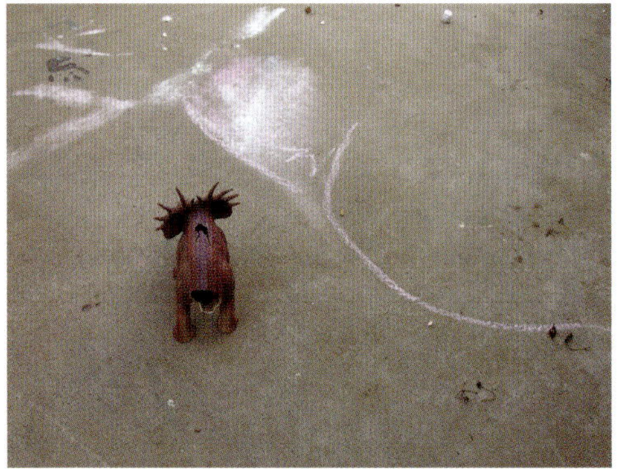

05.09.03

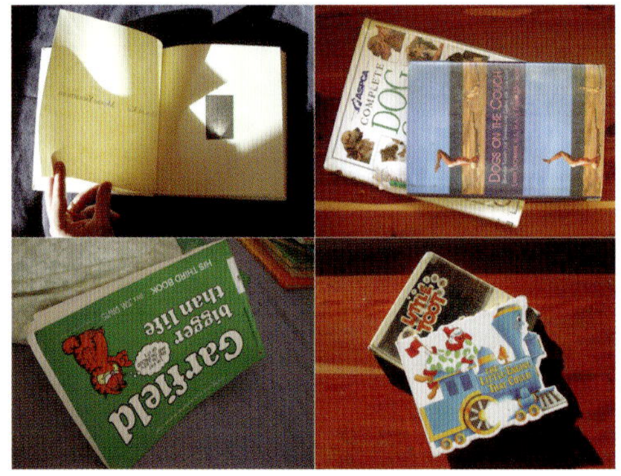


05.10.03

**What the family is reading, second edition**

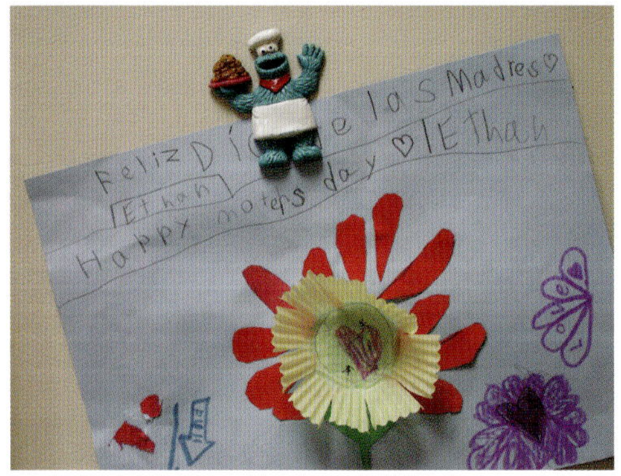


05.11.03

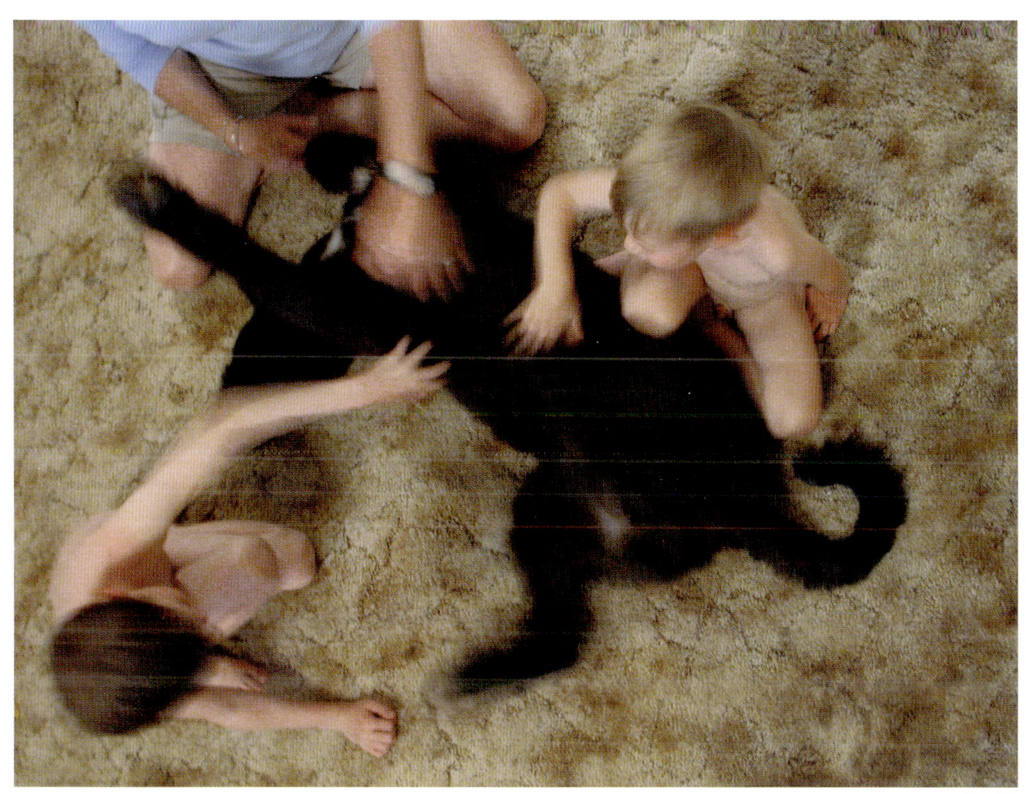

05.12.03

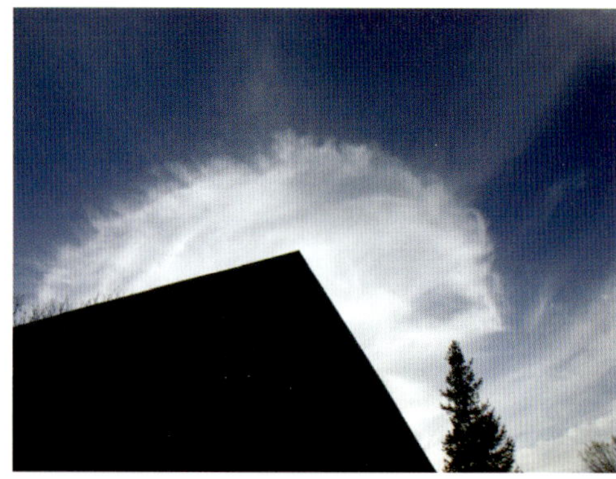

05.13.03
**Nice cloud**

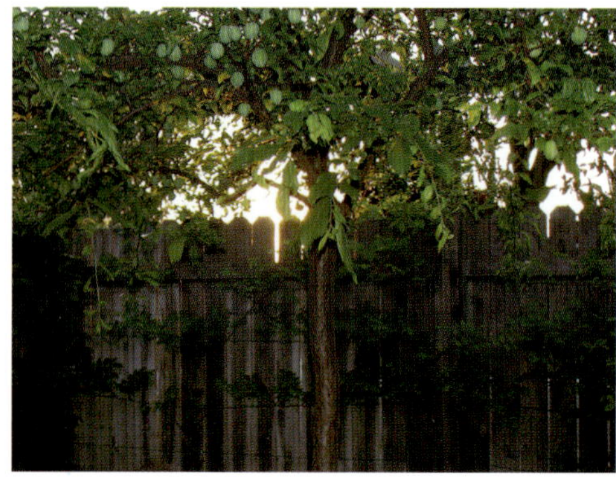

05.14.03
**Sunset at the plum tree**

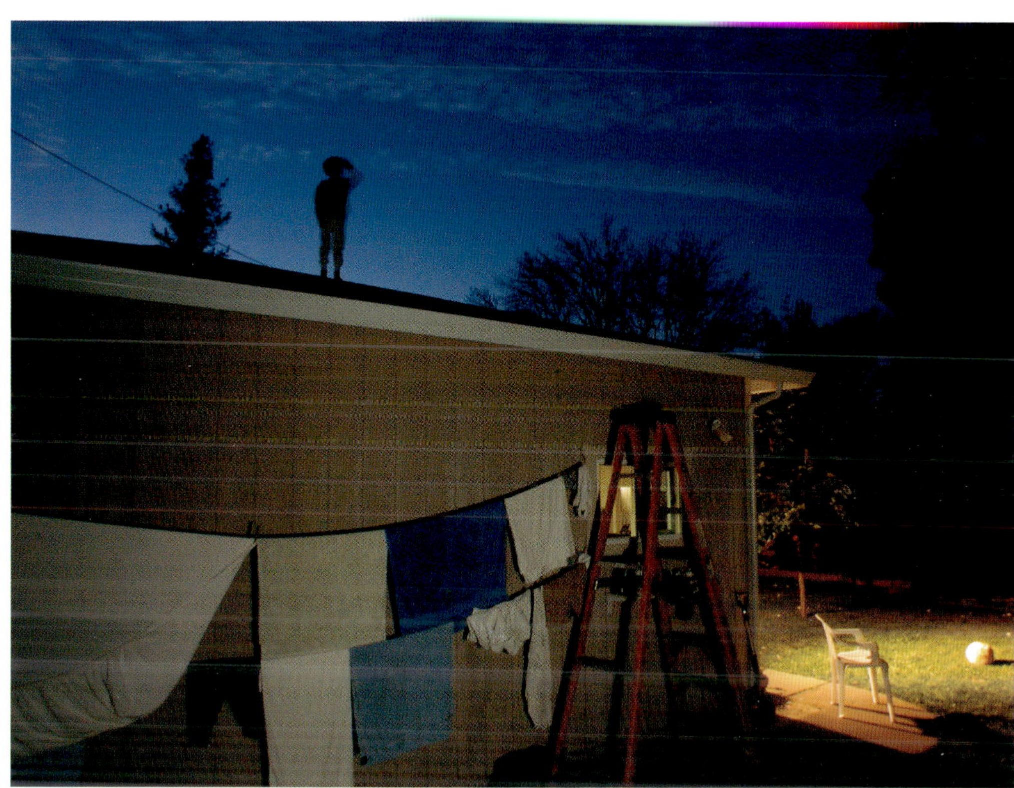

05.15.03

**Total lunar eclipse**

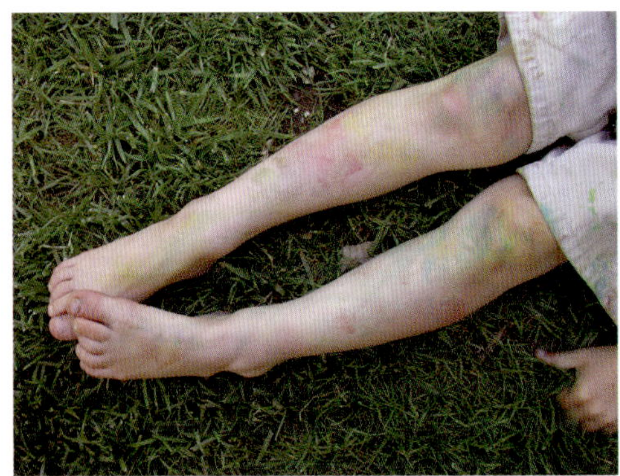

05.16.03

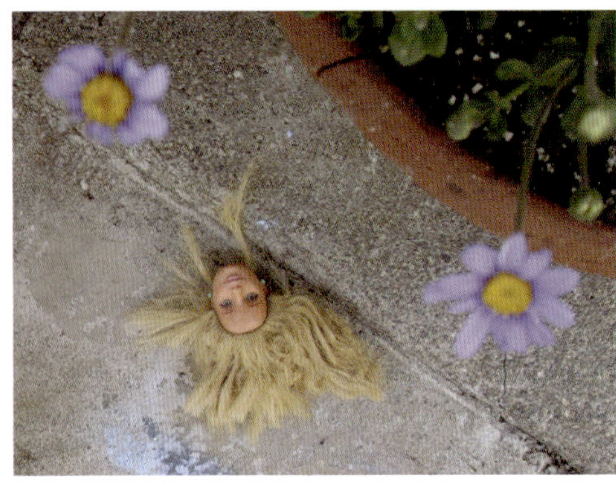

05.17.03

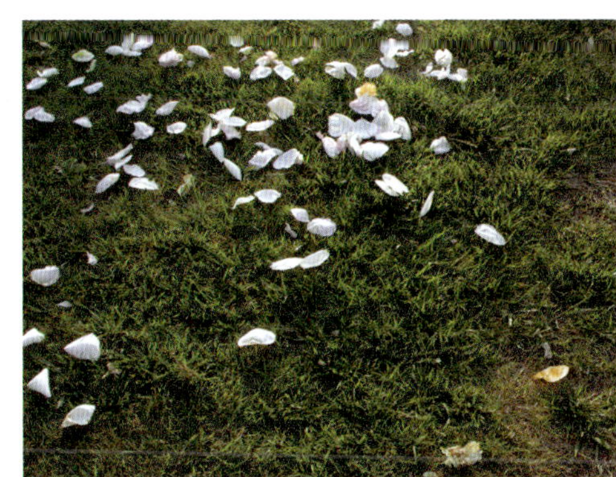

05.18.03

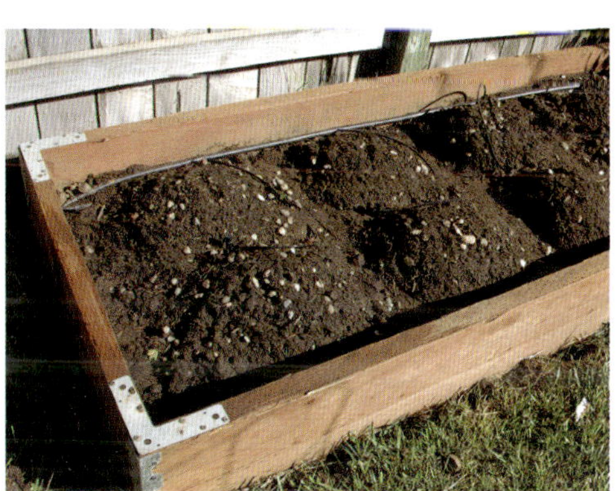

05.19.03

**Watermelons, squash, and pumpkins**

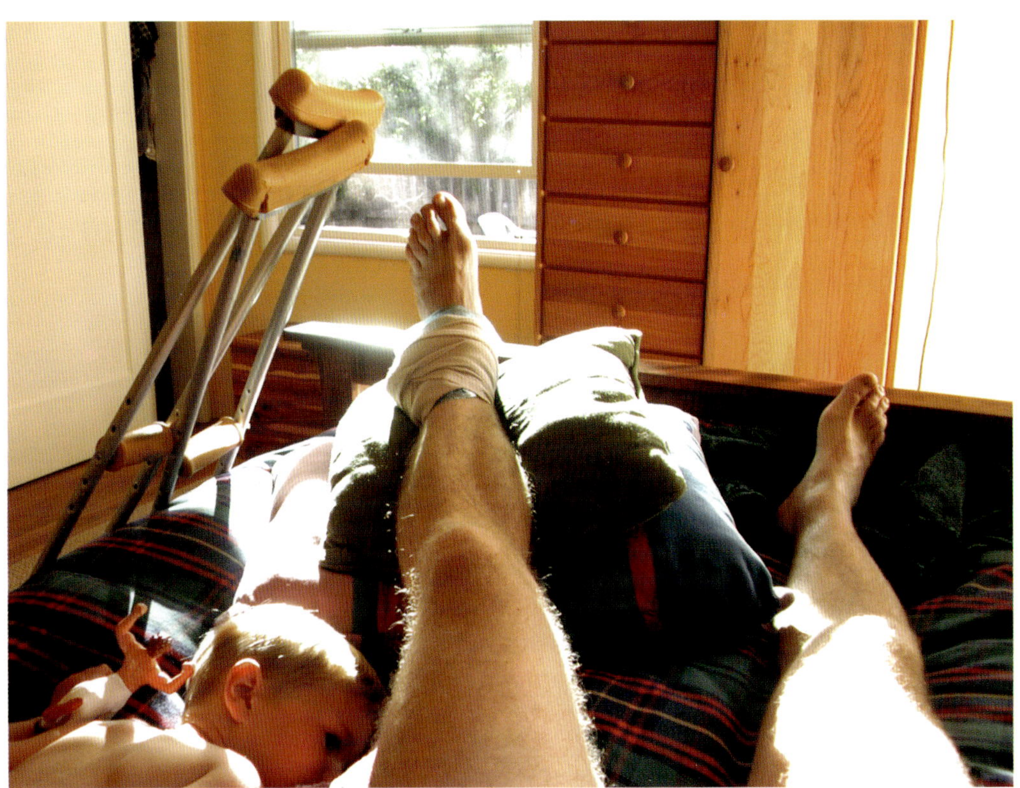

05.20.03

**Basketball**

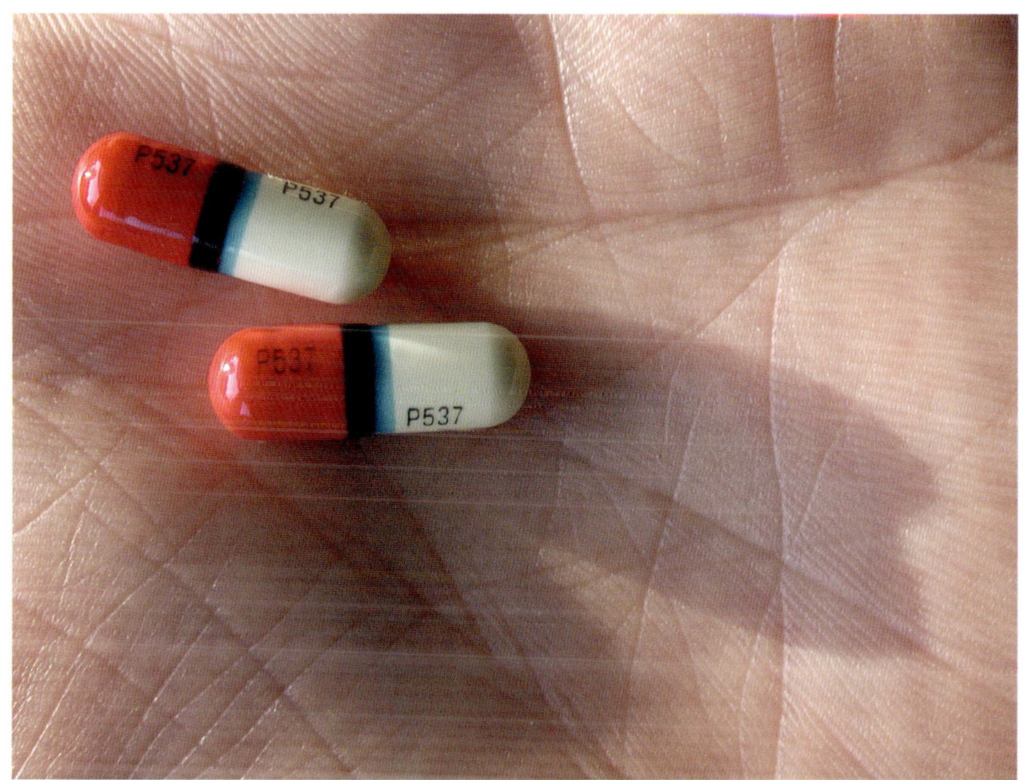


05.21.03

**Tylenol at sunrise**

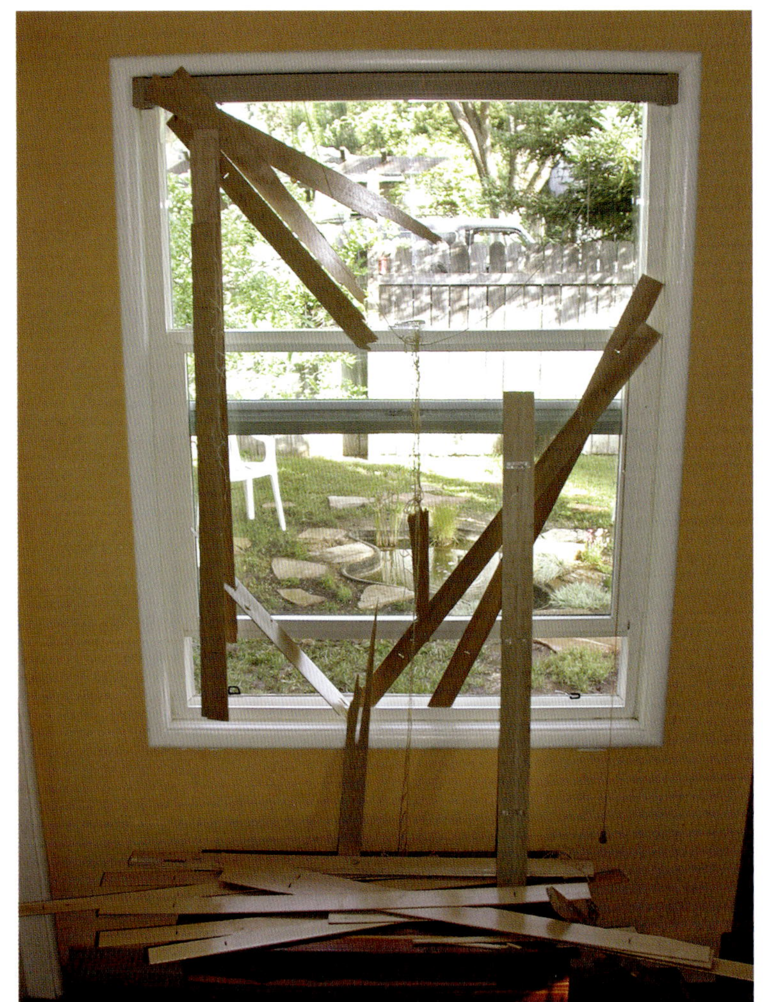

05.22.03

**Canine separation anxiety**

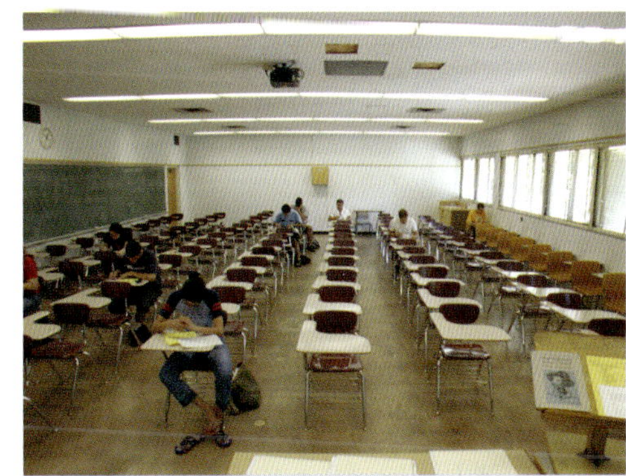

05.23.03
**Last class**

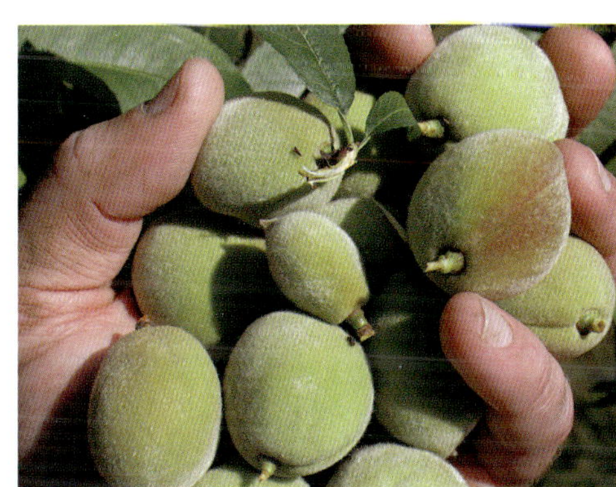

05.24.03
**Thinning the fruit**

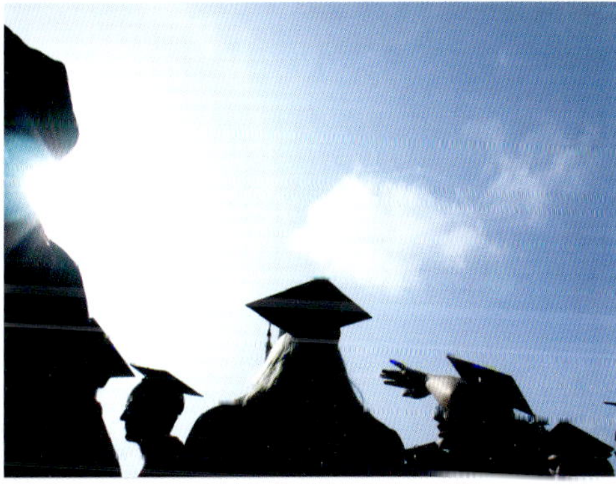

05.25.03

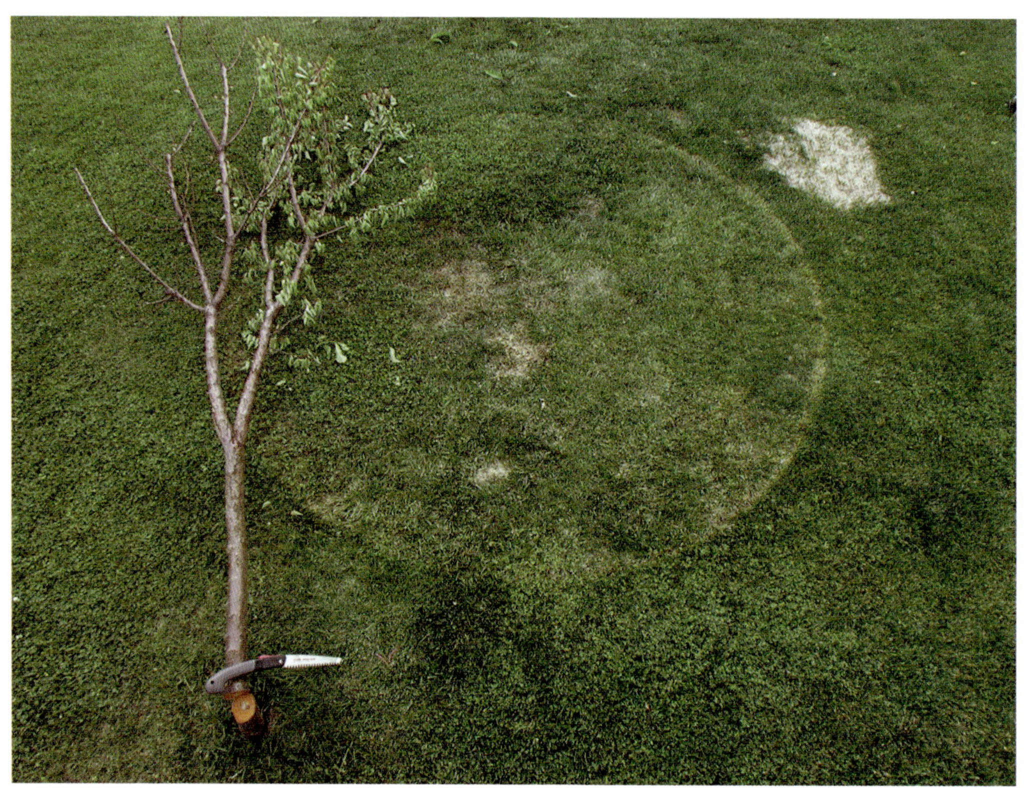

05.26.03

**The apricot tree**

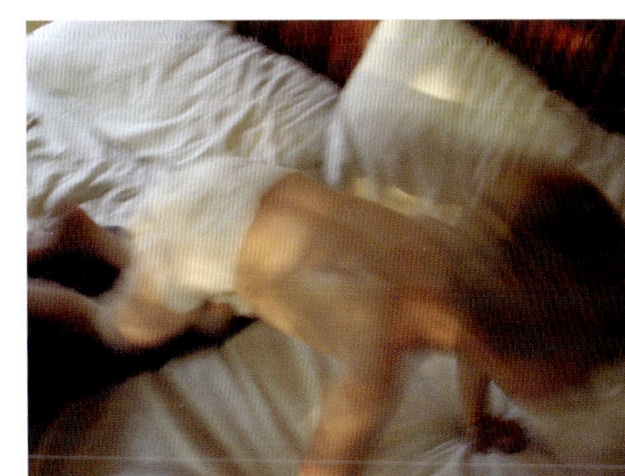

05.27.03

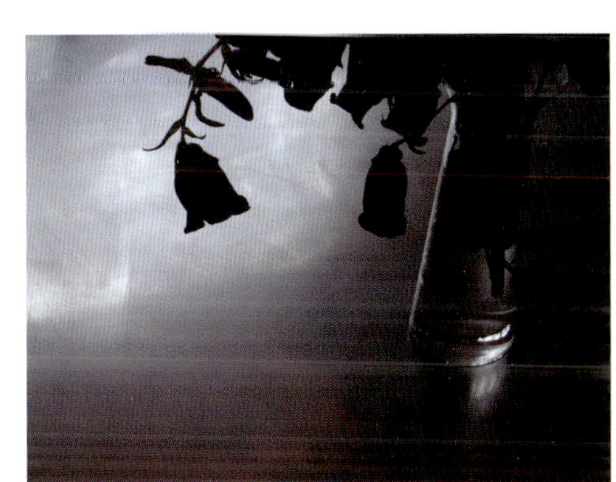

05.28.03

**Canterbury bells**

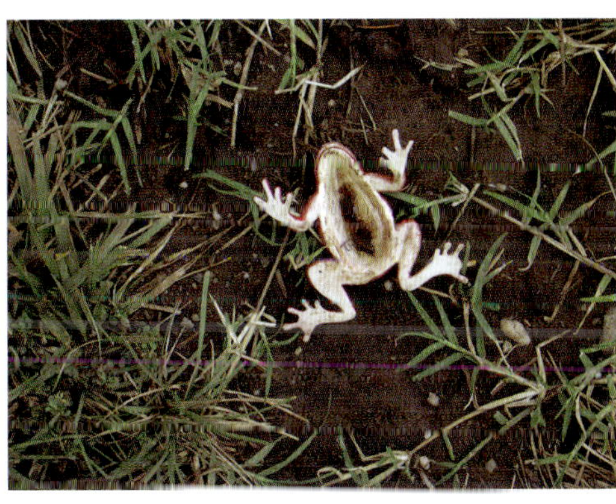

05.29.03

**Frog pond**

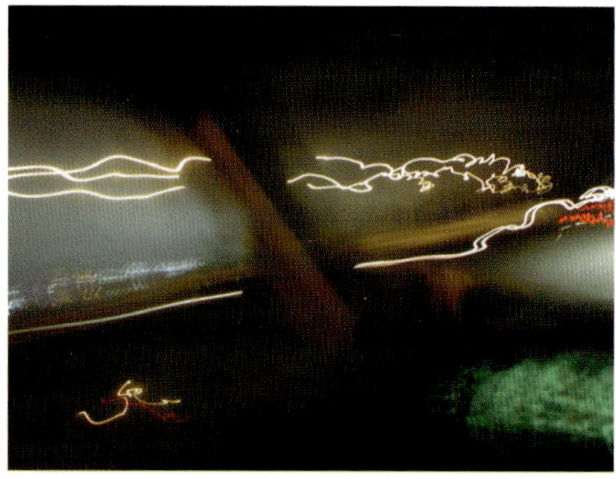

05.30.03

**Driving through San Francisco at midnight**

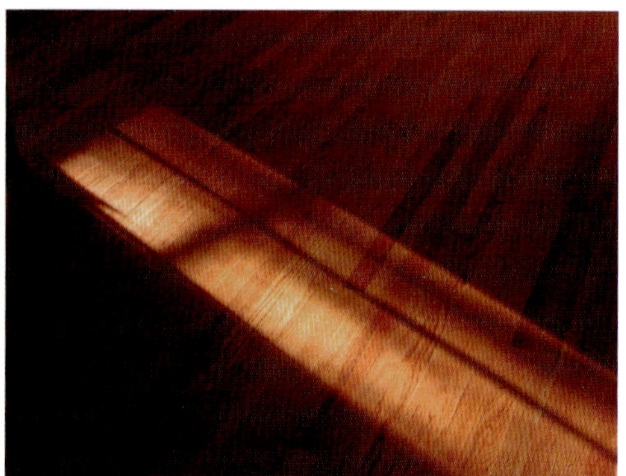

05.31.03

**Back home in Chico**

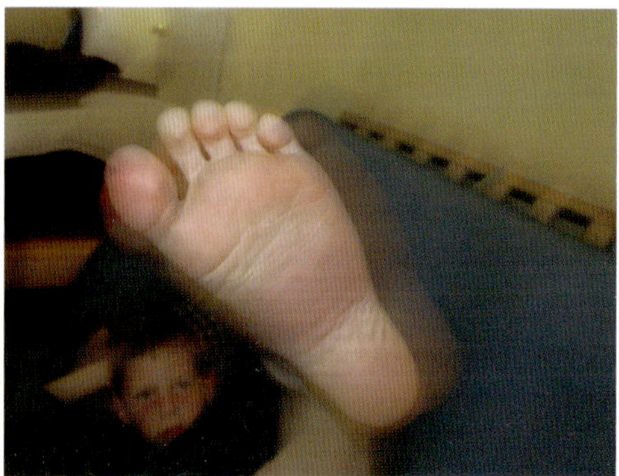

06.01.03

**Bee sting**

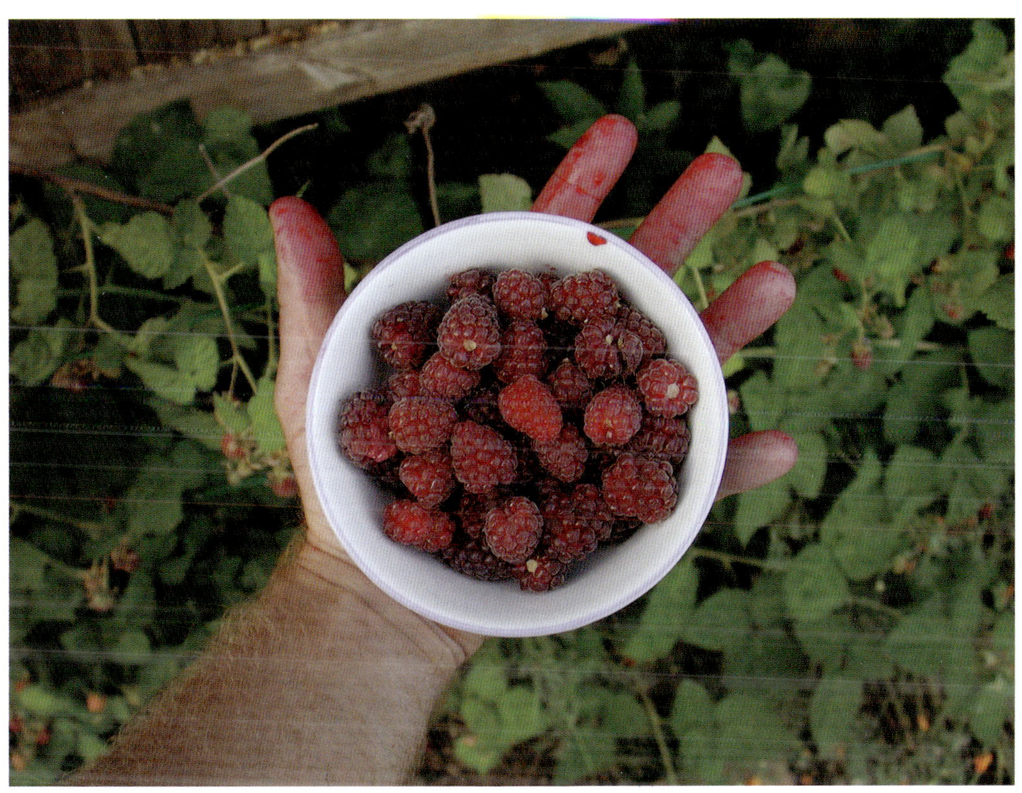

06.02.03

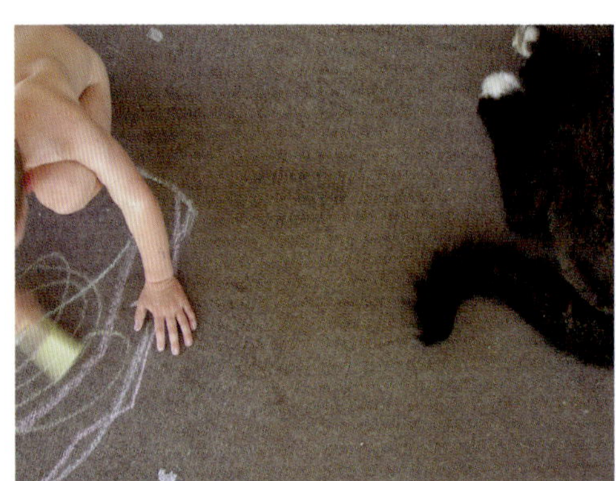

06.03.03

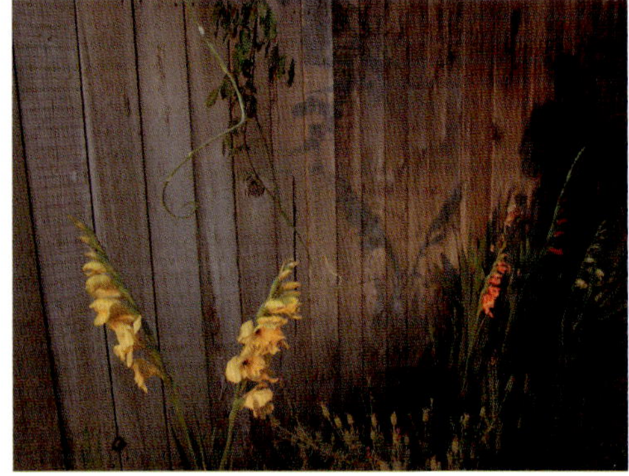

06.04.03

**Evening gladiolus**

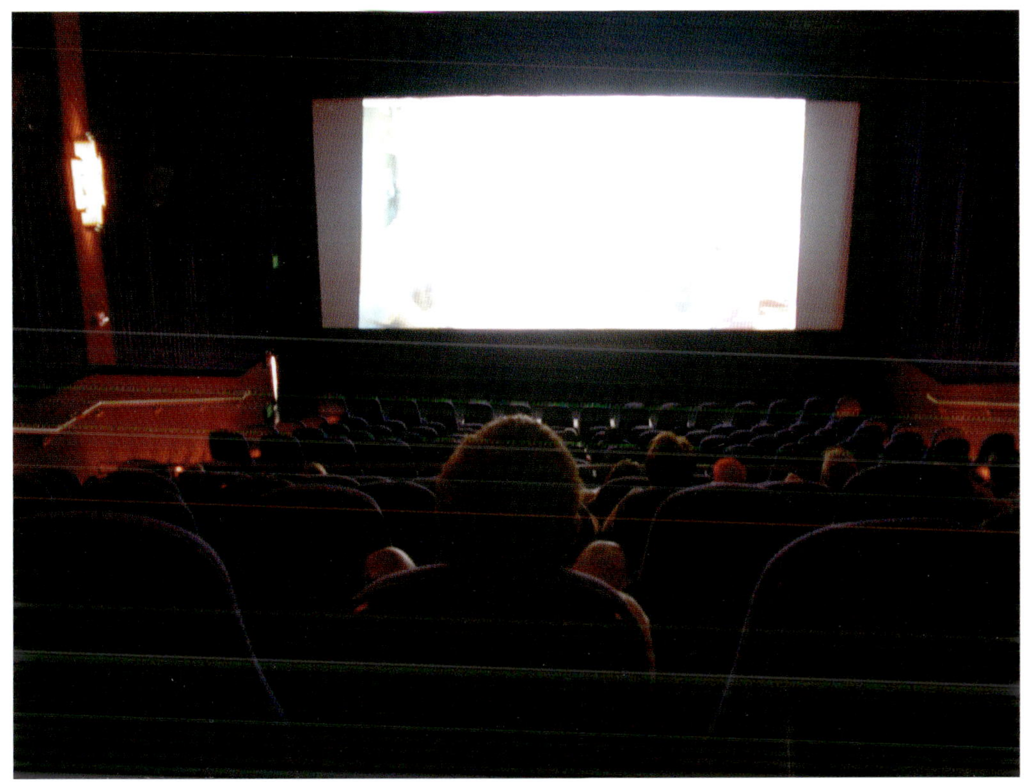

06.05.03

**Summer movie**

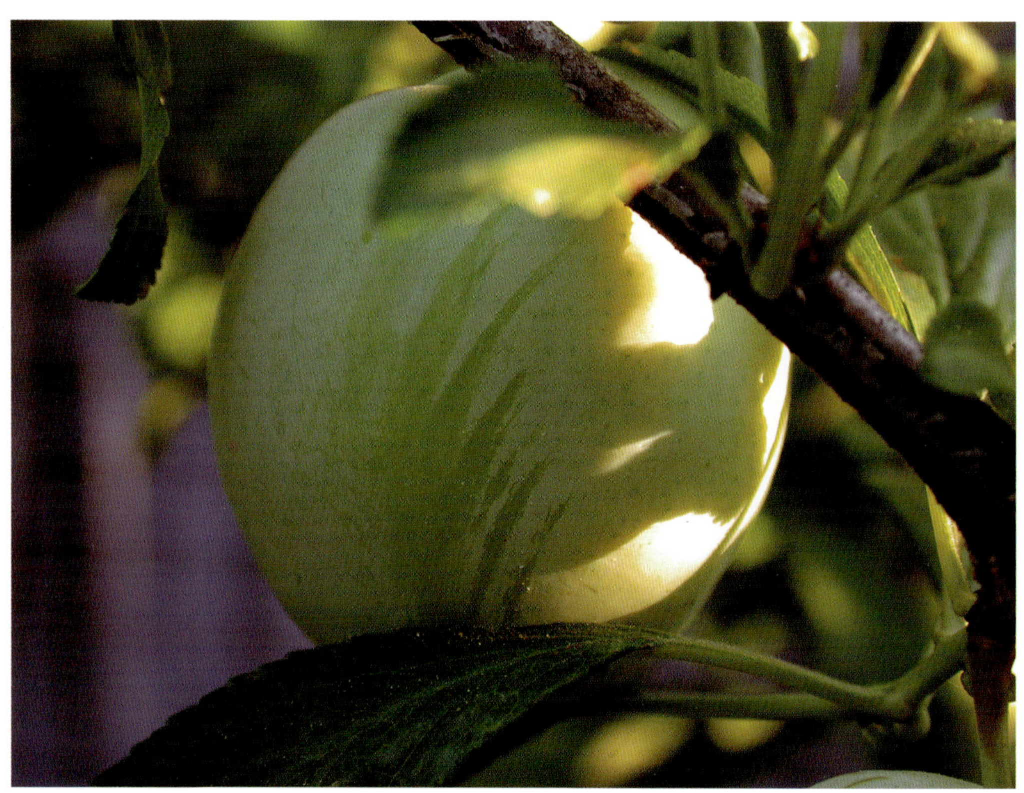

06.06.03

**June plum**

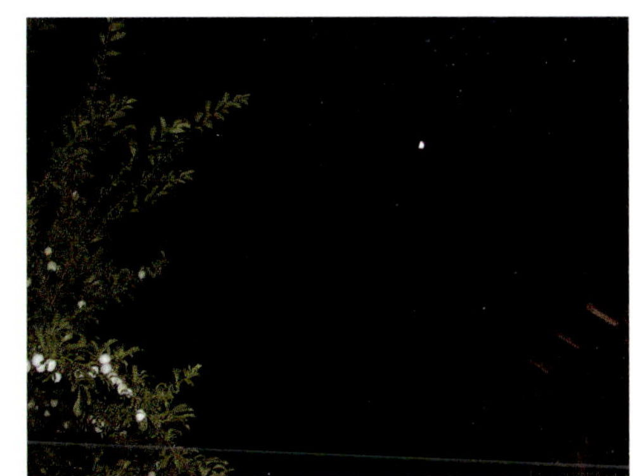

06.07.03
**Half moon**

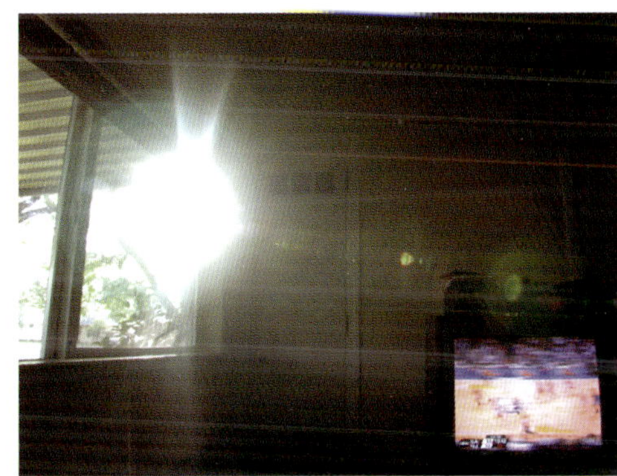

06.08.03
**NBA playoffs**

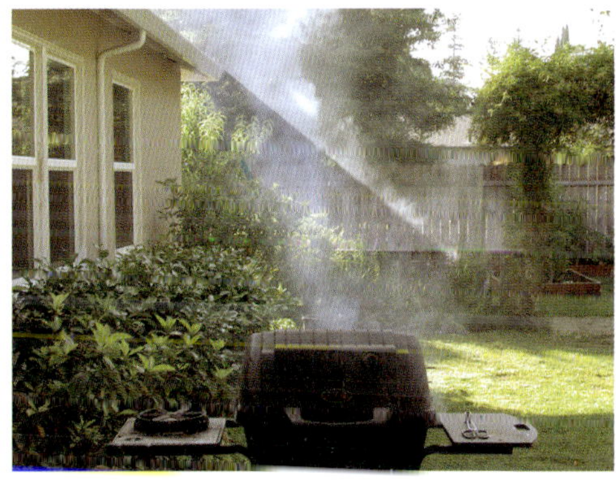

06.09.03

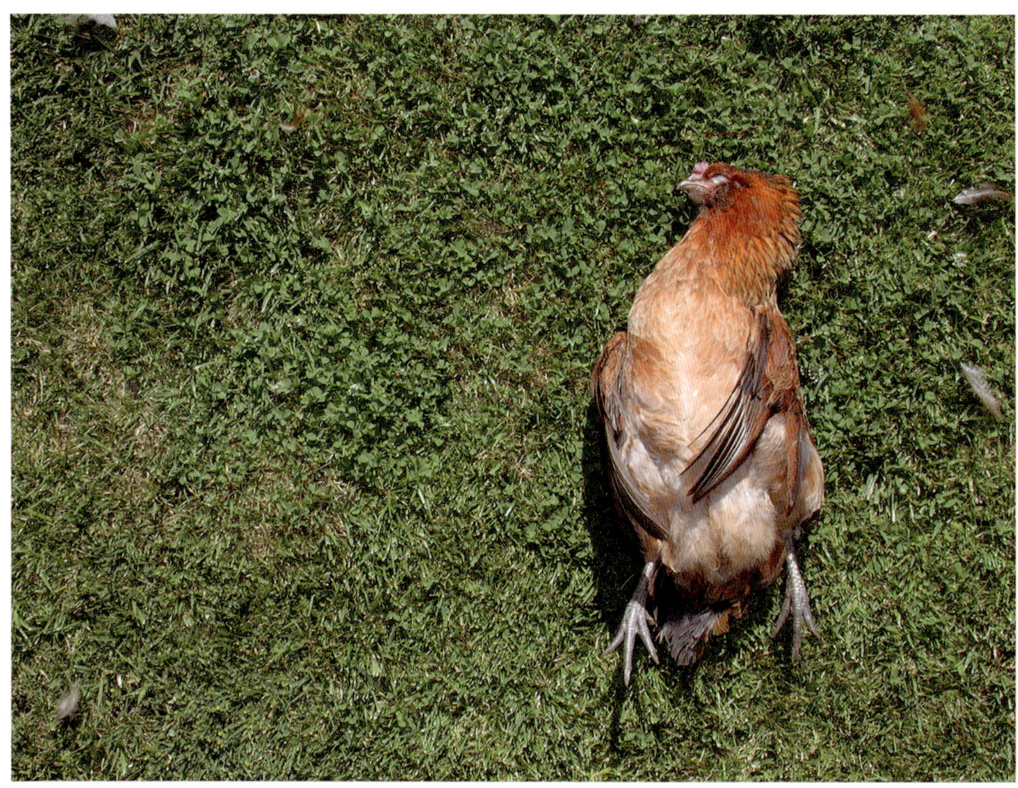

06.10.03

**"Maude," death by canine**

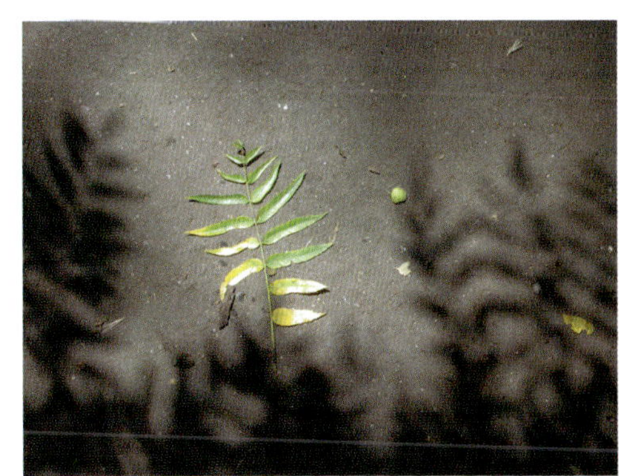

06.11.03

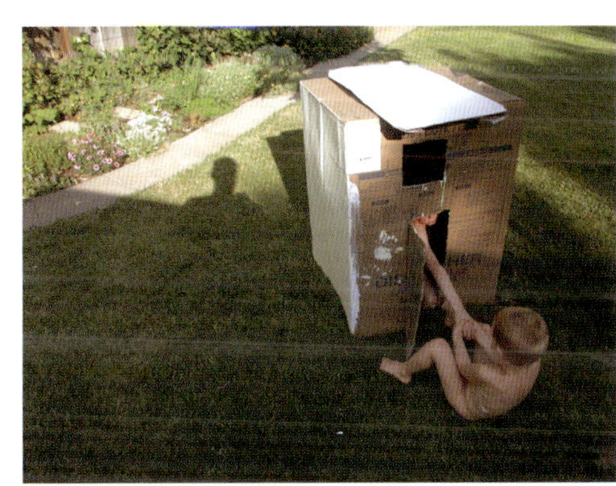

06.12.03

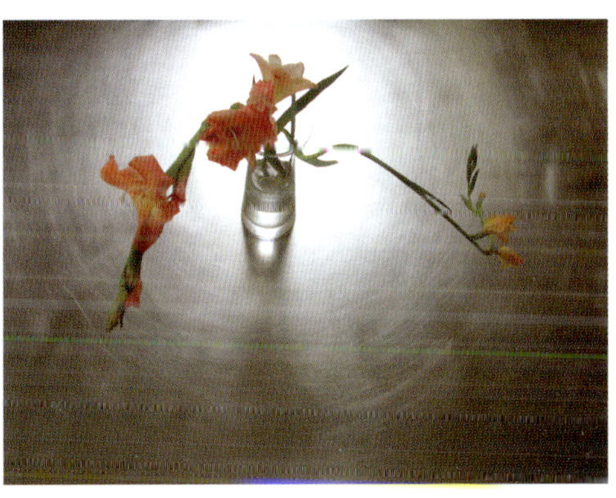

06.13.03

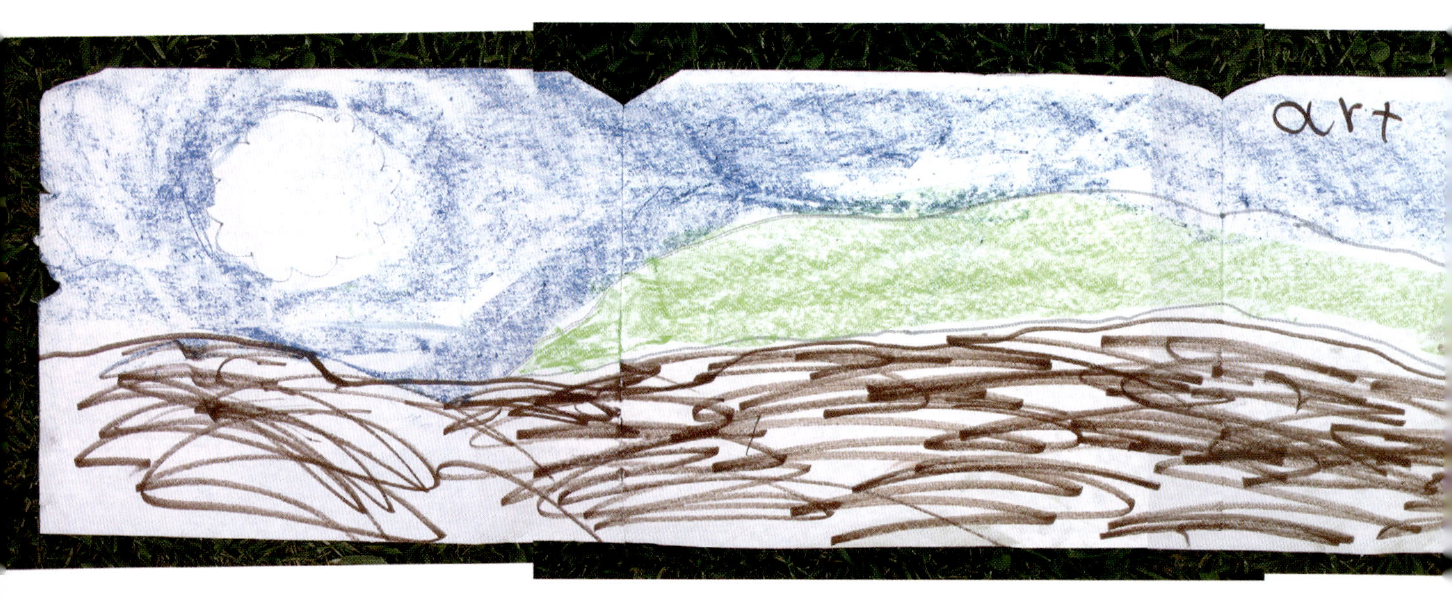


06.14.03

**The allegory of the inattentive art-loving mouse and the landscape serpent ("art can be paneful!")**

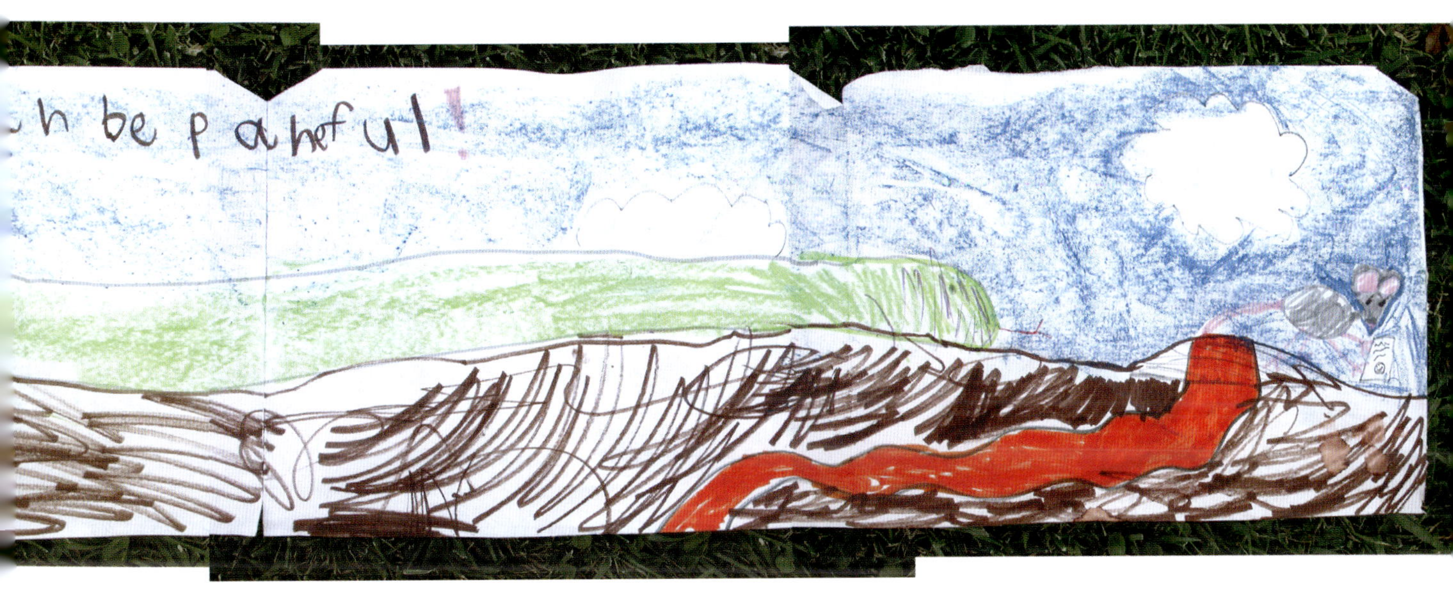
n be pahef ul!

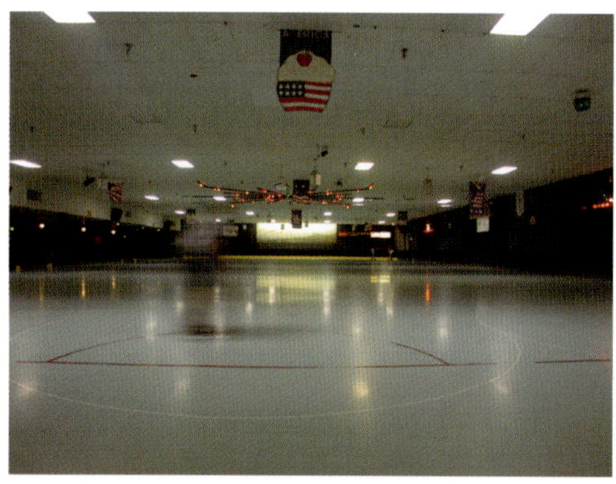

06.15.03

**Father's Day at the local skating rink**

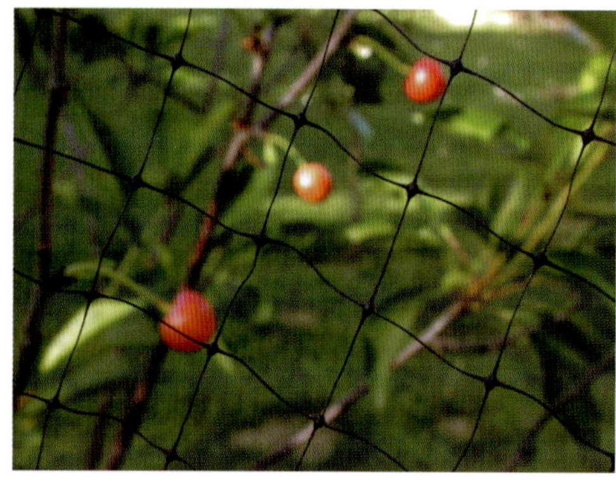

06.16.03

**Cherries 9, 10, and 11**

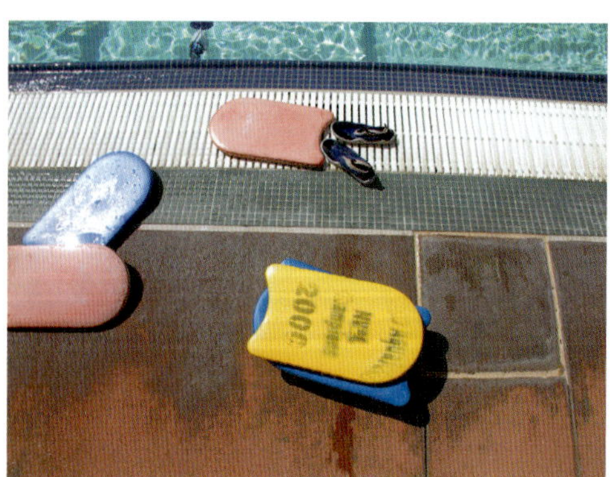

06.17.03

**Swim lessons**

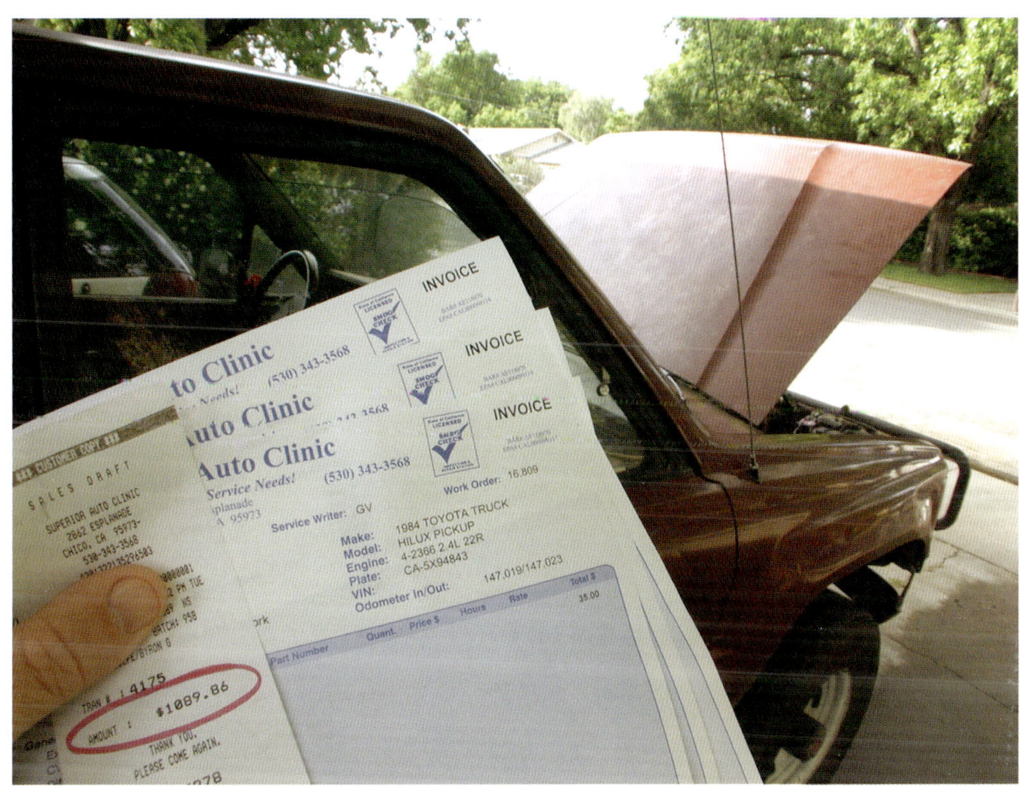


06.18.03

**Why artists long for patrons**

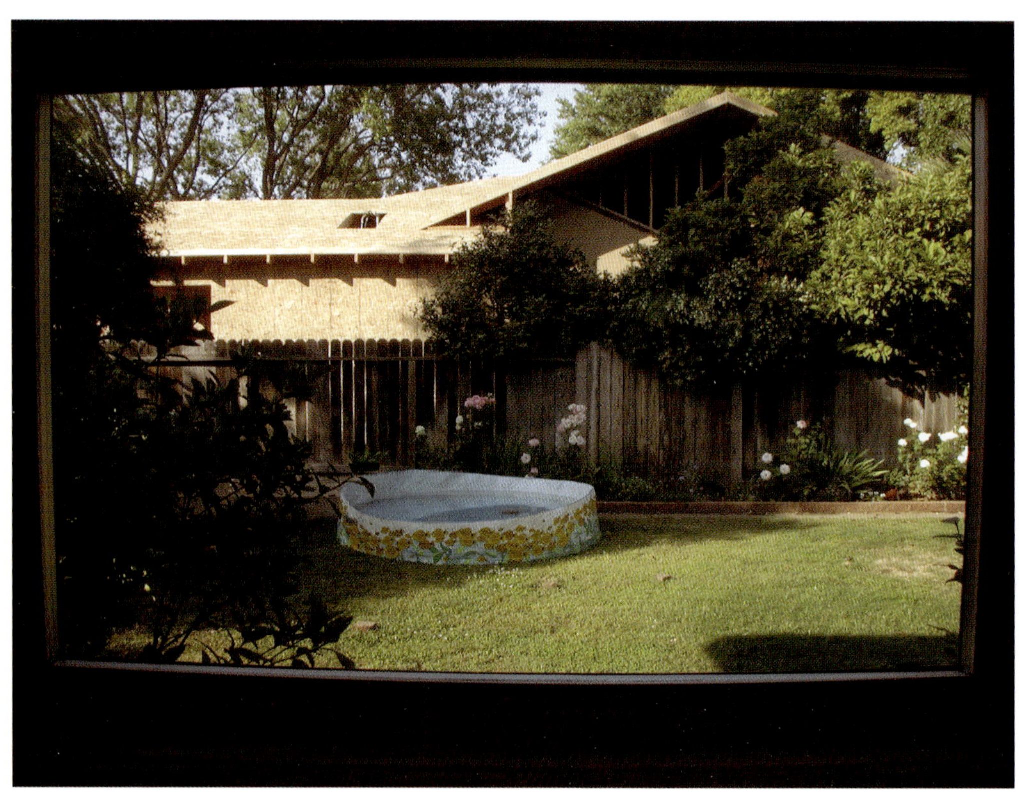

06.19.03

**From my bedroom window that once framed a handsome tree**

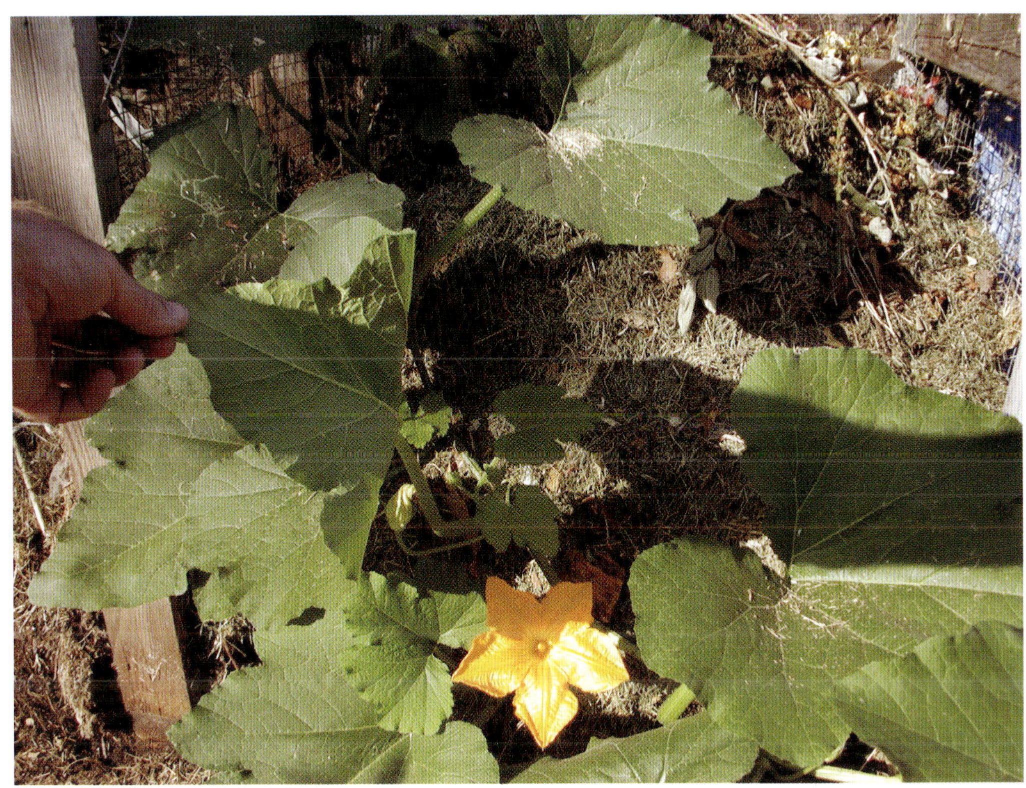

06.20.03

**Pumpkins in the compost patch!**

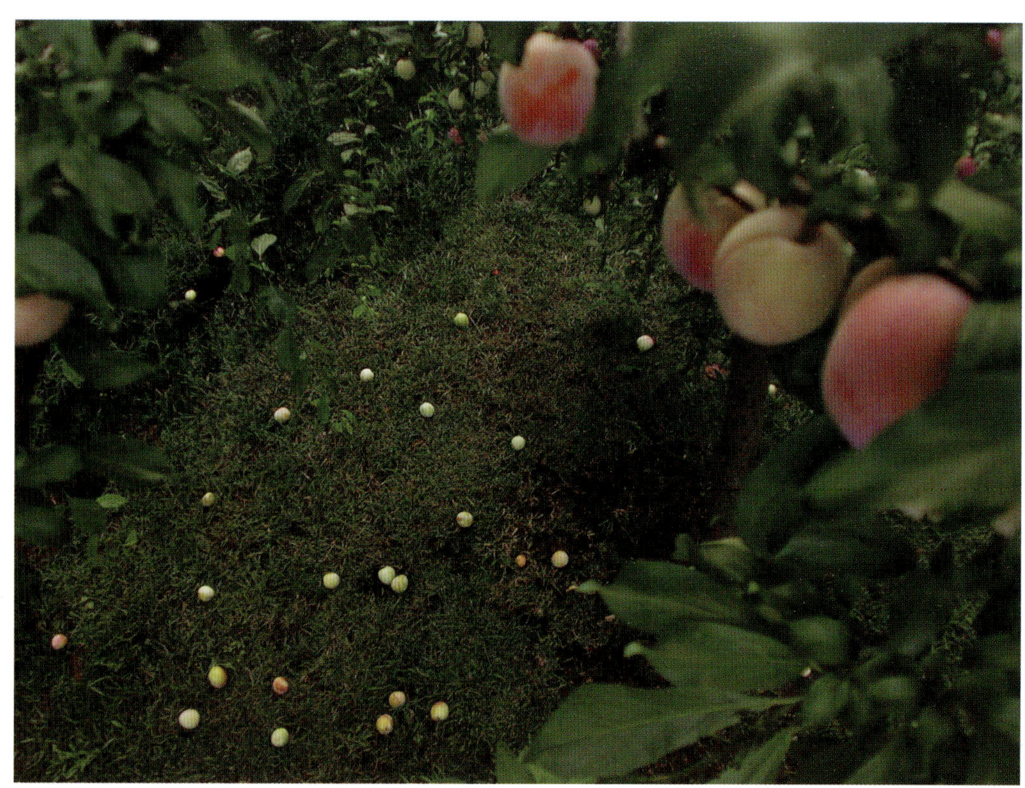

06.21.03

**Longest day: fallen plums from another broken bough**

08.22.03

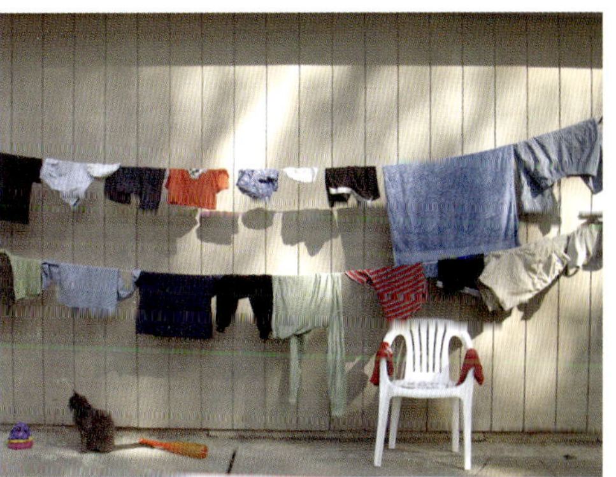

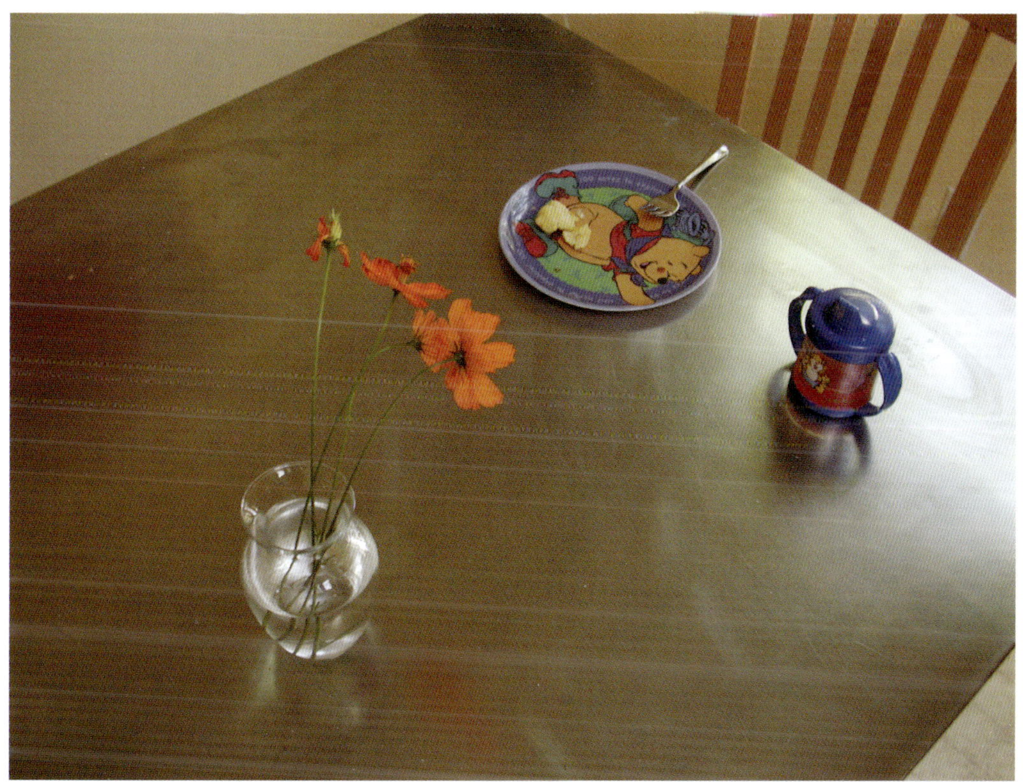

06.23.03

**Last day: I turned thirty-six, it was otherwise ordinary**

## acknowledgments

This book exists largely because of the generosity of others. Over the course of the nearly six years this project has spanned, I have received advice, support, encouragement, and assistance from many—my sincere apologies to anyone I may have inadvertently overlooked in the words that follow. Early on, John Long and the Department of Communication Design at California State University, Chico, provided the camera that made me think this project might actually be possible. The CSU Chico Research Foundation Office of Sponsored Programs provided a grant that helped offset the considerable expense of printing a necessary portion of the nearly 11,000 pictures and various book dummies I created. Julieanne Kost from Adobe Systems provided critical software support. Other invaluable champions of my efforts include friends Alexa Dilworth, Rebecca Solnit, Alan Rellaford, and William Fox. I'm especially grateful to mentors and colleagues Dan Kasser and Mark Klett and I've benefitted immensely from the professional advice and counsel of Joanna Hurley. The Santa Fe Center for Photography's Santa Fe Prize helped in so many ways. It is not an exaggeration to say that without the Center, this book wouldn't have found a home. Thank you to Teri Thomson Randall, Laura Wzorek, Maggie Payne, and to Roy Flukinger at the Harry Ransom Humanities Research Center at the University of Texas at Austin. At Chronicle Books, I'm grateful for Alan Rapp's faith in the project. I have been steadfastly guided through the bookmaking process by Bridget Watson Payne, Brooke Johnson, and Azi Rad. Many of my students helped shape this work in important ways, but Ryan Orcutt, Anthony Fendler, and Mollie Larson were intimately involved in the production and design of early versions of the project and deserve special recognition. Finally, and most importantly, I want to thank my family. For four generations that extend in both directions, you were willing passengers on a journey with an unknown destination. It was a true gift to make something with you and for you.